"ORIGINAL SIN"?

The **Institute of Southeast Asian Studies (ISEAS)** was established as an autonomous organization in 1968. It is a regional centre dedicated to the study of socio-political, security and economic trends and developments in Southeast Asia and its wider geostrategic and economic environment. The Institute's research programmes are the Regional Economic Studies (RES, including ASEAN and APEC), Regional Strategic and Political Studies (RSPS), and Regional Social and Cultural Studies (RSCS).

ISEAS Publishing, an established academic press, has issued more than 2,000 books and journals. It is the largest scholarly publisher of research about Southeast Asia from within the region. ISEAS Publishing works with many other academic and trade publishers and distributors to disseminate important research and analyses from and about Southeast Asia to the rest of the world.

"ORIGINAL SIN"?

Revising the Revisionist Critique of the 1963 Operation Coldstore in Singapore

Kumar Ramakrishna

LSEAS

INSTITUTE OF SOUTHEAST ASIAN STUDIES
Singapore

First published in Singapore in 2015 by
ISEAS Publishing
Institute of Southeast Asian Studies
30 Heng Mui Keng Terrace
Pasir Panjang
Singapore 119614

E-mail: publish@iseas.edu.sg
Website: <http://bookshop.iseas.edu.sg>

The responsibility for facts and opinions in this publication rests exclusively with the author and his interpretations do not necessarily reflect the views or the policy of the publisher or its supporters.

ISEAS Library Cataloguing-in-Publication Data

Ramakrishna, Kumar.
    "Original Sin"? Revising the Revisionist Critique of the 1963 Operation Coldstore in Singapore.
    1.   Political prisoners—Singapore.
    2.   Detention of persons—Singapore.
    3.   Communism—Singapore.
    4.   Communists—Singapore.
    5.   Singapore—Politics and government—1945–1963.
    6.   Singapore—History—1945–1963.
    7.   China—Foreign relations—East Asia.
    8.   East Asia—Foreign relations—China.
    I.   Title.
    II.   Title: Revising the Revisionist Critique of the 1963 Operation Coldstore in Singapore
DS610.6 R16   2015

ISBN 978-981-4620-43-7 (soft cover)
ISBN 978-981-4620-44-4 (e-book, PDF)

Cover photograph: News Coverage of Operation Coldstore in 星洲日報 (*Sin Chew Jit Poh*), 3 February 1963, p. 5.
Reproduced with permission of Sin Chew Jit Poh © Singapore Press Holdings Limited.

Typeset by Superskill Graphics Pte Ltd
Printed in Singapore by Mainland Press Pte Ltd

CONTENTS

ACKNOWLEDGEMENTS

I would like to acknowledge Mr Eddie Teo, Chairman; Ambassador Ong Keng Yong, Executive Deputy Chairman; and Ambassador Barry Desker, former Dean, of the S. Rajaratnam School of International Studies, Nanyang Technological University, for their overall support of this project. I would also like to express my appreciation for the support of the senior management and research staff of the Internal Security Department (ISD) for their willingness to work with me in telling the story of this very important episode in the history of post-war Singapore. Without their encouragement and assistance, this project would never have gotten off the ground. Mr S.R. Nathan, former President of the Republic of Singapore, as well as Mr Benny Lim in the Prime Minister's Office, who has held numerous senior portfolios in the Singapore Government, inspired me with their tremendous enthusiasm for Singapore history, and I hope they will find this volume of interest. Academic colleagues such as Bilveer Singh, Albert Lau, Ang Cheng Guan, Kwa Chong Guan, Mushahid Ali, Ong Weichong, Ho Shu Huang, Tan Tai Yong, Joey Long and Shashi Jayakumar have been sources of good-natured intellectual stimulation on the vicissitudes of Singapore history; while at the Rajaratnam School and its Centre of Excellence for National Security, Damien Cheong, Bernard Loo, Norman Vasu and Yvonne Lee have been wonderful colleagues to work with down the years. Last but not least, I would like to record my appreciation to Ambassador Tan Chin Tiong, Director of the Institute of Southeast Asian Studies (ISEAS); Daljit Singh, ISEAS Senior Research Fellow; and Ng Kok Kiong, Head of the ISEAS Publications Unit, and Rahilah Yusuf, Senior Editor, for their enthusiasm in seeing this project through to publication. It has been a privilege to work together with such dedicated professionals, to further illumine the complexities, of the continually evolving Singapore Story.

INTRODUCTION
The "Alternate" Challenge to the Singapore Story as Context

While the first-ever school textbook on Singapore history — encompassing the period from the founding of modern Singapore by Sir Stamford Raffles in 1819 to independence from the Federation of Malaysia in 1965 — appeared in 1984, the more or less formalized "master narrative" of Singapore's ensuing political evolution, the so-called Singapore Story, "coalesced in the late 1990s". This was "when the key moments in the country's political history as an emerging postcolonial entity were identified and plotted into a national narrative".[1] In 1997, then Deputy Prime Minister Lee Hsien Loong formally launched the National Education (NE) programme, an official attempt to redress the prevailing poor knowledge of Singapore's past on the part of young Singaporeans, many of whom had apparently not even realized that Singapore was once part of the Federation. The ultimate aim of the NE programme was to ensure that future generations of Singaporeans were adequately socialized into the Singapore Story, regarded as "objective history, seen from the Singaporean standpoint".[2] This exercise was by no means idiosyncratically Singaporean. New nations, ever since the emergence of secular nationalism as a potent unifying ideology in Europe in the late eighteenth century, have tended "to rely on skillfully constructing the connections between the past (real or imagined), the present and the future". The purpose of deliberately crafting such national narratives has been "to encourage members of a putative national community to imagine themselves as sharing a special bond and destiny as members of a nation".[3] Hence in Singapore, it is acknowledged that government efforts "at yoking history to the cause of nation-building", even "if particularly insistent and didactic", are not unusual, for a "national history" that possesses "resonance and credibility" helps "foster national identity".[4]

The key themes of the Singapore Story can be summarized via a five-point narrative:[5] first, the founding of modern Singapore by Raffles in 1819 as a British trading post "where there had once been a sleepy Malay village", and the subsequent emergence of the post as a "thriving colony, attracting hundreds of thousands of Chinese immigrants and smaller numbers of Malays and Indians"; second, the wartime trauma of the Japanese Occupation from 1942 to 1945, followed by the British return and planning for a "painless exit strategy" of eventual decolonization to a friendly post-colonial administration; third, the persistence of this colonial strategy of orderly constitutional advance toward self-government despite disruptions by largely Communist-instigated violence in the 1950s, culminating with the election of the nationalist People's Action Party (PAP) government in 1959; fourth, the difficult and ultimately unsuccessful twenty-three-month induction into the Malaysian Federation from 1963 to 1965, originally intended to resolve both the Communist threat as well as ensure Singapore's political and economic viability; and fifth, separation from Malaysia in August 1965 and under the PAP government's steadying hand, the successful management of "racial discord and social disharmony", resulting in the country defying the odds and making the transition "from the Third world to the First". While seminal accounts of the Singapore Story had appeared in the mid-1980s to early 1990s,[6] the publication of founding Prime Minister Lee Kuan Yew's memoirs in 1998 and 2000, together with Albert Lau's account of Singapore's separation from Malaysia in 1998 represented a milestone of sorts in the evolution of the established narrative.[7]

This standard PAP-driven narrative of the Singapore Story has since been challenged. Early criticisms emerged almost immediately, when Singaporean scholars questioned the apparent identification of the Singapore Story with the towering figure of Prime Minister Lee Kuan Yew alone, without due acknowledgement of his PAP Old Guard "lieutenants" such as Dr Toh Chin Chye, Dr Goh Keng Swee, S. Rajaratnam, Devan Nair, Ong Pang Boon and others — including Lee's one-time PAP colleague, eventual chief political rival and alleged Communist, Lim Chin Siong.[8] Other historians, influenced by evolving trends in the discipline of history away from a sole focus on political elites and towards including the previously marginalized lives and voices of ordinary people,[9] have agitated for a "New Singapore History".[10] In the latter case, fresh emphasis is placed on the social and political "paths not taken" by ordinary Singaporeans — workers, students, civil society — since separation from Malaysia, due to post-1965 PAP government policy that is said to have neutered the "dynamism, great political movements, and high aspirations" of pre-independence Singapore.[11] Carl Trocki and Michael Barr argue in this regard that there is a need to articulate a "not-the-PAP" interpretation of "Singapore's recent past and to focus on the positive contributions and efforts of those alternative movements". While they take pains to assure readers that they do not seek to "present an anti-PAP or anti-Lee Kuan Yew approach to the study of Singapore's social and political order", they nevertheless concede that their research suggests that alternative social and political paths not taken in Singapore post-1965 were "often the result of forceful action by those in power". They quip that as one "does not make an omelette without breaking eggs", the "recent history of Singapore is littered with its share of eggshells".[12]

OPERATION COLDSTORE: THE PAP'S "ORIGINAL SIN"?

In this respect the consequences of the major internal security exercise, Operation Coldstore, launched on 2 February 1963 by the Internal Security Council — comprising representatives from the Singapore, Malayan and British Governments — and in which 130 suspected Communists and Communist sympathizers in political parties, unions, rural, educational and cultural organizations were eventually detained,[13] appears to be one of those broken "eggshells" Trocki and Barr had in mind. This episode, which the conventional account records as having been decisive in destroying the subversive threat posed by the Communist Party of Malaya (CPM), appears to have assumed particular importance in the ongoing construction of the alternative "New Singapore History". This history, assiduously being knit together by a group of revisionist historians, political scientists and former political detainees who basically agree on the broad outlines, if not necessarily the finer, granular details — we shall call them "Alternates" for short[14] — appears to generally posit Coldstore as the focal point of perhaps the major "path not taken" post-1965: an ostensibly Progressive Leftist and pluralistic, Barisan Sosialis Singapura (BSS)-led Singapore, with conceivably the principal, charismatic BSS leader Lim Chin Siong as prime minister. Coldstore, in other words, was, according to Alternate historian Thum Ping Tjin, "more than just a footnote in history"; it "made modern Singapore".[15] Hong Lysa, together with Thum and Loh Kah Seng, perhaps the leading Singaporean representatives of the Alternate perspective goes even further, arguing that "the very heart of the PAP myth" that "Operation Coldstore was necessary for national security" represents "the Party's original sin".[16] Against this backdrop, the Alternates make two main attacks on the conventional wisdom concerning Coldstore.

First, rather than targeting potentially violent Communists, Coldstore in fact decimated the "progressive left". The latter has been defined by Thum Ping Tjin as a "pro-labour left-wing movement" comprising a coalition of trade unions, civic societies and student groups united by an anti-colonial platform and agitating for better working conditions, "citizenship rights for Singapore's disenfranchised" and greater democratic freedoms, but was nonetheless committed to peaceful, constitutional processes in achieving political change.[17] In other words, the notion of a dangerous Communist United Front was nothing more than an invention by the PAP authorities — and in fact some senior British colonial officials themselves had deep misgivings about the allegedly weak grounds for the Coldstore detentions.[18] In short, the stock Alternate view is that Coldstore *was mounted not for legitimate security reasons as posterity appears to record, but rather, expedient political ones*:[19]

> The arrests and detentions under the operation were intended to ensure that the British policy of Malaysia was realized, and the PAP was able to achieve dominance in the political sphere of Singapore.

In this view, the defeat of the Progressive Left and the political survival of the pro-Western PAP government was seen by the British as essential for stability in Singapore and the larger Malaysian Federation, which were together regarded as an important "anticommunist bulwark in Southeast Asia in their process of decolonisation during the Cold War".[20] Alternates thus lament that ultimately, "many of the best and brightest of our people were sacrificed in a struggle where the interest of the local population were of little consequence."[21] The Progressive Left in Singapore was thus sacrificed at the altar of Cold War geopolitics.

LIM CHIN SIONG AND WHAT COULD HAVE BEEN

A second, closely related attack by the Alternates on the Singapore Story narrative of Coldstore concerns by far the foremost leading light of the "best and brightest" of the Progressive Left who were politically eviscerated by that operation: Lim Chin Siong, who "appeared like a comet on the Singapore scene" in the early 1950s and who by 1963 "was the dominant political figure in Singapore".[22] Lim consistently publicly denied he was ever a Communist. In the Alternate narrative, Lim, a heroic but ultimately tragic figure who had consistently eschewed political violence in favour of peaceful constitutional struggle, fell victim to the power-obsessed PAP leader Lee Kuan Yew. The latter, anxious over public disillusionment with the PAP's performance in government; internal party dissent at the perceived authoritarianism of the

PAP leadership; and weakening public support as evidenced by the Hong Lim and Anson by-election losses in 1961, was driven to seek political union or Merger with the Federation and the Borneo Territories, principally as a means to eliminate the Progressive Left headed by Lim. The Alternates argue that the Merger Referendum in Singapore in September 1962 was cynically manipulated by the PAP, while the outbreak of the Brunei Revolt in December that year provided the perfect excuse for Lee and his British and Federation allies to mount Coldstore and arrest Lim Chin Siong and the key Progressive Left leaders. Lim was thus "destroyed in the atmosphere of the Cold War".[23] Hong Lysa — with not inconsiderable hyperbole — goes so far as to argue that Lim Chin Siong has in fact been assigned a "timeless pivotal role" as "the other" in the Singapore Story, and the latter's "humiliation is meant to extend beyond Lim's lifetime and into history".[24]

As Singapore approaches the fiftieth anniversary of independence in 2015, elements of the Alternate constituency have intensified their use of the online social media to propagate and defend — at times vociferously — their critiques of Coldstore and the PAP government's role in Lim Chin Siong's allegedly unjustified political demise.[25] The intensity of these debates between the Alternates and "establishment defenders" has not gone unnoticed in the blogosphere.[26] Most significantly, the logical implication of the Alternates' New Singapore History project, that Singaporeans need to collectively consider anew those national political paths not taken, appears to have had increasing resonance since the May 2011 general elections, in which the incumbent PAP fared relatively less well compared to previous electoral contests. While the PAP won 75.3 per cent of the vote in the 2001 elections, ten years later it secured only 60.1 per cent — a drop of fifteen percentage points. This prompted observers to query if "Singaporeans' trust in the PAP government — perhaps the most important commodity in the country's system of elite governance" — had worryingly "diminished"?[27] Sensing and exploiting the shift in the political mood, the Alternate constituency launched a new book attempting to cast the radical Chinese student movement of the 1950s in a fresh light. According to Hong Lysa, one of the book's editors, the late political detainee Tan Jing Quee "had already discerned that this time, it was fine to advertise the book launch widely".[28] Increasing popular interest in the radical student politics of the 1950s — and in particular the career of Lim Chin Siong — appeared to have persisted into 2014, with one young blogger calling upon the younger generation to emulate the example of Lim and his comrades in fearlessly defying the establishment to fight for the good of the common man.[29] Hong, in a November 2014 post, sums up the Alternate position by knitting together Coldstore and Lim Chin Siong's political fate.

She argues that Lim, in his heyday the PAP's "feared political nemesis" has nowadays "become the albatross around the party's neck". This is because any "hint that Lim was not a MCP member", and "not a subversive" would in effect "raise questions about Operation Coldstore", and more to the point, "the morality of how the PAP came to rule Singapore".[30]

It is perhaps tempting therefore to argue that a "Singapore Spring" may be just around the corner, in which the unjustly ignored political heroes of the historical Progressive Left will be rehabilitated, thereby providing the ideological impetus for an ostensibly new, more liberal, democratic and pluralistic path in Singapore politics to be taken. After all, as M. Rajakumar argues, "Singapore's history begins" only when Lim Chin Siong in particular "is given his proper place in its annals".[31] In this sense, the New Singapore History can perhaps be seen as the latest attempt by politically leftist and liberal scholars and activists at home and abroad to critique and delegitimize the almost fifty-year-old political system that Lee Kuan Yew and his Old Guard PAP colleagues set up post-separation, one in which, despite its admittedly unique, non-doctrinaire characteristics, has been widely recognized as having helped Singapore survive and thrive as a viable political and economic entity.[32]

THE ALTERNATES' GREAT TEMPTATION: A GOOD STORY BEFORE FACTS

This book will have brief comments to make on the wider issue of tweaking Singapore's largely successful political system later. The main thrust here, however, is that while the Alternates, and for that matter, other observers are right that a broadening and enriching of the Singapore Story to include the richly textured micro-narratives of ordinary Singaporeans is both necessary and desirable,[33] *one nevertheless has to take care that egregious historical inaccuracies are not uncritically embraced in the process.* As shall be seen, in the eagerness of elements within the Alternate constituency to promote the New Singapore History as an ideological bulwark for political change in Singapore, they arguably do tend to succumb to the old temptation of "not letting the facts get in the way of a good story". Focusing on the case of Operation Coldstore in general and Lim Chin Siong in particular, and employing declassified archival material from the National Archives and other repositories in the United Kingdom, as well as still-classified documents made available by the Internal Security Department Heritage Centre (ISDHC) of Singapore, this book will reiterate that Operation Coldstore was utterly justified because the Communist United Front (CUF) was indeed a real-time threat. It will also demonstrate conclusively that despite his many public protestations down the years, the leading light of the "Progressive Left", Lim Chin Siong, was very much a leading member of the CUF, and hence his arrest as part of Coldstore was fully defensible. What is more, Lim's *own* later painful recantation and repudiation of the all-too-real Communist creed will be revealed. In sum, this book serves as a reminder to heed Spanish philosopher George Santayana's famous warning that those who "do not remember the past are condemned to repeat it".[34] Hence one should not uncritically embrace the often highly politicized output of elements of the Alternate constituency — especially the suggestion that the allegedly "original sin" of Coldstore unjustly deprived Singaporeans of supposedly glorious liberal democratic, socialist, egalitarian "paths not taken".

PLAN OF THE BOOK

The rest of this book is divided into five chapters. First, it will defend in some detail the employment in this study of formerly classified records, including the old colonial Police Special Branch as well as more recent still-classified ISD reports, in the process anticipating and debunking the usual but at times self-contradictory Alternate objections to their use. Second, it will examine the theory behind the CUF, something given surprisingly short shrift by Alternate historians — and with the necessary detail and granularity — examine how the CUF emerged and evolved in Singapore in the mid-1950s. The basic question to ask is: are the Alternates right in arguing that there was actually no evidence of the fabled "Communist Tiger" of PAP lore? Third, the book will show that Alternate attempts to rehabilitate Lim Chin Siong as a Progressive Leftist leader whose political career was cruelly cut short by his politically opportunistic detention under Coldstore are wide off the mark. It will be seen that Lim was instead very much the central CUF leader in Singapore.

Fourth, the book will re-evaluate the actions of Lee Kuan Yew and his non-Communist PAP faction in its internal struggle with the pro-Communists within the Party — who later split off to form the BSS, in the years leading up to Coldstore. The issues to explore here are: were Lee's actions really those of a power-obsessed opportunist as the Alternates allege and that Coldstore was mounted for crass political rather than legitimate security reasons? Fifth and finally, because the current debate on Operation Coldstore shows that a wider popular appreciation of Singapore's history is sorely needed, the book will outline four key strategies for buttressing a systematically "pluralized" *Singapore Story 2.0*, so to speak, that embraces not just the perspectives of the political elites but also of ordinary Singaporeans. In the final analysis, in 2015 the nation will celebrate its fiftieth anniversary of independence. Thus a Singapore Story that is seen as consensus-sustaining and widely embraced by the public — particularly the increasingly politically influential "Generation Y" of cosmopolitan, well-travelled and social media-savvy Singaporeans — would appear to be very much a *sine qua non* of the utterly ventilated city-state's continued stability and vitality amidst a globalized, fast-paced and not infrequently dangerous world.

Notes

1. Hong Lysa and Huang Jianli, *The Scripting of a National History: Singapore and Its Past* (Singapore: NUS Press, 2008), pp. 5, 14.
2. Ibid., pp. 6–7, 21.
3. Michael D. Barr and Zlatko Skrbis, *Constructing Singapore: Elitism, Ethnicity and the Nation-building Project* (Copenhagen: NIAS Press, 2008), p. 20; Benedict Anderson, *Imagined Communities: Reflections on the Origins and Spread of Nationalism* (London: Verso, 1991).
4. Hong and Huang, *Scripting of a National History*, pp. 2, 15.
5. Barr and Skrbis, *Constructing Singapore*, pp. 21–23.
6. For instance, John Drysdale, *Singapore: The Struggle for Success* (Sydney: Allen & Unwin, 1984); Dennis Bloodworth, *The Tiger and the Trojan Horse* (Singapore: Times Books International, 1986); Alex Josey, *Lee Kuan Yew: The Crucial Years* (Singapore: Times Books International, 1980); Ernest C.T. Chew and Edwin Lee, eds., *A History of Singapore* (Singapore and New York: Oxford University Press, 1991); C.M. Turnbull, *A History of Singapore, 1819–1988* (Singapore and New York: Oxford University Press, 1989).
7. Lee Kuan Yew, *The Singapore Story: Memoirs of Lee Kuan Yew* (Singapore: Singapore Press Holdings and Times Editions, 1998); idem, *From Third World to First: The Singapore Story 1965–2000. Memoirs of Lee Kuan Yew* (Singapore: Singapore Press Holdings and Times Editions, 2000); Albert Lau, *A Moment of Anguish: Singapore in Malaysia and the Politics of Disengagement* (Singapore: Times Academic Press, 1998).
8. Lam Peng Er and Kevin Y.L. Tan eds., *Lee's Lieutenants: Singapore's Old Guard* (St Leonard's: Allen and Unwin, 1999); Loh Kah Seng, "Within the Singapore Story: The Use and Narrative of History in Singapore", *Crossroads: An Interdisciplinary Journal of Southeast Asia Studies* 12, no. 2 (1998): 8, n. 3.
9. Richard J. Evans, *In Defence of History* (London: Granta, 1997).
10. For a discussion of how a New Singapore History is needed to act as a "counterhegemonic programme to preempt the PAP's self-celebratory propaganda on the eve of Singapore's 50th anniversary as an independent state", see <http://

akikonomu.blogspot.sg/2014/07/living-with-myths-i-singapore-story.html> (accessed 7 August 2014).

11. Michael D. Barr and Carl A. Trocki, "Introduction", in *Paths Not Taken: Political Pluralism in Post-War Singapore*, edited by Michael D. Barr and Carl A. Trocki (Singapore: NUS Press, 2008), p. 3.

12. Ibid., pp. 3–4.

13. Lee Ting Hui, *The Open United Front: The Communist Struggle in Singapore, 1954–1966* (Singapore: South Seas Society, 1996), p. 257.

14. "Alternate" or "New Singapore History" output has become a broad church, spanning the gamut from scholarly works and the memoirs of former detainees, to online blogs, videos and articles. A broadly representative sample would include, *inter alia*, Hong and Huang, *Scripting of a National History*; Barr and Trocki, eds., *Paths Not Taken*; Barr and Skrbis, *Constructing Singapore*; Tan Jing Quee and K.S. Jomo, eds., *Comet In Our Sky: Lim Chin Siong in History* (Kuala Lumpur: INSAN, 2001); Poh Soo Kai, Tang Jing Quee and Koh Kay Yew, eds., *The Fajar Generation: The University Socialist Club and the Politics of Postwar Malaya and Singapore* (Petaling Jaya: Strategic Information and Research Development Centre, 2010); Said Zahari, *Dark Clouds at Dawn: A Political Memoir* (Kuala Lumpur: INSAN, 2001); Poh Soo Kai, Tan Kok Fang and Hong Lysa, eds., *The 1963 Operation Coldstore in Singapore: Commemorating 50 Years* (Petaling Jaya and Kuala Lumpur: Strategic Information and Research Development Centre and Pusat Sejarah Rakyat Malaysia, 2013); Thum Ping Tjin, "The 1963 Operation Coldstore in Singapore", 16 November 2013 <http://www.youtube.com/watch?v=GwviaaULeiY> (accessed 7 August 2014). While some observers may question the need for labelling, it seems apposite to remind one and all that the Alternates have already traversed the labelling path themselves, referring to historians that defend the Singapore Story as "gatekeepers": see for example, Loh Kah Seng and Liew Kai Khiun, eds., *The Makers and Keepers of Singapore History* (Singapore: Ethos Books and Singapore Heritage Society, 2010) and Hong and Huang, *Scripting of a National History*. The current writer himself has been called an "establishment defender": See Geoff Wade, "Singapore's History Wars", 30 April 2014 <http://www. eastasiaforum.org/2014/04/30/singapores-history-wars/> (accessed 7 August 2014).

15. Thum Ping Tjin, "Merger, Acquisition, or Takeover? Singapore's Progressive Left, Merger and the Enduring Consequences of Operation Coldstore", talk delivered at Oxford University, U.K., 31 January 2014.

16. Hong Lysa, "They Do Say the Darnest Things: What a To-Do About Operation Coldstore", 29 September 2014 <http://minimyna.wordpress.com/2014/09/29/ they-do-say-the-darnest-things-what-a-to-do-about-operation-coldstore/> (accessed 2 October 2014).

17. Thum Ping Tjin, "*The Fundamental Issue Is Anti-Colonialism, Not Merger: Singapore's 'Progressive Left', Operation Coldstore, and the Creation of Malaysia*"

(Singapore: Asia Research Institute Working Paper 211, November 2013), pp. 3, 21.

18. Ibid., pp. 5, 15–16; Geoff Wade, "Operation Coldstore: A Key Event in the Creation of Modern Singapore", in *The 1963 Operation Coldstore in Singapore: Commemorating 50 Years*, edited by Poh Soo Kai, Tan Kok Fang and Hong Lysa (Petaling Jaya and Kuala Lumpur: Strategic Information and Research Development Centre and Pusat Sejarah Rakyat Malaysia, 2013), pp. 38–40.

19. Wade, "Operation Coldstore", in Poh, Tan and Hong, eds., *The 1963 Operation Coldstore in Singapore*, p. 68.

20. Ibid., p. 67.

21. M.K. Rajakumar, "Lim Chin Siong's Place in Singapore History", in Tan and Jomo, eds., *Comet in Our Sky*, p. 111.

22. Ibid., p. 98.

23. Ibid. See also Poh Soo Kai, "Living in a Time of Deception", in Poh, Tan and Hong, eds., *The 1963 Operation Coldstore in Singapore*, p. 191; Greg Poulgrain, "Lim Chin Siong in Britain's Southeast Asian De-Colonisation", in Tan and Jomo, eds., *Comet in Our Sky*, p. 123; Thum, *"The Fundamental Issue Is Anti-Colonialism, Not Merger"*, pp. 17–19.

24. Hong and Huang, *Scripting of a National History*, p. 38.

25. On Lim Chin Siong, see the debate between the author and the Alternates Thum Ping Tjin and Hong Lysa: Thum Ping Tjin, "Lim Chin Siong was Wrongfully Detained", *The Online Citizen*, 8 May 2014 <http://www.theonlinecitizen.com/2014/05/lim-chin-siong-was-wrongfully-detained> (accessed 7 August 2014); Kumar Ramakrishna, "Lim Chin Siong and that Beauty World Speech: A Closer Look", *IPS Commons*, 4 June 2014 <http://www.ipscommons.sg/index.php/categories/featured/177-lim-chin-siong-and-that-beauty-world-speech-a-closer-look> (accessed 7 August 2014); and Hong Lysa's somewhat startling riposte: "What is History: A Glance at 'Lim Chin Siong and that Beauty World Speech: A Closer Look'", 10 June 2014 <http://minimyna.wordpress.com/2014/06/10/what-is-history-a-glance-at-lim-chin-siong-and-that-beauty-world-speech-a-closer-look/> (accessed 7 August 2014). The author's defence of the orthodox Coldstore narrative had drawn fire from Hong as well: Kumar Ramakrishna, "Revising the Revisionists: Operation Coldstore in History", *IPS Commons*, 19 February 2014 <http://www.ipscommons.sg/index.php/categories/featured/159-revising-the-revisionists-operation-coldstore-in-history> (accessed 7 August 2014); Hong Lysa, "A Tale Outrageously Told: Days of Rage on the Hock Lee Riots", 23 February 2014 <http://minimyna.wordpress.com/2014/02/23/a-tale-outrageously-told-days-of-rage-on-the-hock-lee-riots/> (accessed 7 August 2014). Hong's reactions to the author's Coldstore piece come after her comments on the Hock Lee riot documentary.

26. Geoff Wade, "Singapore's History Wars", 30 April 2014 <http://www.eastasiaforum.org/2014/04/30/singapores-history-wars/> (accessed 7 August 2014); Tan Bah Bah, "The Lim Chin Siong Story: Clash of the Singapore

Historians", *The Independent* (Singapore), 13 June 2014 <http://theindependent. sg/blog/2014/06/13/lim-chin-siong-story-clash-of-the-singapore-historians/> (accessed 7 August 2014).

27. Donald Low, "What Went Wrong for the PAP in 2011?", in *Hard Choices: Challenging the Singapore Consensus*, edited by Donald Low and Sudhir Vadaketh (Singapore: NUS Press, 2014), p. 168.

28. Hong Lysa, "In Memory of Tan Jing Quee", *The Online Citizen*, 14 June 2014 <http://www.theonlinecitizen.com/2014/06/in-memory-of-tan-jing-quee/> (accessed 7 August 2014). The book launched was *The May 13 Generation: The Chinese Middle Schools Student Movement and Singapore Politics in the 1950s* (Petaling Jaya: Strategic Information and Research Development Centre, 2011). It was edited by Tan Jing Quee, Tan Kok Chiang, and Hong Lysa. The book was launched a week after the May 2011 elections.

29. Ariffin Sha, "Youth of Singapore: It's Time to Rise", 31 July 2014 <http:// ariffin-sha.com/arise-young-singaporeans/> (accessed 7 August 2014).

30. Hong Lysa, "The Battle for Merger Re-Staged: SG50 and the Art of Shadow Boxing", *The Online Citizen*, 7 November 2014 <http://www.theonlinecitizen. com/2014/11/the-battle-for-merger-re-staged-sg-50-and-the-art-of-shadow-boxing/> (accessed 8 November 2014).

31. Rajakumar, "Lim Chin Siong's Place in Singapore History", in Tan and Jomo, eds., *Comet in Our Sky*, p. 113.

32. Singapore's political system has long been the subject of intense debate in the comparative politics domain. Conventional political modernization theories posit that a country as affluent as Singapore should have become a Western-style liberal democracy a long time ago. Scholars variously label Singapore's current system, *inter alia*, as "soft authoritarian", "semi-democratic", "communitarian", "corporatist", "illiberal democratic", and a "networked autocracy". See respectively, Gordon P. Means, "Soft Authoritarianism in Malaysia and Singapore", *Journal of Democracy* 7, no. 4 (Oct 1996): 103–17; William F. Case, "Can the 'Half-way House' Stand? Semidemocracy and Elite Theory in Three Southeast Asian Countries", *Comparative Politics* 28, no. 4 (July 1996): 437–64; Chua Beng Huat, *Communitarian Ideology and Democracy in Singapore* (London: Routledge, 1997); David Brown, *The State and Ethnic Politics in Southeast Asia* (London: Routledge, 1996), chapter 3; Hussin Mutalib, "Illiberal Democracy and the Future of Opposition in Singapore", *Third World Quarterly* 21, no. 2 (2000): 313–42; and Cherian George, "Networked Autocracy: Consolidating Singapore's Political System", in *Political Change, Democratic Transitions and Security in Southeast Asia*, edited by Mely Caballero-Anthony (London: Routledge, 2009), chapter 7.

33. Chua Mui Hoong, "Many Singapore Stories, One Resilient Nation", *Straits Times*, 3 August 2014.

34. <http://www.brainyquote.com/quotes/quotes/g/georgesant101521.html> (accessed 2 October 2014).

1

GOVERNMENT SOURCES
Who Uses Them, and the Alternates'
Unarticulated Ideological Outlook

THE ALTERNATES' COMPLAINT ABOUT
GOVERNMENT SOURCES

In constructing the New Singapore History in general and their version of
Coldstore in particular, the Alternates advance the argument that the original
Singapore Story is flawed and "deeply partial". This is not just because the
prevailing master narrative has been written by the winning PAP side, it has
also been based on previously classified official documents — confidential
correspondence between London, Kuala Lumpur and Singapore, minutes
of meetings, position papers and handwritten notes — said to be deeply
permeated by "the rhetoric of counterinsurgency" that reflects "Cold War
imperatives" and is "dominated by its stark political categories".[1] This "prose
of counterinsurgency", argues T.N. Harper, is manifested in the "plausible
yet Olympian language of the intelligence abstract; the measured tone of
the despatch; the bureaucratic-passive tense"; and allegedly a "'careless and
impressionistic' use of the evidence". He asserts that not only have most
"journalists and observers" providing the historical record "unquestioningly
embraced its assumptions", much of the prevailing accounts have "back-
projected categories of counter-insurgency that were not so hard or discrete
at the time".[2] According to such logic, mainstream accounts of the Singapore
Story in general and the Malayan Emergency and Operation Coldstore in
particular, such as, *inter alia*, the works by John Drysdale, Dennis Bloodworth,
Aloysius Chin and Lee Ting Hui, precisely because they are "based on Special

Branch sources", are *eo ipso* problematic.[3] At the time of writing, incidentally, Hong Lysa warned of the pitfalls of reading the work of the "poisonous and scandalous Dennis Bloodworth", presumably because he was given access to *inter alia*, "ISD [Internal Security Department] records".[4]

Such sentiments are misleading. Contemporaneous and knowledgeable observers who watched the Singapore Special Branch in action in 1956 declared that it was "unquestionably the world's greatest authorities on Communism in Asia".[5] At any rate, a related charge by elements within the Alternate constituency is that those historians and other observers who attempt to defend the Singapore Story, in particular those employed by national security think-tanks linked to the Singapore government, are *ipso facto* themselves suspect of having an immutable counter-insurgency/national security and pro-government bias. Hong Lysa for example, in attacking the author's online defence of the prevailing orthodoxy on Coldstore in February 2014, not only parrots the old refrain that one cannot ignore "the prose of counterinsurgency" that permeates official British records — what she dismisses as "a Special Branch speciality" — she draws attention to the author's employment in the Centre of Excellence for National Security at the S. Rajaratnam School of International Studies, a government-linked institution.[6] As we shall soon see, however, this tactic of diverting attention from the substance of a writer's argument, by focusing attention on his or her institutional or class affiliation, is a well-rehearsed one amongst writers of a particular ideological bent.

CONTRADICTIONS WITHIN THE ALTERNATES' POSITION

Because the Alternates are critical of mainstream historians as well as their use of government records,[7] it is important to address this issue before proceeding further as this book also makes extensive use of government sources. There are several problems with the Alternate critique of the use of government records. First and most obviously, they certainly use them themselves. Greg Poulgrain, for instance, in seeking to "illustrate how the colonial authorities had conspired to ensure Lim Chin Siong did not attain leadership of the PAP", freely indicates, without any qualifying caution whatsoever, that all documentary evidence is "from the Public Record Office in London".[8] As we shall see, moreover, in making their case for the supposed perfidy of Lee Kuan Yew in manipulating matters to destroy the alleged Progressive Left, other Alternates make exhaustive use of declassified government records, the "rhetoric of counterinsurgency" with its supposedly ominous "bureaucratic-passive tense" notwithstanding. The reasons, of course, are obvious to both Alternates and mainstream historians and researchers. Keith Windschuttle reckons that only "a minority of the evidence used by historians is that which has been deliberately preserved for posterity", and that the "biggest single source of evidence comprises the working records of the institutions of the past, records that were created, not for the benefit of future historians, but for contemporary consumption and are thus not tainted by any prescient selectivity"; thus, most of these government records "retain an objectivity of their own".[9] Little surprise then that even the Alternate historian Geoff Wade himself concedes that the "British papers, and particularly the records of the Internal Security Council, are valuable in that they were written not for public consumption and thus reflect quite 'raw' accounts of the events as the British officials and their informants perceived them."[10] Quite true: the bedrock assumption underlying secret and confidential government records is that one might express one's frank assessments without fear of being found out by the wrong audiences. This is precisely why the "Wikileaks"[11] and Edward Snowden scandals[12] (whatever one may personally think of the merits or otherwise of these cases is tangential to the point being made here) have caused such consternation to governments worldwide.

IT'S *HOW* YOU USE THE SOURCES, STUPID

The point of course, is not whether such sources are used or who uses them — be they Alternates or historians in national think-tanks for instance — but rather, how such sources are used. The British historian Richard J. Evans reminds us:[13]

> We ask who has written the document, and why, and to whom the document is addressed, and why, we check it out for internal consistency and consistency with other documents relating to the same subject, and if it contains information derived from other sources, we ask where this information comes from and do our best to check it out too.

Official government records — declassified or otherwise — should therefore be subject to careful source criticism and cross-checks with other types of sources along the lines suggested above. Following the wise counsel of G.R. Elton, while the careful historian studying the circumstances surrounding Coldstore should indeed avoid "childlike trust" in the official documents, he or she should simultaneously avoid the other extreme of a reflexive "excessive scepticism", as both these attitudes spring from the same problematic wellspring of "insufficient thought".[14] In fact if the Alternates take a closer look at Lee Ting Hui's painstakingly constructed pioneering study of the Communist United Front (CUF) in Singapore, they would encounter a meticulous historian who takes

Elton's advice to heart: Lee's bibliographic section runs into more than forty pages, and he takes pains to explain the strengths and limitations of the different types of Special Branch records he peruses for his book.[15] Lee's assessment of three types of official classified documents is worth summarizing as they are relevant to the present study: first, he opines that CPM documents intended by their originators for purely internal consumption by the Party faithful are "the best guides or clues to the mysteries of the Communist movement".[16] Second, confidential governmental assessments of various aspects of the CPM and of individual personalities — while not entirely error-free — are generally reliable simply because government officers had to make decisions and carry out real-world action based on these assessments, and consequently were "in no position to mislead themselves by telling misshaped tales".[17] Third, a very important — if potentially tricky — third category of government records are "unpublished security statements" made by the detainees themselves. Lee admits that such sources had to be handled with "great circumspection" and cross-checked with other sources, including the views of officials familiar with the character and circumstances of the respective detainees. Lee concludes however, that once the veracity of such detainee statements have been cross-checked for "internal consistency", "consistency with statements of other persons, or consistency with yet other sources", they represent "a good guide to understanding Communist activities".[18] The current study employs declassified and still-classified materials along the lines suggested by Lee.

THE "BUREAUCRATIC SCHOLAR" ARGUMENT

Furthermore, it has to be said that certain elements of the Alternate constituency overestimate at best and caricature at worst the degree to which national security think-tanks in Singapore reflect official perspectives. This, one hastens to add, is by no means an original argument. They appear to toe a line promulgated by the political scientists David Martin Jones and Michael L.R. Smith, who have charged that in modernizing Southeast Asian states including Singapore, "the bureaucracy and the local scholarly community" have become "indistinguishable", with the result that so-called "scholar-bureaucrats" nurtured by government-linked think-tanks such as the "Institute of Southeast Asian Studies and the Institute of Defence and Strategic Studies in Singapore and their Malaysian, Indonesian, Thai and Philippine equivalents" have essentially promoted the developmental state's goals and ruling ideology. In short, such think-tanks function chiefly as a "department of government in an organically incorporated body politic".[19] The views of Smith and Jones — and near-ideological bedfellows like some amongst the

Alternates — that national security-related scholarship in Southeast Asia in general and Singapore in particular is inescapably "bureaucratized", are not merely tendentious and sweeping, they are substantively inaccurate. Hong's argument for instance that "privileged access" to government archives in Singapore has been granted only to "a handful of journalists, selected historians and other academics" is overblown.[20] Privileged access is not all it's cracked out to be. The renowned policy-oriented terrorism scholar Alex Schmid, on the other hand, is much more realistic, nuanced and fine-grained in his assessment. He assesses that by and large, it is only government in-house analysts with the necessary security clearances that have access to "top secret" information, while as a rule, academic researchers in think-tanks, even if in regular contact with government, largely have to make do with "open sources" only. Sharing of sensitive classified information with academics, even "trusted" ones, is the exception rather than the rule, because of genuine cultural differences between government and academia not just in Singapore but everywhere:[21]

> Academics want to conduct thorough studies while governments want results at short notice. The questions that interest academics are often not the same for which governments seek answers. Academics are afraid that they will have to give up some of their cherished intellectual independence when working, with or for, governments. Governments, on the other hand, expect that research results will not be used to openly discredit existing government policies when access is granted to privileged information, especially when academic research is government funded.

The current author, in being granted limited access to ISD's still-classified documentation for the purpose of this work, is certainly not the first to be granted such a privilege. As mentioned others, such as Lee Ting Hui, John Drysdale and Dennis Bloodworth, have had "exceptional access" to interviews and sources in the past as well, and such access made for "compelling and authoritative reading".[22] In fact, while the current study was shown to ISD officials for comments and clarification of certain points, the author was at no time instructed in any way to uncritically and fawningly present any form of what Hong Lysa derisively terms "ISD-speak"[23] — quite simply because that would have been the fastest way to undercut the credibility of both the author and that of his academic institution. Essentially, both ISD and the author were in general agreement that it would be beneficial to the public for much of the facts about Coldstore and Lim Chin Siong to be released, so as to correct the serious errors being promulgated for several years now by elements of the Alternate constituency. It is worth noting, moreover, that some Alternates appear to adopt the tactics often used by the acolytes of the French postmodernist historian Michel Foucault; that is, "to refute a speaker, one simply identifies his class position and ignore what he actually says"; and "the focus is directed to the way what is said reflects the prevailing 'discursive formation' or how it is a form of knowledge that serves the power of the authorities concerned."[24] Hence open-minded readers should judge for themselves if, for example, Hong's dismissive comment about the credibility of the current author — simply by virtue of his current employment in the government-linked Rajaratnam School — should perhaps be viewed in this light.

THE GHOST OF FOUCAULT AND THE POSTMODERNIST TURN

This brings us to the thinly veiled ideological/political programme of some key elements within the Alternate constituency: it is worth noting that in 2006 Hong argued for a perspective that sees not one but several Singapore "histories" or more precisely, "discourses, each with political and other motives".[25] She has also argued that "power precedes the narrative proper, contributing to its creation and its interpretation".[26] In other words, she is saying that there can be no objective history, merely a discourse that reflects the interests and ideological preferences of the ruling class. Her colleague Thum Ping Tjin, for his part, adopts a broadly similar outlook, arguing that the eminent student of Singapore history, C.M. Turnbull, was inescapably "part of the British establishment" and hence her "values colour her evaluation" of the historical record.[27] For his part, Loh Kah Seng likewise reminds his Facebook following that despite its international image of a "global city", Singapore is actually "a little town" that is "managed by a local elite, all the way down from the apex of political power to the lower rungs of the bureaucracy and to institutions like the schools and universities"; hence it "is impossible to separate the ideas and policies from the people who manufacture and implement them".[28] Loh, Hong and Thum hence appear — though they at no time articulate this explicitly upfront — to have been significantly influenced by the radical ideas of Foucault, who has argued that history can never be objective but merely represent a "form of knowledge that serves the power of the authorities concerned."[29] While this is not the place to go into a comprehensive discussion of the postmodern turn in history, a few key observations should be made. Granted, the postmodern turn has certainly been very useful in restoring "individual human beings to history" where "social science approaches had more or less written them out". This should be applauded.[30] However, the *ultimate logic* of the postmodernist, Foucaldian approach to history — it should equally be apprehended — is deeply self-defeating: for it suggests that all history is essentially "partisan history" at best and at worst "fiction" — and the historian cannot help but be a "political activist".[31] However, if "political or moral aims become paramount in the writing of history", then, as Richard Evans warns, "scholarship suffers":

> *Facts are mined to prove a case; evidence is twisted to suit a political purpose; inconvenient documents are ignored; sources deliberately misconstrued or misinterpreted.* If historians are not engaged in the pursuit of truth, if the idea of objectivity is merely a concept designed to repress alternative points of view, *then scholarly criteria become irrelevant in assessing the merits of a particular historical argument* (my emphasis).

In fact, Evans shows that some postmodernist-inclined historians actually take the position that rather than "believe in the absolute truth" of what they are writing, they instead "must believe in the moral or political position" they adopt. This, he rightly hints, is not history at all but rather, propaganda.[32] It is not insignificant therefore that the implicit postmodernist orientation of Loh compels him to adopt an inescapably partisan standpoint, arguing almost as an article of faith that the New Singapore History must focus on "rendering power visible in all its forms and ways" in Singapore, with a view to expose the country's "institutional failings".[33] Meanwhile, Hong and Thum have similarly eschewed the once-hallowed value of studied scholarly detachment in favour of high-profile political activism through their very visible and vocal canvassing of support — through heavy and strategic use of the social media — for the Coldstore and other detainees.[34] This is precisely why Hong's attempts to construct an analytical distinction between a purely "academic" history — which she claims she and her postmodernist-inclined Alternate colleagues are merely producing for professional peers — and the "polemical" works by former detainees, appear unpersuasive.[35] Moreover, by further blurring the supposed distinction by working together with the former detainees on high-visibility book projects on the 13 May 1954 Generation (2011) and Operation Coldstore (2013), can she and her like-minded historian colleagues blame dispassionate observers for conceiving of all of them as a largely undifferentiated agenda-driven constituency?

CONTRADICTIONS WITHIN THE FOUCAULDIAN APPROACH AND THE TRADITIONALIST BACKLASH

Hong Lysa suggested in September 2014 that the historian's "political intent" should never overwhelm his or her "scholarship".[36] Despite this, however, we shall see later how certain postmodernist-inclined elements within the Alternate constituency have nevertheless appeared to have succumbed to the stock postmodernist temptation to privilege one's respective moral/political position as the overriding consideration in their interpretation of Coldstore. At this juncture however, it suffices to observe that the postmodernist approach to history has inspired a furious backlash from empirically-minded traditionalist historians who assail it for its internal contradictions. Windschuttle thus correctly points out that Foucault himself, despite his denial of any possibility of objective history, nevertheless makes use of "evidence as though it is given by the historic record" in constructing his own arguments — inadvertently if implicitly conceding therefore that "factual information" does reside at the core of history; and more to the point, that "history remains a search for truth and the construction of knowledge about the past."[37] As we shall see below, Foucauldian-inclined Singaporeans and other Alternates likewise tend to sift the historical record — the notion of any possibility of a historical truth being a pietistic fiction conveniently laid aside for the moment — for material to augment their preferred narratives. This seems to be a kind of backhanded concession that when all is said and done, some kind of objective history is possible after all. To reiterate the great British empirical historian G.R. Elton, therefore:

> Historical method is no more than a recognized and tested way of extracting from what the past has left the true facts and events of the past, *and so far as possible their true meaning and interrelation*, the whole governed by the first principle of historical understanding, namely that the past must be studied in its own right, for its own sake, and its own terms…*Its fundamental principles are only two, and they may be expressed as thus: exactly what evidence is there, and exactly what does it mean?* Knowledge of all the sources, and competent criticism of them — these are the basic requirements of a reliable historiography (my emphasis).[38]

The traditionalist, empirical approach to the Singapore Story in general and to Operation Coldstore in particular adopted in this book, openly and at the outset, acknowledges the current author's own inherent subjectivity. One certainly need not be a postmodernist to recognize this reality. In the final chapter the implications of the current writer's own stance for the current analysis will be further and explicitly fleshed out. Elton reminds us that good historians "constantly regard their own preconceptions in order to minimise the effects these might have on the operation". The careful historian is consequently aware of and guards against the temptation to "sculpt the evidence rather than derive from it".[39] This self-recognition of one's inherent subjectivity impels the current writer to "approach a reconstruction of past reality that may be partial and provisional, and certainly will not be objective, but is nevertheless true".[40] Joyce Appleby, Lynn Hunt, and Margaret Jacob make a similar point, arguing that rather than "underlining the impossibility of total objectivity or completely satisfying causal explanation, we are highlighting the need for the most objective possible explanations as the only way to move forward".[41] In the final analysis, the underlying — and thoroughly unapologetic — assumption of this work is that history, as a discipline that straddles both the humanities and the social sciences, retains its three time-honoured objectives: "it aims to record the truth about what happened in the past"; it seeks to "build a body of knowledge about the past"; and pursues the study of the past "through a disciplined methodology, using techniques and sources" that as a rule, "are accessible to others in the field".[42]

Notes

1. T.N. Harper, "Lim Chin Siong and the 'Singapore Story'", in Tan and Jomo, eds., *Comet in Our Sky*, pp. 6–7.
2. Ibid., pp. 13, 21–22.
3. Ibid., p. 49, n. 8.
4. Hong, "The Battle for Merger Re-Staged".
5. J.B. Perry Robinson, cited in C.M. Turnbull, *A History of Singapore*, p. 263.
6. Hong, "A Tale Outrageously Told: Days of Rage on the Hock Lee Riots". See also her "What is History: A Glance at 'Lim Chin Siong and that Beauty World Speech: A Closer Look'", 10 June 2014 <http://minimyna.wordpress.com/2014/06/10/what-is-history-a-glance-at-lim-chin-siong-and-that-beauty-world-speech-a-closer-look/> (accessed 7 August 2014).
7. As mentioned, government records employed in this study from the U.K. National Archives/Public Record Office and the Rhodes House Library, Oxford have been declassified. Records from the ISD Heritage Centre though remain classified.
8. Greg Poulgrain, "Lim Chin Siong in Britain's Southeast Asian De-Colonisation", in Tan and Jomo, eds., *Comet in Our Sky*, pp. 116–17.
9. Keith Windschuttle, *The Killing of History: How Literary Critics and Social Theorists are Murdering Our Past* (New York: The Free Press, 1996), p. 221.
10. Geoff Wade, "'Operation Cold Store': A Key Event in the Creation of Malaysia and in the Origins of Modern Singapore", paper presented at the 21st Conference of the International Association of Historians of Asia, 21–25 June 2010.
11. See <https://wikileaks.org/About.html> (accessed 2 October 2014).
12. For an interesting interview with Snowden, see James Bamford, "The Most Wanted Man in the World", *Wired.com*, 22 August 2014 <http://www.wired.com/2014/08/edward-snowden/> (accessed 2 October 2014).

13. Evans, *In Defence of History*, p. 110.
14. G.R. Elton, *The Practice of History* (London: Fontana Press, 1987), p. 105.
15. Lee Ting Hui, *The Open United Front: The Communist Struggle in Singapore, 1954–1966* (Singapore: South Seas Society, 1996), pp. 353–96.
16. Ibid., p. 353.
17. Ibid., p. 354.
18. Ibid.
19. David Martin Jones and M.L.R. Smith, *ASEAN and East Asian International Relations: Regional Delusion* (Cheltenham: Edwar Elgar, 2006), pp. 33–34. The Institute of Defence and Strategic Studies was renamed the S. Rajaratnam School of International Studies in January 2007.
20. Hong Lysa, "Time to Understand Singapore's History in All it Complexity", *The Online Citizen,* 25 March 2014 <http://www.theonlinecitizen.com/2014/03/time-to-understand-spores-history-in-all-its-complexity/> (accessed 7 October 2014).
21. A.P. Schmid, "Terrorism Research and Government", International Center for Counter-Terrorism (ICCT) Commentary, 18 April 2014.
22. Historian Albert Lau makes this point. See Lam and Tan, eds., *Lee's Lieutenants*, p. 232, n. 1.
23. Hong, "A Tale Outrageously Told: Days of Rage on the Hock Lee Riots".
24. Windschuttle, *Killing of History*, p. 132.
25. Karl Hack, "Framing Singapore's History", in *Studying Singapore's Past: C.M. Turnbull and the History of Modern Singapore*, edited by Nicholas Tarling (Singapore: NUS Press, 2012), p. 19.
26. Hong and Huang, *Scripting of a National History*, pp. 15–16.
27. Thum, "The Limitations of Monolingual History", in Tarling, ed., *Studying Singapore's Past*, p. 104.
28. Loh Kah Seng, "Singapore Histories: Titles, Reputations, Bosses and Subordinates in a Little Town", 1 October 2014 <https://www.facebook.com/notes/kah-seng/singapore-histories-titles-reputations-bosses-and-subordinates-in-a-little-town/10152729122973887?pnref=lhc> (accessed 1 November 2014).
29. Windschuttle, *Killing of History*, p. 132. The "postmodernist perspective", of Hong Lysa for example, has not escaped the notice of other scholars, although the fuller implications of this stance are unexamined. See Lam Peng Er and Kevin Y.L. Tan, "Introduction", in Lam and Tan, eds., *Lee's Lieutenants*, p. xviii.
30. Evans, *In Defence of History*, p. 248.
31. Windschuttle, *Killing of History*, pp. 136–37.
32. Evans, *In Defence of History*, p. 219.
33. Loh, "Singapore Histories: Titles, Reputations, Bosses and Subordinates in a Little Town".
34. For instance, Thum and Hong participated in a roundtable in November 2013 commemorating the launch of the book *The 1963 Operation Coldstore in*

Singapore: Commemorating 50 Years, edited by Poh Soo Kai, Tan Kok Fang and Hong Lysa (Petaling Jaya and Kuala Lumpur: Strategic Information and Research Development Centre and Pusat Sejarah Rakyat Malaysia, 2013) <https://www.youtube.com/watch?v=GwviaaULeiY> (accessed 2 October 2014).

35. See Hong Lysa, "Rejoinder on 'Alternative Narratives: The Danger of Romanticising the Other'", *RSIS Commentary* 117/2010, 17 September 2010 <http://www.rsis.edu.sg/wp-content/uploads/2014/07/RSIS11720103.pdf> (accessed 7 October 2014). Hong was responding to a commentary by RSIS colleague Ong Weichong, "Alternative Histories: The Danger of Romanticising the Other", *RSIS Commentary* 113/2010, 14 September 2010 <http://www.rsis.edu.sg/wp-content/uploads/2014/07/RSIS11320103.pdf> (accessed 7 October 2014).

36. Hong, "They Do Say the Darnest Things".

37. Windschuttle, *Killing of History*, p. 154.

38. Elton, *Practice of History*, pp. 86–87.

39. "G.R. Elton", in *The History Debate*, edited by Juliet Gardner (London: Collins and Brown, 1990), pp. 6–8.

40. Evans, *In Defence of History*, p. 249.

41. John Tosh, ed., *Historians on History* (Harlow, Essex: Pearson Education, 2000), p. 311.

42. Windschuttle, *Killing of History*, p. 185.

2

WAS THERE *REALLY* A DANGEROUS COMMUNIST UNITED FRONT?

While Alternates like Thum Ping Tjin go so far as to declare that the "historiography is clear on the lack of evidence of communism"[1] in Singapore's post-war history, most voices within the Alternate constituency argue instead that while the Communist Party of Malaya (CPM) organization was "central to the left", and its "cadres played a pivotal part in trade unionism and popular front politics", its role has nevertheless been exaggerated in the Singapore Story.[2] T.N. Harper for instance argues that the insurrection "now seems like a concatenation of forces from below", over which the CPM "exercised little direction".[3] For their part Loh Kah Seng and Michael Fernandez insist that it is "simplistic to blame the violence" perpetrated by leftist unions in the mid-1950s "solely on communist instigation".[4] The former leftist Dominic Puthucheary, challenging the oft-quoted metaphor in the Singapore Story that Lee Kuan Yew had to "ride the Communist Tiger" to power in Singapore, articulated the Alternate position well:[5]

> Was there really a tiger? Did the tiger want to swallow anybody? Or was there a movement with a wide range of political views from extreme left to social democratic right which attempted to create an alternative to a colonially-designed society, an embryo for creating a new Malaya?

The sum total of the Alternate position, therefore, is that while there certainly was an anti-colonial Progressive Left movement in Singapore in the 1950s to early 1960s, this was not necessarily one that was closely directed by the CPM behind the scenes. Hence Harper suggests that the "very idea of a 'Communist United Front' is perhaps a misnomer: most of the groups caught up in leftist popular radicalism" were "neither communist, united, nor a front for anybody but themselves".[6] Michael Barr and Carl Trocki echo this assessment, arguing that while the CPM "could offer moral and spiritual leadership, the party on the ground in Singapore had little influence over everyday events", and that "[s]tudent and labour movements, strikes and demonstrations were often the result of spontaneous actions by the individuals directly involved". They thus challenge the conventional notion that the CPM "posed a serious threat to Singapore's established order".[7]

The Alternates' position is fraught with problems. They as a whole pay scant attention to the actual mechanics of the Communist United Front (CUF) and its symbiotic relationship with armed struggle, either in theory, or in practice in Singapore in the 1950s. This is unsurprising given how published writings by leading CPM personalities such as Chin Peng[8] and Fang Chuang Pi[9] scarcely appear to systematically and sufficiently inform Alternate assessments of the nature of the Communist threat. Without a detailed and somewhat forensic understanding of the way the CUF evolved in theory and then developed and operated in Singapore in the period under review, the rationale for Coldstore can never be understood. Furthermore, we shall see that the CUF was a living, breathing, stubbornly resilient and constantly evolving entity in Singapore. While it is true that the CUF was not always able to exercise fine-grained control over key events throughout the tumultuous 1950s, this is not the point. Its demonstrated potential, if CUF leaders so decided, for fomenting violence — and the ominous implications for political and ethnic harmony in the new Malaysian Federation — was never in serious doubt. Hence the CUF was fully a "serious threat to Singapore's established order".

THE COMMUNIST UNITED FRONT IN THEORY

Communism, as envisaged by German philosopher Karl Marx (1818–83), sought to resolve an ancient dilemma that had befuddled generations of European thinkers for centuries — the seeming contradiction between a "philosophy and religion which teach that all men are brothers, and an economic system which organizes them as masters and servants". Marx's theoretical solution — which he claimed derived from scientific principles applied to the study of history — was to create via a revolution led by the "new fourth estate of the industrial workers", a "classless society in which all the means of production, distribution, and exchange will be owned by the community, and from which the State — conceived as an instrument of coercion and oppression — will have disappeared".[10] In classic Communist theory, between the final "revolution that abolishes the capitalist order and this communist society" is a transitional phase known as the "dictatorship of the proletariat" or Socialism. Marx's Russian disciples agreed with him that while in the final stage of the Communist utopia, the guiding principle would be "from each according to his ability, to each according to his needs", in the transitional stage of Socialism it would have to be "from each according to his ability, to each according to his work". As R.N. Carew Hunt points out, the essential difference between Socialism and Communism is over means, not ends. Hence while the "socialists hold that they can both introduce and maintain their system by democratic methods", the "communists hold that neither is possible".[11] While Marx had expected proletarian revolts to break out in Europe, these did not materialize. The great Russian Marxist disciple Vladimir Lenin (1870–1924) soon proffered an interpretation. He explained that living conditions had improved under capitalism, partly because the European bourgeoisie had founded overseas colonies including in Asia, which had generated great wealth to be expropriated back to Europe to be distributed amongst European workers, thereby dulling their revolutionary potential. Lenin thus assessed that besides inciting European workers to overthrow the bourgeoisie, much effort was also needed to "agitate the subject peoples in the European colonies and dependencies to stand up and overthrow colonial rule". Hence while Communism as a modern international movement began in the mid-nineteenth century in Europe, following Lenin's victory in the Bolshevik Revolution in Tsarist Russia in October 1917, he set up the Third International, better known as the Comintern, whose aim was to spread Communism throughout the world, including Asia. It was the Comintern that brought Communism to Singapore and Malaya.[12]

Practical real-world difficulties in seizing political power via armed revolution meant that Communists had to be flexible in their strategies employed; sole reliance on violence was not always possible especially from a position of material weakness. In setting up the Comintern in March 1919, Lenin had decried the "abstract communism" of the younger revolutionaries, which "had not matured to the point of practical mass political action". Insisting that rejecting compromise on principle is "childish", he urged his acolytes to know how to "combine the strictest loyalty to the ideas of communism with an ability to make all the necessary practical compromises — to tack, make agreements, zigzags, retreats, and so on". Hence was born the strategy of the united front. Carew Hunt most presciently explains:[13]

The object of all communist parties is to capture the masses; and in their struggle for power their real enemies are not the right-wing parties (with whom they will deal at their own leisure after the revolution has been achieved), *but the socialists, who are competing with them for the goodwill of the workers.* But while the communists thus regard the socialists with an especial bitterness, it is precisely with them, or with their leaders, that the tactics of the united front require them to cooperate, *though the ultimate end of this cooperation is to drive them off the field.* As the socialists are perfectly aware of this, and have themselves no love for the communists, the employment of united-front tactics…*calls for considerable ingenuity* (my emphasis).

In Communist theory, the united front strategy took two forms: "united front from above", in which the Communists "established contact with the masses" by collaborating with the leaders of non-Communist organizations, or "united front from below", which meant "appealing to the rank-and-file members of such organizations over the heads of their leaders".[14] Significantly, Lenin added that "Communists must be able to agree to sacrifices and even if need be to resort to all sorts of stratagems, manoeuvres, illegal methods, evasions and subterfuges in order to achieve their end".[15]

CUF ORIGINS AND OVERALL STRATEGY IN SINGAPORE

The CPM came into being in April 1930, when the Comintern splintered the existing Nanyang Communist Party that had had jurisdiction beyond Malaya over neighbouring countries, such as Thailand, into various national parties, including the CPM. The CPM was placed under direct control of the Far Eastern Bureau of the Comintern. It was really from October 1936, following the arrival of several seasoned Communists from Amoy, China, that the CPM became more active in united front work; enjoying a "vast increase" in "membership, financial resources and influence" in the next three years by capitalizing on anti-Japanese zeal amongst Malayan Chinese in the wake of the Japanese attack on China in 1937.[16] The CPM's stock enjoyed a further uptick during the Japanese Occupation as it mounted — in the guise of the Malayan People's Anti-Japanese Army (MPAJA) — the only serious armed resistance against Japanese forces, due in no small part to the arms and training its mainly Chinese guerrillas received from the British.[17] From the start, the CPM was compelled to operate clandestinely as its aim was after all to overthrow the colonial British authorities. Having read with diligence the works of Russian and Chinese Communists, the CPM leadership understood the need to be flexible in the approach adopted for seizing power.

In terms of strategies of armed struggle, they noted that while Marx had urged European workers to fight the bourgeoisie without stressing the need for alliances with other classes, Lenin had advocated a "worker-peasant alliance" to pursue the "socialist revolution", something the CPM in fact adopted in Malaya up till 1940.

However, Mao Zedong became more influential in shaping CPM leaders' thinking after 1940. The Party thereafter, following Mao, broadened Lenin's original united front to a "four-class alliance" of workers, peasants, "petty bourgeoisie" or the middle class, and the "national bourgeoisie", to achieve not so much a socialist but rather a "new democratic revolution". The CPM also identified students, women, and youth as potentially potent social forces to be tapped for the revolution. The composition of the united front aside, the CPM adopted a general policy of armed struggle from its very beginnings to the end of the Japanese Occupation; from 1948 to 1954, and then from 1961 onwards.[18] Historian Lee Ting Hui however notes that the CPM also adopted a strategy of "peaceful politicking" or "peaceful struggle" in the periods 1945–48 and 1954–61. While the peaceful struggle between 1945 and 1948 was the brainchild of Lai Tek, the CPM Secretary-General from 1939 to 1947, the Soviet leader Nikita Khrushchev was the inspiration for the CPM's peaceful struggle from 1954 to 1961.[19] From 1951 onwards — with the intensification of geopolitical and ideological competition between the nuclear-armed Western and Eastern blocs — both the Soviet and Chinese Communist Parties influenced the CPM's strategic thinking, thereby integrating the latter within the wider Cold War conflict.[20] By 1960, however, the CPM had come firmly under the control of the Chinese Communists, whose consent was required or else "nothing could move".[21]

In any case, be it armed or peaceful struggle, the united front approach was always used by the CPM. As Lee Ting Hui memorably put it, "one could say that the CPM was a person and the armed or peaceful struggle, and the united front were his two arms with which he did combat with his enemies."[22] The logic behind the CPM's united front strategy was as follows:[23]

> *A better policy was to form an alliance with all other political forces...which also happened to share the same enemy, and confront the enemy with this combined strength.* This way, victory in the struggle would be more assured. *The other political forces thus befriended, or made use of, might also be, fundamentally speaking, one's enemies. However, for the time being, conflicts with such must be set aside.* Principal contradictions must take precedence over subsidiary ones. Only after the arch enemy had been disposed of should secondary enemies be dealt with. Of course, amongst the secondary enemies, there

are also the greater and lesser ones. When the opportunity came to deal with them, they had also to be categorized into principal and subordinate targets... *Thus in the long-run, all enemies could be eliminated one by one. This method of dealing with enemies was the tactic of the united front* (my emphasis).

Furthermore, in the case of a united front employing the peaceful struggle strategy, the CPM, unsurprisingly, much preferred to operate openly and legally, as this enabled them to easily "make contact with workers, peasants and so on, and recruit them into their organisations".[24] However, the period 1945–48 was the only time when it enjoyed legal status, and could function openly and legally. That is, the CPM had an open office, which established ties with other parties, as well as an underground section — the Singapore Town Committee — that controlled overall operations and secretly infiltrated men into such parties.[25] This was always the ideal state of affairs for the Communists. Nevertheless, the open and legal status was always only a means to an end. Yeong Kwo, CPM Deputy Secretary-General, put it succinctly:[26]

> We are no believers in legality and are certainly not content with an open and legal struggle. *Our aim is to cover up and support an illegal struggle by means of open and legal activities.* Open and legal activities are used to create the conditions in preparation for a struggle to overthrow the enemy with illegal revolutionary methods (my emphasis).

In the peaceful struggle period 1954–61, however, because the CPM failed to secure legal recognition, particularly at the abortive Baling Peace Talks of December 1955 (see below), it had no choice but to execute its peaceful struggle strategy underground and illegally, and hence "supervise mass and united front movements in an indirect manner" in the "form of infiltration".[27] From 1954, therefore, when the CPM Central Committee led by Secretary-General Chin Peng switched from the failed armed struggle strategy launched in 1948 to a policy that acknowledged the error of neglecting "masses work" and henceforth pursued a peaceful — but clandestine — struggle, a "closely-knit complex" — the CUF of yore — gained significant ground in Singapore.[28] A secret CPM directive laid out the *modus operandi* of the CUF:[29]

> The progressive forces should formulate plans and make arrangements to assign cadres and Party members to *infiltrate factories, mines, villages, streets, schools and people of all strata*, use all kinds of ways and means to unite and organize the broad masses and assign personnel to join all kinds of public bodies, take part in them with the *aim of seizing control* so that the Party and the people will have extensive contact and therein press on

with the efforts to recruit Party members and continually expand the Party organization (my emphasis).

The basic aim — Chin Peng himself averred later in 1963 — was that CUF organizations could "undermine public order and create political crises in the country" through "skillful exploitation of controversial issues and public grievances, genuine or otherwise", so as to "fan hatred toward the Government". Thereafter, by exploiting the ensuing instability, the CUF could "take over state power through a well-planned and ably directed insurrection".[30] Hence the Alternate constituency's view of the mass disturbances of the 1950s as being merely an inchoate "concatenation of forces from below" is quite simply, inaccurate. In the CUF strategy, the Party "stood above the rest", acting as the vanguard of the unions, peasant societies and other mass organizations in its sway. The CPM's control over the CUF was exercised in one of two ways: either the Party deployed members in various organizations to form their leadership, or it "recruited their leaders to become members of the Party". Of course from the CPM perspective, the ideal situation was "naturally to secure as strong a leadership as possible over the subordinate sections", but in practice, this was not always feasible. Hence if the leadership in the penetrated organization was strong, control was ensured, but if weak, CPM "influence would be only marginal".[31] Aloysius Chin, a former senior Malaysian Special Branch officer and acknowledged CPM expert, also made the important point that Communist elements working in the CUF knew how to keep their heads down to avoid detection:[32]

> Agents infiltrated into organizations ... *took the greatest care to conceal their connections with the CPM and might work for several years in this way without being exposed. Being trained communists they did not require frequent direction from the Party.* They were able to interpret events, and any published statements that might be made by the Party, in the correct Party manner, and unless something went wrong *there was no need for them to have any contact for long periods with their superiors in the Party.* The organizations themselves might often not realize the manner in which they were being exploited and in the meantime their members were being subconsciously indoctrinated with communist ideas (my emphasis).

As we shall see, such security-obsessed Communist tradecraft was precisely one key reason why it was so difficult in the period leading up to Coldstore to identify hard evidence of CUF machinations beforehand, thereby leading the Alternates to argue — wrongly — that there was *ergo* no such thing as a Communist conspiracy at all. We shall return to this all-important theme in a future chapter.

THE EVOLUTION AND ACTIONS OF THE CUF
IN SINGAPORE

Phase 1: 1945–48

The secret CUF apparatus in Singapore was controlled by the Singapore Town Committee (CPMSTC) which, following the Japanese surrender in September 1945, was led by the then CPM Secretary-General Lai Tek.[33] Lai Tek's successor, Chin Peng later asserted that the CPMSTC enjoyed a "high level of autonomy" from the Central Committee of the Party.[34] Capitalizing on post-war Singapore's inclement socioeconomic conditions, which included inadequate official rice rations, insufficient housing, high rents, overcrowding, high cost of living and low wages, and fully exploiting its new above-ground, open and legal status — the reward for wartime collaboration with the British — the CPMSTC rapidly rebuilt its old networks that had been destroyed by the Japanese. It set up Directing Committees that in turn oversaw Branch Organizations that penetrated youth groups, peasants' groups, womens' associations, and unions in the transport, rubber, handicraft, naval base and other industries. Of note, the CPM-dominated Malayan General Labour Union organized a two-day strike in January 1946 involving 150,000 workers. The three-man Branch Organizations — the basic CUF building block — disseminated propaganda, recruited new blood, maintained discipline and collected subscriptions from members as well as donations from supporters. The CPMSTC also set up so-called Party Corps, basically CPM members under direct CPMSTC control, to infiltrate various organizations and capture key portfolios such as chairman, secretary, general affairs officer etc. The task of the Party Corps officials was to discreetly steer the policies of penetrated bodies in the general direction of CUF policy. The CPMSTC, equally keen to reach out to the "English-speaking masses", penetrated the Malayan Democratic Union (MDU), an English-educated, left-wing, anti-colonial political party as well.[35]

Under CPMSTC direction, a united front was formed with political parties from the three main ethnic groups: the Malay Nationalist Party (MNP), The Malayan Indian Congress (MIC), and the MDU. The MNP also had a Malay-based network called Pusat Tenaga Rakyat (PUTERA). After the Malayan General Labour Union split in 1946 into the Singapore Federation of Trade Unions (SFTU) for Singapore island, and the Pan-Malayan Federation of Trade Unions (PMFTU) for the peninsula, the CPMSTC brought the PMFTU together with its other front organizations, the New Democratic Youth League (NDYL),[36] the Women's Federation, the MPAJA Ex-Service

Comrades Association, the MDU and MIC to form the All-Malaya Council of Joint Action (AMCJA). This was later merged with PUTERA to form the AMCJA-PUTERA united front against the British. As Lee Ting Hui argues, the CPMSTC cooperation with the MDU, MIC and MNP represented a "united front from above". At the same time, because the CPMSTC had infiltrated its members into leadership roles within the MNP and MDU, this was an example of a "blocs within" approach.[37] So successful were the CPM's post-war efforts that its Secretary-General Chin Peng even publicly observed in 2003 that by 1947 the "CPM controlled labour unions throughout Malaya and Singapore" and pointedly, "[o]ur political influence and following had never been stronger".[38]

Phase 2: 1948–54

The onset of the Emergency in June 1948 ended the open and legal, peaceful struggle phase, and the CPM — somewhat caught on the back foot — embarked on armed struggle.[39] This move severely disrupted the CPMSTC and its network in Singapore, with most CPM members going underground, or withdrawing to the Malayan jungle to join the Malayan People's Anti-British Army (MPABA — later renamed the Malayan National Liberation Army or MNLA). The CUF in Singapore all but collapsed as the CPMSTC's various front organizations, including the SFTU, PMFTU, the NDYL and others, were banned under the newly enacted Societies Ordinance and the Trade Union Ordinance; the MDU on its part dissolved itself after Emergency was declared. Mass arrests also took place in June 1948.[40] It was only in August 1948, that Lau Kwong and four other ranking Communists steadied and reorganized the CPMSTC, slowly resuscitating the CUF network on the island, reconstituting District Committees and Branches amongst Chinese middle-school students, factory, naval base and rural workers. In particular, the District Committees were soon rationalized into the Trades Committee, Rural Committee, and Students' Committee, "that oversaw the work of Communist cadres in factories in the Chinatown and North Bridge Road areas, rural factories and villages, and the Chinese middle schools respectively".[41]

Of particular importance was the setting up in late 1948 of the Singapore People's Anti-British League (ABL), based on the format of the old Anti-Japanese League during the Occupation.[42] While Alternate historians at times appear to diminish the ABL's CPM signature, even arguing that it could be seen as a "legitimate vehicle for democratic socialism",[43] this is really misleading. The ABL was a full-fledged "underground peripheral organization" led by the CPMSTC, and contributed much to CPM ranks, through associated bodies such as the important Students' ABL, an organ directed by the Students' Committee, which maintained penetration of the strategic "student masses".[44] This way, the CPMSTC was able to start up secret cells within leading Chinese middle schools like Chinese High School, Chung Cheng High School, Nan Chiau Girls' High School, Chung Hwa Girls' High School, Yock Eng High School, and Nanyang Girls' High School, among others.[45] The ABL's functions were to strengthen the anti-British independence struggle, safeguard the core leadership of the CPM, and build up the latter's influence.[46] ABL members were "considered sympathisers of the MCP and on probation to become full MCP members should they be considered up to the mark".[47] In particular, ABL members were evaluated based on their willingness to make sacrifices such as engaging in "illegal activities and violence" before they could be considered for absorption as CPM members.[48] The ABL also started an important English-speaking Branch, drawn from the ranks of former MDU members, led by the brilliant if enigmatic Raffles College graduate Eu Chooi Yip, or ECY, as Chin Peng apparently called him, who was regarded by befuddled Special Branch officers as "slippery as the eel" and adept at adopting "numerous living covers" to "remain elusive and free from security dragnets and clampdowns".[49] The ABL greatly helped CPM recruitment through its propaganda work, in particular through putting out the clandestine Chinese vernacular newsletter *Freedom News*, as well as two English publications, *Freedom* and *Battlefront*.[50] Such documents like *Freedom News* were only for CPM/ABL members' internal consumption.[51] In fact, to be caught with a copy of *Freedom News* in one's possession in the open meant "instant arrest".[52] Because the slippery ECY was also effectively bilingual in English and Chinese, and was known to have a "quick, incisive pen", he became the chief editor of *Freedom News* in January 1949 when it was restarted by the CPMSTC.[53]

At any rate, by December 1948, Chin Peng and the CPM Central Committee had decided to follow "Mao's blueprint for revolutionary warfare to the letter", to achieve the ultimate goal of a "People's Democratic Republic of Malaya".[54] In this connection, Chin Peng clarified that in this phase of armed struggle, "the main principle" is that "the armed struggle is the main form of struggle", and that the "underground and legal struggle should co-ordinate with the armed struggle".[55] It is worth emphasizing that the Alternate constituency has failed to appreciate this very important point: the CUF existed to complement the armed struggle — and Chin Peng himself regarded armed struggle "as inevitable".[56] Singapore was hence seen as "strategic zone of action" within which CUF elements could "distract part of the enemy forces" from the latter's main counter-insurgency effort in the Malayan jungles up north. Accordingly, from February 1950 the CPMSTC employed the so-called Workers' Protection Corps — under the direction of the CPMSTC's Trades Committee — in a "campaign of violence and intimidation" in Singapore, including burning of taxis owned by British companies, extorting wealthy contractors and businessmen, to shootings, arson, and grenade attacks — including a grenade attack on the British Governor at Happy World Park. The CPM hoped that apart from its desire "to pin down troops that might otherwise be sent to Malaya to suppress" MNLA units, the efforts of the Protection Corps would boost recruitment efforts in Singapore, especially of young Chinese.[57] The CPMSTC's violent campaign in Singapore, however, proved counter-productive. First, it "scared away" the upper- and middle-class Chinese, thereby preventing their induction into the CUF and enhancing the latter's access to material resources and numbers. Second and worse, it provoked a strong counter-reaction from the British, which resulted in another major round of arrests and disruption of the network on the island in 1951.[58]

In fact, the CPMSTC itself had already been disrupted by December 1950.[59] Overseen since January that year by Central Committee Member (CCM) Hor Lung of the CPM South Malaya Bureau, who was based across the Causeway in Johore, the CPMSTC virtually collapsed when three leading members were all arrested throughout the year: Deputy Secretary Tan Swee Hiong @ Chen Xia was picked up in April, while Secretary Tay Ah Meng and Committee Member Guo Ren Huey were detained in December. Thereafter from early 1951 onwards Wong Mau Choong @ Wan Fung of the CPMSTC's Students' Committee became the *de facto* CUF leader in Singapore. He reported briefly to CPM Central Committee Member (CCM) and Deputy Secretary-General Yeong Kwo, and subsequently to Hor Lung in Johore. However, Wong Mau Choong himself was arrested in January 1954, with the result that leadership of the CPMSTC on the island itself passed over to Wong Meng Keong, a deceptively "unremarkable" young Chinese man who was a "compulsive womaniser" and who had multiple aliases, *inter alia*: Ng Meng Chiang, Ng Meng Keong, Chow Kwang (or Zhou Guang), and most colourfully, Comrade D. Following the 1951 police crackdown in Singapore, Chin Peng had passed instructions to the remaining key CPMSTC leaders to withdraw to safer locations. While in the next two years some left for China, ECY and others fled south to the Indonesian Rhio Islands and also Jakarta, establishing themselves there for more than a decade and turning the Rhios into the key staging area for the "Singapore urban guerrillas". Between 1951 and 1957, Yeong Kwo (till his demise in August 1956, at which point Hor Lung stepped in) tenuously kept the Indonesian-based ECY in touch with CPM Central Committee policy directives, while the latter in turn kept a strategic watching brief over the battered CPMSTC apparatus in Singapore. However, until 1957, operational direction of the CUF within Singapore itself was in the hands of Comrade D. The latter was notably assisted by a highly dedicated young man named Fang Chuang Pi, later to be known more famously as the Plen, a collaborator with ECY on *Freedom News*, who had narrowly escaped arrest in mid-1951 by dramatically diving into the pond of a pigsty during a police raid on the secret production site of the newspaper.[60]

Phase 3: 1954–56

By late 1951, the CPM began to realize that the armed struggle strategy was flawed and the insurgency effort in Malaya was flagging. Chin Peng himself admitted that the terror campaign launched by the CPM when the Emergency started had been counter-productive, as it had antagonized the masses. Hence in October 1951 a new set of directives were issued, emphasizing that "no unnecessary acts of terror should be used against the masses" and that instead, "every attempt should be made to win over the masses".[61] Chin Peng also conceded that a big mistake by the CPM in June 1948 had been "the withdrawal of all its underground and United Front cadres into the jungle", which had "brought about the immediate collapse of the CPM front organizations and revolutionary masses movements". It was felt that henceforth through "CUF tactics, the CPM would be able to penetrate open and legal organizations" which would "provide excellent cover for the CPM elements", thereby preventing "early exposure and arrests" while mobilizing "popular support from all sectors of the population".[62] This policy stance was affirmed by CPM Politburo members Zhang Lingyun @ Siao Chang and Chen Rui, who were based in China and who following a thorough review of the operational situation in Malaya and Singapore, observed that the problem was "neglecting masses work". They emphasized that "Revolutionary Masses Movement and United Front Work" were of equal importance to "Revolutionary Armed Struggle". They thus stressed the need for expanding CUF activities "in order to acquire majority support" and "to establish some firm foothold in masses front organizations".[63] In particular, given the inclement operational circumstances in the Malayan jungles, Singapore island by 1954 was seen as an "offshore sanctuary and supply base, a springboard for the future subversion of the mainland".[64] Due to disrupted communications following the colonial authorities' crackdown on the CPMSTC in Singapore, the CPM's so-called October 1951 Directives took a while to "to filter down to the scattered, semi-autonomous lower-level cells on the island". Hence some cells heard of the injunction to suspend "acts of disturbance and sabotage" and instead "step up the lawful struggle in the open united front", only in early 1953, others even later.[65]

In any case, beginning in 1954, CUF work in Singapore experienced a significant uptick. This was partly facilitated as well by the implementation of the British-sponsored Rendel Commission findings in February, ushering in constitutional reforms as a step towards eventual self-government. The Rendel reforms expanded the Singapore electorate fourfold through the automatic registration as eligible voters of all British subjects born in Singapore and introduced a new Legislative Assembly, of which twenty-five members would be elected, six nominated and three ex-officio. While there would also be six elected members out of a governing council of nine ministers, the key portfolios of chief secretary, financial secretary and the attorney-general would still be in British hands.[66] While the Rendel reforms were certainly cautious, making provision for — in reality — only partial self-government in Singapore after the upcoming April 1955 elections, its scope did imply a lifting of some aspects of the tough Emergency Regulations in place since June 1948, allowing for the "easy formation of political parties, trade unions and other organizations, and minimum restrictions on propaganda". As Lee Ting Hui points out, the "CPM decided to take advantage of the opening" afforded by the fortuitous Rendel reforms; "it could go in strength into mass and united front work".[67]

At any rate the centerpiece of the CUF struggle by 1954 was the Chinese middle schools. The CPMSTC Students' Committee and under it, the Students' ABL had survived the harsh crackdown of 1951 and since then had in effect been the "emergency nerve centre" of the CUF on the island.[68] A hot-button issue that cropped up at this time was National Service. The British colonial authorities had introduced National Service (NS) Bills in Malaya and Singapore in 1952, identifying males aged between eighteen to fifty-five years as liable for compulsory service, either in the armed forces, the police or civil defence. The National Service Ordinance was subsequently passed in December 1953, targeted at males aged between eighteen and twenty. Registration was to occur in April and May 1954. Comrade D, as seen, was at the time the directing figure of the CUF on Singapore island — overseeing the "development of the various mass organisations and the united front" and tasked to resolve "all the problems which these faced".[69] As he controlled the Students' Committee of the CPMSTC, he immediately saw the NS issue as an ideal way to jumpstart the open united front struggle. He thus issued a directive on 30 March 1954 calling for an all-out effort to oppose the NS Bill. Hence throughout March and April 1954 a variety of pamphlets, posters and cartoons was disseminated to ABL/CPM members. This included a special *Freedom News* supplement of 27 March 1954 exhorting students to "boycott recruitment and refuse to be sent to death" and further warnings that NS was an "evil intrigue" of the British to trick the local people to fight for the perpetuation of colonial rule.[70]

Moreover, rather than matters fermenting "spontaneously", as the Alternates seem to believe, "specially selected" personnel were sent to schools and factories where there were young males liable for call-up to actively mobilize them against the bill. In particular, at Chung Cheng High School, ABL members Lim Hock Koon[71] and Lim Kim Chuan[72] were instructed by their immediate superior, Woo Chong Poh @ Comrade R[73] to form an Action Committee with three other Chung Cheng High students with ABL/CPM links, to spearhead the anti-NS campaign in the school. This Chung Cheng High Action Committee planned, coordinated and directed the campaign at school level, as well as organized protest meetings with other Chinese middle schools, gathering signatures to petition British Governor William Goode against NS enlistment. The committee even organized lorries to ferry students to the demonstration site at King George V Park, and briefed students on how to counter police actions and the use of tear gas. The Chung Cheng High School Action Committee also worked closely with four representatives from Chinese High School to later organize camp-ins at both schools to continue the anti-NS protests. The classified sources consulted for this study, it is worth reiterating, indicate that the anti-NS disturbances, rather than being a spontaneous development, reveal clear signs of attempted orchestration. The CPM man said to be in overall charge was one Chiam Chong Chian @ Gao Lao,[74] while at the school level a Chinese High student, one Xie,[75] reportedly formed another seven-man Action Committee comprising students of Chinese High School, Chung Cheng High School, Nanyang Girls' High School, Chung Hwa Girls' High School, and Nan Chiau Girls High School.[76] No less a figure than the chairman of the powerful CPM-penetrated Singapore Chinese Middle School Students' Union (see below) himself, Robert Soon Loh Boon,[77] confirmed years later in an interview that the students were being manipulated and directed from behind the scenes:

> Because we are Chinese school students, we also read books about Communist Party, we know that *definitely there were instructions*, and especially when at that time, *it was quite rife*, every morning you go, you will find in your school desk, there are Communist literatures (sic) put in for you to read. So I, out of curiosity, out of my sympathy towards them, I read those articles secretly, so from then on, *I know there were instructions, and also through meetings you can see those people who are under the guidance or leadership of the Communists* and the way they present things (my emphasis).[78]

Incidentally, the involvement of CPM and ABL elements in the unrest was confirmed further in a book published by former ABL/CPM members in 2013.[79] To reiterate, this thoroughly Communist-engineered agitation — rather than "spontaneous" as the Alternates suggest — culminated in the infamous 13 May riots that broke out between 500 Chinese middle-school students, mainly from Chung Cheng High, and the police. Twenty-six people were injured and forty-eight students arrested.[80]

The CPM saw the anti-NS agitation, while unsuccessful in scuttling the NS Bill, as nevertheless a "great success". Lim Chin Siong commented that the episode exposed the "intrigues of the British Colonial Master" and helped the "awakening" of the students to the importance of "unity".[81] Comrade D felt that this agitation "was the most successful student struggle ever since the Emergency Regulations".[82] Comrade D, working as usual behind the scenes, capitalized on this momentum. Following a discreet electoral pact between students' representatives and David Marshall's left-wing Labour Front party that subsequently won the April 1955 elections held under the Rendel constitution, the ad hoc anti-NS registration student committees set up to manage the ongoing agitation coalesced into and were formally registered six months later as the permanent Singapore Chinese Middle School Students' Union (SCMSSU). The powerful open-front SCMSSU, embracing ten Chinese middle schools with a total student population of 16,000, was fully able, much to the CPMSTC's great satisfaction, to easily engage in "open and legal acts" as it led the pro-Communist student mass movement.[83]

Not content to rest on his laurels, Comrade D next turned to the unions. To be sure, since the formation of the CPM in 1930, much of its strength had been in the unions, through open-front organizations like the Malayan General Labour Union (MGLU). As noted in 1946, the MGLU split into the Pan Malayan Federation of Trade Unions (PMFTU) in the peninsula and Singapore Federation of Trade Unions (SFTU) on Singapore island itself. By 1947 the SFTU had 72 affiliated unions with 56,000 members out of a total of 126 unions in Singapore. By April 1948, the SFTU was involved in many strikes in Singapore, but with the onset of the Emergency in June, it and its affiliates were eventually deregistered by the end of the year. However, following the Rendel constitutional reforms of 1954, the political space opened up once again and Comrade D, through the instrumentality of the CPMSTC's Workers Movement Committee, made inroads in the labour field, with the result that rural resident associations, hawker associations, old-boys' associations, cultural associations and other unions sprang up.[84] In 1955, of the 300,000-strong labour force, 140,000 were unionized.[85] In particular, the Singapore Factory and Shop Workers' Union (SFSWU) was set up in May

1954 with Yong Koh Kim as President. Yong was a former CPM/MPAJA member who was arrested in July 1955 and banished to China. Two months earlier, however, a young and charismatic left-wing activist called Lim Chin Siong had become the General Secretary of the SFSWU — he had joined as a member in 1954 — and soon the union experienced tremendous growth in membership, exploding in numbers from about 1,350 in 1955 to 37,000 by 1956, and controlling over a hundred branches in various industries. In addition, by that time, other unions had joined the SFSWU, making it the largest single union in Singapore, representing a third of the estimated 140,000 unionized workers on the island.[86] Little wonder that the SFSWU was said to be to labour what the SCMSSU was to the students.[87]

The SFSWU was thus well-placed to spearhead the widespread labour disturbances that dogged Singapore in 1955, a year which saw 275 strikes or the loss of 946,354 man-days, a huge spike in industrial unrest since the late 1940s just before the British clamped down on CPM-controlled unions. Moreover, as in the case of the anti-NS agitation, this was no mere "spontaneous actions by the individuals directly involved".[88] Rather the wave of 1955 strikes were in fact initiated behind the scenes by the CPMSTC, in an attempt to better integrate the labour movement into the CUF via exploiting genuine worker grievances over low pay and bad working conditions.[89] This was the background to the infamous Hock Lee bus riots, by far the most serious industrial dispute in 1955. The Hock Lee bus strike began in April 1955 and paralysed the bus network, which was Singapore's main transportation system at the time. It was spearheaded by Fong Swee Suan,[90] Secretary of the Singapore Bus Workers' Union (SBWU), who persuaded three-quarters of the workers in the Hock Lee Bus Company to form a branch of the SBWU. The Hock Lee management, who apparently had a Kuomintang background, opposed the action, dismissing two workers responsible for starting the SBWU Hock Lee branch, and even started its own union to absorb other workers who could be deployed in case the SBWU Hock Lee workers went on strike.

Following weeks of disputes, Fong led the SBWU in instigating a strike by SBWU Hock Lee workers to protest against the dismissal of 200 employees who were their own union members, as well as poor working conditions, long hours and low pay. Tellingly, Fong instructed the workers not to disperse even if the police arrived.[91] On 23 April 1955, the striking workers stopped buses from leaving the depot and crippled the city's entire bus system. Fong's close friend and fellow unionist, Lim Chin Siong of the SFSWU — concurrently an "advisor" to the SBWU — then rallied other unions such as the Singapore Tractor Company Employees Union (STCEU) to support their Hock Lee counterparts. On 1 May at a rally, Lim told 8,000 attendees — including 2,000 Chinese middle school students — that the workers must unite against the Emergency Regulations and fight to the end, while Fong himself unhelpfully added that "bloodshed was inevitable in a revolution". After the rally, lorryloads of workers and students were led by Lim Chin Siong to "comfort" the Hock Lee workers, while the students also sang Communist songs in a show of sympathy for the workers' struggles.[92]

The ensuing agitation and stand-off at the Hock Lee depot and in the Alexandra Road/Tiong Bahru area between the strikers, students, other workers and the police, peaked in intensity between 10 and 11 May, finally culminating in riots between the afternoon of 12 May and the morning of 13 May — by no means coincidentally — the first anniversary of the 13 May anti-NS incident of the previous year. Thirty-one persons were injured and there were four deaths: Detective Corporal Yuen Yau Phang was burnt to death when rioters set fire to his car, while Andrew Teo Bock Lan, a constable with the Volunteer Special Constabulary, was severely beaten by rioters and died in hospital. Gene D. Symonds, an American press correspondent was also badly beaten and died from head injuries. Most horrifying was what happened to the fourth person who died: sixteen-year-old student Chong Lon Chang, who suffered a gunshot injury. Instead of rushing him immediately to hospital, the rioters paraded his body for over two hours to further incite the crowd. After the boy died, the Communists planned to turn his funeral into another demonstration, but this was frustrated. Chong was nevertheless, pointedly buried in a grave next to former CPMSTC Secretary Lim Ah Liang, who had himself been injured in anti-British riots in 1946 and jailed. Lim died in August 1947, soon after release, and was considered "a great martyr in the Communist movement".[93] It is worth noting that in his own analysis of the Hock Lee incident, Alternate historian Thum Ping Tjin failed to mention the actions of the mob in preventing Chong from receiving immediate medical attention — an act that may have potentially saved the young boy's life. This omission in effect produces a simplistic two-dimensional portrait of ostensibly anti-Chinese and evil British officials out to crush a principled CPM leadership committed to "peaceful constitutional change". Readers may want to reflect at this point: is this quite significant omission perhaps yet another example of how some Alternates cannot quite resist the temptation to ensure that the facts do not get in the way of a good story?[94]

To be sure, C.C. Chin notes that the CPM did place "its cadres in leading positions" in episodes such as the Hock Lee incident, but suggests that "they were unable to control the development of events".[95] While a CPM observer at the time of the Hock Lee riot echoed this sentiment, complaining that "the procession headed by the wounded student on the stretcher" indeed had "no organised leadership", he took pains to underscore that had there been such leadership "the affair would have become more serious and the government would find great difficulty in dealing with it".[96] This suggests that the Alternates, in downplaying the agency of the CPM and playing up the supposed random spontaneity of the 1950s Singapore disturbances, miss the point. As the violent consequences of the Hock Lee riots just described show, while minute-by-minute, tactical direction of the incidents may not always have been possible as this was a clandestine, behind-the-scenes struggle, the strategic intent of creating an explosive situation that could be set alight and thereafter exploited — as C.C. Chin himself puts it, like a "match thrown into explosives" — was all the Communists needed.[97] At any rate, the CPM certainly considered the unrest a success. Celebrating the "victorious ending of the Hock Lee incident" and denouncing the "barbarous British Imperialists", *Freedom News* declared that "[an] economic struggle has been precipitated into becoming a political struggle" that "enabled the political awakening of the workers and the broad masses". It trumpeted that the "victorious settlement of the Hock Lee labour unrest" was also a "victory for [all] workers and the people throughout Singapore and Malaya".[98] Moreover, in 2013, former ABL/CPM members publicly confirmed that the "Hock Lee strikes were carried out under the direct leadership" of "Commander Lu Yexun".[99] Again, like the anti-NS registration agitation of a year earlier, the Hock Lee episode was no spontaneous event as the Alternates suggest, but rather instigated from behind the scenes by CUF elements.

Throughout 1955, the British gradually became increasingly worried about the ability of Chief Minister David Marshall to preserve order in Singapore — the *sine qua non* as far as London was concerned of any advance towards full self-government. Following the Hock Lee incident, Marshall had wanted three Chinese schools whose students had been involved in the episode to expel the culprits on threat of closure. In defiant response, starting on 18 May, 600 Chung Cheng High and 1,000 Chinese High students staged a weeklong sit-in, organized by the "Committee for the Protection of Chinese Education". Unsurprisingly, they were supported by Lim Chin Siong's SFSWU and Fong Swee Suan's SBWU. Marshall backed down, concerned about the possible adverse electoral consequences of using the police to forcibly disperse the students, with the recent violence still fresh in his mind. The CPMSTC was apparently pleased with the "success" of the students.[100] That's not all. On 12–13 June 1955, at the instigation of Lim and Fong, workers from the SFSWU, SBWU and the Federation of Coastal Workers, by Communist estimates around 60,000–70,000 in number, struck in support of the Singapore Harbour Board Staff Association (SHBSA) in its dispute over working conditions and pay with the Singapore Harbour Board (SHB) — an impasse that had been ongoing in fact since 30 April. The June strike had an adverse effect on the postal service and all passenger transport in Singapore. In the tense build-up to the strike, between 11 and 13 June, the British had arrested seven persons, including Fong. However once Marshall announced that the cases of these detainees would, as per the Emergency Regulations, be considered within two weeks of the arrests, Lim called off the strike on 17 June. Subsequently, by the following month, six of the seven arrested, including Fong Swee Suan, had been unconditionally released. As *Freedom News* gushed, never before had "persons arrested under the Emergency Regulations been let out of prison unconditionally" — implying that "the Government had succumbed to pressure from the Communist movement".[101]

Marshall had indicated during the campaign leading up to the April 1955 general elections that he would abolish the unpopular Emergency Regulations introduced in 1948, and on assuming office he ordered a review of the relevant legislation. To be fair, he was no appeaser of Communism,[102] hence by August, when new laws were introduced to replace the Emergency laws, two in particular stood out for their potentially onerous implications for the CUF: the Preservation of Public Security Ordinance (PPSO) and the Criminal Law (Temporary Provisions) Ordinance — which prevented strikes and lockouts in the essential services. These were to come into effect by October 1955. However, again following the prompting of Lim Chin Siong, a Trade Union Working Committee Representing 95 Trade Unions in Opposition to the Public Security Legislation and the Trade Disputes Ordinance, in short, the Singapore Trade Union Working Committee (STUWC), was set up to fight the bills. The STUWC organized protest campaigns against the bills and during a meeting in early October 1955, Lim apparently made inflammatory speeches, arguing that the new laws would give the police more powers to arrest trade unionists and students, and variously condemned the bills, the government, the police, and Special Branch. The STUWC continued the agitation even after the bills became law.[103] In short, by the time Marshall resigned in June 1956, following his failure to win a "full loaf of independence" for Singapore from the sceptical British at the London constitutional talks a couple months earlier, the CUF appeared to have made great gains: in October 1955, the SCMSSU had been formally registered and thus able to function openly amongst the schools,[104] while the SFSWU was in a position, according to worried Special Branch assessments of the time, to significantly "disrupt the economic life of Singapore and cause great inconvenience to the vast majority of the population".[105]

Ironically, it was at this very time, after June 1955, that elements within the CUF began to urge restraint and patience so as to ensure long-term victory, because "the extremism which had been followed since the anti-National Service movement in 1954 might now be counter-productive". As such, the remainder of Marshall's term till his resignation in June the following year proved relatively uneventful. To be sure, in March 1956, a gathering at Kallang Airport to show support for Marshall's fight with the British for constitutional advance did degenerate into clashes with police, but unlike the other episodes addressed thus far, this was indeed a genuine "spontaneous outburst" rather than "the result of machinations by the Communists".[106] The new Labour Front Chief Minister, Lim Yew Hock, however, came to office in June 1956 determined to win British confidence that he could be tough on Communist agitators and thus be entrusted with self-governance. Accordingly, he set the government on a collision course with the CUF. As early as 19 September 1956, he deregistered the pro-Communist Singapore Womens' Federation and the Chinese Brass Gong Musical Society, arrested six CUF leaders, including the SFSWU president and three activists linked to the Chinese middle schools, among whom was the chairman of the Singapore Chinese Primary School Teachers' Association, who was banished to China. Lim then followed up five days later with the banning of the SCMSSU, the arrests of its chairman Robert Soon Loh Boon, as well as, a week later, Chia Ee Tian,[107] an SFSWU official and concurrently a member of the Central Executive Committee of the PAP (see below). The Labour Front government explained that the SCMSSU had been banned for persistently flouting the injunction not to engage in politics and working with other CUF organizations to organize political protests.[108]

The SCMSSU deregistration, unsurprisingly, triggered mass protests by 5,000 students across the Chinese middle schools. On 28 September, Lim Chin Siong reportedly led a delegation to meet Chief Minister Lim to lodge a protest and that same evening, the former, together with prominent pro-Communist union leaders like Jamit Singh, Devan Nair, Fong Swee Suan and James Puthucheary formed the Civil Rights Convention of 95 Unions to protest the dissolution of CUF-linked organizations and arrest of its leaders. Protests spiked on 10 October when Lim Yew Hock arrested four more SCMSSU leaders and told the management committees of Chung Cheng High School and Chinese High School to expel 142 students on grounds of subversion. In response, some 1,000 Chinese High School and 3,000 Chung Cheng High School students staged a camp-in at their respective school premises. They demanded the restoration of the registration of the SCMSSU, the release of arrested students, and for the expulsion orders for the 142 students to be rescinded. On 12 October, Lim Yew Hock ordered the closure of the schools, but the students did not budge, and as always, received strong moral and material backing from the SFSWU and its affiliates, whose members supplied them with food and other essentials. It was obvious to contemporary observers that this support was a show of solidarity as the previous year the students had aided the workers during the Hock Lee incident. The political and emotional impact of the school closure order should not be underestimated, as Chinese High School and Chung Cheng High School were regarded as "the Eton and Harrow of the Chinese-speaking world in Singapore and Malaya".[109] Then on 22 October, the CUF initiated actions to enforce a general strike by students in Singapore. Large crowds of Chinese High and Chung Cheng High students visited other schools for a few days to persuade students there to skip class. Female students from Nan Chiau Girls' High School and Chung Hwa Girls' High School boycotted their classes in support.[110]

That same day, Fong Swee Suan, in a speech at the Civil Rights Convention, called on the unions to support the students with a general strike. On 23 October, Lim Chin Siong's speeches and those of others were "more inflammatory than usual in nature". Finally, a day later, Lim Yew Hock issued an ultimatum for parents to take their children out from Chung Cheng High and Chinese High by 8 p.m. on 25 October, or else he would send in the police to clear the schools. At the same time the Chief Minister dissolved four cultural associations linked to the two schools and arrested eight persons connected with them. On 25 October evening, about two hours before the expiry of Chief Minister Lim's ultimatum, Lim Chin Siong spoke at a PAP rally at Beauty World Park to "protest peacefully" against the banning of the organizations and the arrests. In fact, Lim's speech was "seditious and inflammatory", and it appeared to have enraged the crowd, some of whom were reportedly then ferried to nearby Chinese High where a crowd of 4,000 had built up. Sometime after the 8 p.m. deadline, clashes broke out when the crowd attacked the police. Rioting subsequently spread to Chung Cheng High School at Goodman Road where a 400- to 500-strong mob clashed with the police, and also attacked Tanjong Katong Post Office and Geylang Police Station. Riots later spread to Rochor Road and other parts of Singapore.

On 26 October morning the police forcibly dispersed the students in Chung Cheng High and Chinese High with batons and tear gas, while that same morning left-wing unions launched an islandwide sympathy strike involving 7,000 workers in the bus and mine manufacturing industries. Rioting carried on throughout the day across the island, again at Chung Cheng High and Chinese High. In Jurong, moreover, members of the Singapore Farmers' Association (SFA) burnt down an English school and attacked a police station. That evening left-wing unionists met at the SFSWU headquarters to discuss plans to spread the rioting, but the police suddenly imposed a midnight curfew. During the early hours of the next day, the police mounted simultaneous raids on SFSWU headquarters, four of its branches and the SFA, arresting by some estimates, 259 people, under the PPSO. Police separately detained about 1,000 people, including 235 secret society gangsters, for rioting, breaking the curfew and other offences. Finally, by 30 October, with the help of 600 Gurkha troops from Malaya, as well as the support of army helicopters and armoured cars, the disturbances were quelled. In the end, 13 people were dead, 123 injured, 70 cars destroyed, two schools razed, two police stations damaged.[111]

The so-called "October Revolution" actually proved very costly for the CUF in Singapore. Fourteen PAP pro-Communist members and unionists, including Lim Chin Siong (SFSWU Secretary-General); Fong Swee Suan (SBWU Secretary-General); James Puthucheary (SFSWU Secretary); Devan Nair (Singapore Traction Company Employees' Union advisor); and S. Woodhull (Naval Base Labour Union Secretary) were arrested. Moreover, as noted while the SCMSSU had been deregistered in September 1956, in February 1957, the SFSWU was dissolved as well. *Freedom News* complained of the wrong policy of "leftwing adventurism" — "the error of fomenting revolution without carefully ascertaining the readiness of, and preparing the masses to revolt; as well as not heeding the guidance of the M.C.P". The net result was the severe loss of CUF manpower, resulting in a "state of inactiveness of the M.C.P. network".[112] However, the fact of the matter was that despite some key arrests, most of the persons nabbed in the Lim Yew Hock sweep of late 1956 "were not members of the CPM or even of the SPABL [Singapore People's Anti-British League]", the majority of whom had taken care to remain underground. Lee Ting Hui explains the significance of this fact:

> If the CPM and the SPABL remained intact, fresh blood could be recruited to start the various mass movements once again. The organisations and the publications which were banned were also important but their loss could be tolerated. Replacements could be created. *The ordinary members of the mass organisations and such organisations themselves were like the leaves of the lallang whereas the underground components of the movement were like the roots. The leaves could be destroyed, but, if the roots were untouched, new leaves would grow again when conditions were right* (emphasis mine).[113]

In fact, the highly resilient CPMSTC "roots" began regenerating and by August 1957, worried authorities noted that their "recovery had become significant".[114] A Labour Front government white paper of that month noted that "strong Communist Front groups are again forming and manoeuvring to gain control in important and typical Communist fields of activity as they did in 1955/56."[115] The authorities were right to be concerned. By 1959 — the year the PAP came to power in Singapore — the unions remained very much under CPM influence. Chin Peng himself alluded to this when he made the following telling comment about the labour scene in 1959 in his memoirs: "I can certainly say that most of [Singapore's] workers sympathised with the left-wing trade unions and members of these unions well appreciated they were under the control of the CPM."[116] However, by 1959 the CPMSTC had also fully recognized that due to evolving circumstances, the "business end", so to speak, of the CUF had to change from the students and workers to a new sphere of action: that of politics, and in particular, the PAP.

Phase 4: 1956–61

As noted, Comrade D had become the CPMSTC's chief directing figure in Singapore itself in January 1954 and while ECY attempted to provide strategic oversight from his Indonesian hideout, the former — the man on the spot — tried to steer the CUF through the period 1954–56. As seen, this was a truly tumultuous period, encompassing the anti-NS registration disturbances, the Hock Lee riots and the running battles with the Lim Yew Hock Labour Front government that ultimately, however, resulted in severe losses for the CUF during the "October Revolution" of late 1956. The same year, ECY was summoned to Beijing for a meeting with the CPM's China-based leadership. On briefing CPM Central Committee members Zhang Lingyun @ Siao Chang and Chen Rui on the situation in Singapore up to that point, ECY was instructed to assert greater control of the CUF action in Singapore. CCM Chen Rui even separately "lectured" ECY on how to best conduct underground work, including conducting CUF work through "multiple lines". Subsequently, in early 1957, ECY, back in Indonesia, summoned Fang Chuang Pi, as noted Comrade D's right-hand man in Singapore, who was at the time running *Freedom News* and other underground propaganda, and informed him that a three-man Singapore directing cell was being set up, involving ECY, Comrade D — who was to be withdrawn to Indonesia — and Fang, who would remain forward deployed in Singapore.

The Singapore-based Fang nominally had to report to ECY and Comrade D in Jakarta. Nevertheless, it would turn out that from 1957 onwards, due to communications difficulties, to all intents and purposes Fang would enjoy near "absolute control" of the CUF in Singapore itself. At any rate, ECY told Fang at a 1957 Jakarta meeting that the CPM Central Committee had reaffirmed that "the struggle in Singapore should be regarded as an integral part of the struggle in Malaya" and had "taken a positive view of the widespread development of the open mass movement in Singapore and sent its praises". However, due to the losses suffered by the CUF because of the sin of "leftwing adventurism" — apparently one reason why Comrade D was being pulled out — henceforth the "guiding principle of mass work in Singapore would be to bring colonial rule in Singapore to an end by substituting illegal activities with open legal struggles, and expanding and consolidating the anti-colonial united front". Fang, given his background in propaganda work, was seen as a natural choice to coordinate the new emphasis on "open propaganda work" with "open organizational work". Apart from the unions and student associations, ECY also directed Fang to "penetrate grass-roots organizations" such as "Country People's Associations, the newly launched Nanyang University, and Old Boys' Associations". Significantly, the meeting also "formally decided that the PAP and Lee Kuan Yew would be a subject of our united front co-operation in the left-wing anti-colonial struggle in Singapore".[117] In his own memoirs, Fang confirmed the existence of a "three-member working group" comprising himself, ECY and Comrade D.[118] Fang recalled drafting a resolution that

> contained these sentiments: exploiting the conditions and opportunities available in the united front with the PAP to develop the mass movement, obtain overall leadership of all mass organisations and groups, consolidate and strengthen our position in the PAP, and expand the strength of the left-wing in preparation for any unforeseen event.

He confirmed that he was appointed to "assume overall leadership of the struggle in Singapore and to implement the resolution of the working group".[119]

ECY's views were unsurprisingly consistent with the sentiments of his own CPM superiors in the peninsula. In early 1956, CPM Deputy Secretary-General Yeong Kwo had written to CCM Hor Lung in the South Malayan Bureau in Johore to complain of the violent tactics of the student movement during the anti-NS registration and Hock Lee episodes. He had warned that the "students were only giving themselves away". Hor Lung subsequently sent word to Singapore that increased emphasis "must definitely be given to the legal and open mode of struggle".[120] In April 1957, therefore, the CUF in Singapore underwent a significant transformation. Regional Committee Secretary Ah Ann of the South Malayan Bureau ordered the dissolution of the ABL, and while outstanding and loyal ABL activists were immediately absorbed into the CPM fold, others were told to infiltrate the PAP and other legal and open left-wing bodies, including political parties — principally the

Workers' Party and the Partai Rakyat Singapura (PRS) — unions, peasant organizations, cultural associations and old boys' associations. In addition, publication of *Freedom News* and all underground propaganda was terminated, and "open publications" were to be used henceforth for CPM propaganda. All connections, moreover, "however faint", with the CPM and ABL were to be immediately cut to drastically reduce operational signatures. As C.C. Chin noted, the CPMSTC by April 1957 was required to give "full support" to the PAP.[121]

Not that the PAP was unfamiliar with the CPM: it had been formed in November 1954 with the help of CUF elements, after all. Lee Kuan Yew himself declared in his memoirs that the world of the "Chinese-educated communists" was one "full of vitality, of so many activists, all like jumping beans, of so many young idealists, unselfish, ready to sacrifice everything for a better society". He was "convinced" that if he could "not harness some of these dynamic young people" to the PAP cause, "we would never succeed".[122] Lee had first met Lim Chin Siong, Fong Swee Suan and Robert Soon Loh Boon in 1954 at the former's Oxley Road home. They introduced themselves as from the SBWU, and Lee was duly impressed with the "[k]eenness and dedication" shown "in every line of their faces and in every gesture". After discussions, Fong Swee Suan agreed to join the PAP as a convening member — Lim Chin Siong did not become a convenor but became a member — and Lee observed that with Fong's presence, "the new party would have a reasonably broad working class base", and would be balanced in composition, with "the English-educated, the Malay blue- and white-collar workers", and "the Chinese clan associations, trade guilds and blue-collar workers" represented as well.[123] At the April 1955 elections won by David Marshall's Labour Front, the PAP secured four seats. Lim Chin Siong won on a PAP ticket in Bukit Timah ward and entered the Legislative Assembly, together with Lee who won in Tanjong Pagar.[124] The relations between the Lee and Lim factions in the PAP did not stay cordial for too long, however. Ideological differences emerged very early. Fong Swee Suan later admitted that "Lee and company were disposed toward the Fabian-type of socialism while Lim, Devan Nair and he favoured a more radical approach."[125]

The student and worker-driven violence of May and June 1955 and October 1956 further strained relations between both camps, forcing the PAP's non-Communist leaders to publicly distance themselves on numerous occasions from the rough-and-tumble antics of their pro-Communist colleagues like Fong and Lim who were as seen deeply immersed in these episodes.[126] S. Woodhull,[127] firmly in the Lim Chin Siong PAP camp, and who regarded Lee as "not left enough", "not ideologically deep enough" and hence "not one of us", observed that Lee was upset because the Lim faction in short order began to act independently in the labour field without consulting him. At this point, however, the pro-Communists felt there was no need to move against Lee. Woodhull recalled that:

> We were quite happy to let Lee go on. There was no attempt to clip his wings or oust him ... because we knew the organization was not in his hands. The trade unions, the street bodies, farmers ... you name it. He had not the men to control the ground but we had the capacity to organise that. So, never for one moment did he trouble us too much.

In fact, non-Communist PAP members even formed the impression that Lim Chin Siong "ruled the party" with Lee Kuan Yew as his advisor.[128]

The failure of the CPM at the Baling Peace Talks in December 1955 however was to have an impact on the power configuration within the PAP. In May of that year the British authorities in Kuala Lumpur had received the so-called "Ng Heng" letter, which called for discussions to end the Emergency. Ng Heng was a pseudonym for CPM Secretary-General Chin Peng, who, worried about rapidly declining MNLA morale given the evident failure of the shooting war in the Malayan peninsula, now sought to lay down arms — but on Communist terms. Then in July 1955, the Alliance Party led by United Malays National Organization (UMNO) leader Tunku Abdul Rahman, won the federal elections that were constitutionally mandated as a step towards eventual Malayan independence. As Malaya's first Chief Minister, the Tunku — with British agreement — proceeded to counter Chin Peng's peace feelers with an amnesty offer. The amnesty was inaugurated on 9 September 1955 and included a promise of immunity for all Surrendered Enemy Personnel (SEP), regardless of crimes committed under Communist direction, as well as repatriation for all those who wished to return to China. Kuala Lumpur, however, retained the right to investigate SEP who wished to remain in Malaya but at the same time refused to recant Communist ideology. A meeting to clarify the amnesty terms at Baling, in the Malayan State of Kedah, was agreed to between the parties, following which Chin Peng shrewdly nullified the impact of the amnesty by persuading his rank and file to "wait and see", because at Baling he would secure better exit terms. When the Tunku and Marshall met Chin Peng in Baling, Kedah in late December 1955, Chin Peng dug his heels in further, countering that the CPM would only lay down arms if — like the period 1945–48 — it was granted legal recognition, so it could fully operate above ground in the open. The CPM Secretary-General also insisted on "no detention, no investigation and no restriction of movement". The Tunku — to the relief of his nervous British sponsors — rejected these demands and the talks collapsed. However, the "wait-and-see" posture of the MNLA rank and file meant that the amnesty achieved limited results and the Tunku scrapped it on 8 February 1956.[129]

Chin Peng's failure at Baling to secure legal recognition for the Party, however, was a crucial development. It meant that any hope of "a return to the pre-Emergency days, with the CPM recognized and able to operate politically", was stillborn. Chin Peng was said to have been "frustrated and dejected".[130] Moreover, the importance of having an alternative open and legal political vehicle to pursue its aims in Malaya and Singapore — both territories always seen in Communist eyes as a political unity — became more urgent than ever. From 1956, therefore, the pro-Communist faction in the PAP began to seek greater control of the PAP Central Executive Committee (CEC), to better shape party policy while retaining the non-Communists led by Lee Kuan Yew as front men. The pro-Communists made their first move at the Third Party Conference in July 1956, capturing four out of twelve seats in the CEC. Lim Chin Siong, Chia Ee Tian, Goh Boon Toh[131] and Devan Nair were elected. However, as a result of the October Revolution that year, the Lim Yew Hock Labour Front government arrested Lim, Chia and Nair. Undeterred, the Lim faction regrouped and made a stronger attempt to capture the PAP CEC at the next Party Conference on 4 August 1957. This time they won six out of twelve posts, and assumed the posts of chairman and secretary-general when Lee Kuan Yew and his group refused to take office. They achieved this — in line with the classic Leninist dictum to employ "all sorts of stratagems, manoeuvres" and "illegal methods" — partly through fraud: they obtained PAP admission cards to the conference and duly packed the meeting with pro-Communist trade union members. Toh Chin Chye admitted in an interview years later that he was surprised at the large turnout of people, many of whom he could not recognize. He began to realize that "tickets were handed out freely to people who might not even have been party members". Toh conceded moreover that another problem was that the PAP was too loose an organization at that point; because it wanted to be a mass party, for only two dollars a year in subscriptions, "we just let in anybody".[132] For his part Lee kicked himself, acknowledging that the non-Communists had been "fools" for believing in the notion of "playing fair" and "let's leave it to the good sense or good choice of the members", rather than recognizing that by doing so they had exposed themselves to being manipulated by the pro-Communists, who had quite obviously exploited the situation to their benefit.[133] As we shall see, this incident was to leave a deep and lasting impression on the future prime minister.

The six pro-Communists who won were Tan Chong Kin @ Chan Chong Keen (Chairman); T.T. Rajah (Secretary-General); Tan Kong Guan; Chen Say Jame; Goh Boon Toh and Ong Chye Ann. However, while Lee and the five other non-Communists were refusing to take their places on the CEC in protest at the nature of the election, the Lim Yew Hock government launched another sweep targeting unions and the PAP that saw five of the six newly elected pro-Communist PAP CEC office holders detained under the PPSO. Lim Chin Joo, younger brother of Lim Chin Siong, later wrote to Lee in 1959 — which Lee made public the following year — to express regret for having played a role in the attempted leftist "coup" of August 1957. In any case, the PAP non-Communists soon responded to the August 1957 episode by amending the party constitution so as to entrust the election of CEC members to only a core group of proven and trusted cadre members, and not the ordinary members as before. They also assessed that the August 1957 coup attempt was a "wild and reckless move by a gang of 'left-wing adventurers' acting unilaterally or acting on a wrong reading of what their masters wanted". This was not an inaccurate assessment, as it turned out. From detention, Lim Chin Siong and Fong Swee Suan had apparently tried to contact their compatriots to warn them not to oust the non-Communists led by Lee, as they were needed as "cover". Moreover, rumours of secret collusion between Lee and Lim Yew Hock in the August 1957 arrests of the five leftist PAP CEC members were not substantiated.[134]

As seen, following ECY's instructions to alter the CUF strategy in Singapore by ceasing all clandestine activities and instead focusing on penetration of open organizations, Fang Chuang Pi moved to draw the PAP more fully into the CUF orbit, so as to emplace "leftists and MCP underground members in the PAP structure, both in the party and in any future government". To this end he recognized that he had to mend relations with an angry Lee Kuan Yew following the abortive takeover attempt of the PAP CEC in August 1957 by the rogue pro-Communist elements.[135] As such, in March 1958, Fang made discreet contact with a wary Lee and assured him that the troubles created in 1956 and 1957 by Lim Chin Siong, Fong Swee Suan and Lim Chin Joo within the PAP had been due to the CPM's difficulty in getting instructions across to Lim Chin Siong and the CUF leaders, who did not understand the Communist policy of the united front, who were "over-zealous" but had meant well and wanted to bring about a revolution in Malaya. Between that first meeting and May 1961, Fang, whom Lee dubbed "the Plen" — short for "plenipotentiary" — secretly met Lee five times.[136] Another reason for the CPMSTC to intensify its cultivation of Lee was that following the second and third

London constitutional talks in March 1957 and May 1958, in British eyes the latter's stock had been rising in inverse proportion to that of Labour Front Chief Minister Lim Yew Hock.

The All-Party Mission led by Lim — but in which Lee's guiding influence was increasingly plain for the British to see — had made plans for Singapore to attain full self-government in all areas except for foreign affairs, defence and internal security. A new constitution — apparently significantly shaped by Lee — was thereby finalized in May 1958, which granted the British final say in these three core areas. Of particular interest and relevance to Operation Coldstore — still a few years away — the new constitution provided for an Internal Security Council (ISC), with Singaporean, British and Malayan representatives, and chaired by the British Commissioner in Singapore. The ISC would start functioning upon the city attaining self-government in 1959. The net effect of the finalized constitutional proposals was that Lee succeeded in establishing a united front of his own with the other non-Communist members of the delegation and the British — against the CPM — a fact that the latter fully recognized to its chagrin. This merely confirmed British intelligence assessments of Lee, that by about 1956, were concluding that not only was he not Communist as initially thought, he — rather than Lim Yew Hock — was "the best bet" to lead a self-governing Singapore.[137] Rather than being a "crypto-communist", one British official later observed, London began to realize that Lee was in fact the complete opposite: a "crypto anti-communist".[138]

The PAP as expected, swept along on the strength of CUF control of the grassroots organizations, won by a landslide in the May 1959 general elections. However, as a precondition for taking power, Lee demanded that eight left-wing leaders detained in the security sweeps of 1956 and 1957, be released. Lim Chin Siong, Fong Swee Suan, Devan Nair, S. Woodhull, James Puthucheary,[139] Chen Say Jame, Chan Chiaw Thor and Tan Chong Kin were all duly released on 4 June 1959. While in doing this Lee was keen to burnish his left-wing political credentials for the consumption of the CUF masses, he had quietly secured the agreement of the eight detainees beforehand — as a *quid pro quo* to get them released — to sign a statement, "The Ends and Means of Socialism". Drafted by Devan Nair — who by his release had reportedly given up Communism — the statement required the group to pledge their "commitment towards achieving an independent, democratic, non-communist socialist Malaya by peaceful means". Moreover, these men were not allowed to take part in the 1959 elections. Lee, however, sensed that Lim Chin Siong in particular, unlike the rest, had not been sincere in signing the declaration, seeing it only as a tactical move to secure his release — and appeared later to succeed in persuading Woodhull and Fong to return to the Communist path.[140]

Lee's wariness towards Lim was not without foundation. As early as a week after his release, Lim apparently confided in his PAP faction that it was not the right time to "go against the moderate faction led by Lee Kuan Yew, which is now at the height of its power" and hence "the leftist faction will tag along until such time when it is appropriate for the leftists to take over the leadership in the PAP from the moderates."[141] Lee sensed this. In a calculated effort to keep a check on the pro-Communist leaders within the PAP following their release from detention, he ensured that Lim, Fong, Woodhull, Puthucheary and Nair were given positions as "political secretaries" in various ministries with no real power and hence "designed to neutralise them".[142] Lee had also ensured that the next party CEC was elected for a new term before the detainees were released, to preclude the possibility of their being elected to it. They were not permitted to become cadre members of the party either.[143] This fact was not lost on Lim Chin Siong, who was appointed Political Secretary to the Minister for Finance, Dr Goh Keng Swee. A deputy secretary in the ministry, George Bogaars,[144] recalled later that Goh had instructed him to give Lim "stuff to do" to keep him occupied so he would stay "out of mischief" and away from "his old trade union buddies", but Lim "never appeared physically in the Ministry so that he could be given things to do".[145]

This was because Lim was busily building a new power base with his "old trade union buddies", in particular within the Singapore General Employees' Union (SGEU). Following the demise of the SFSWU in 1957, the SGEU had been captured by ex-SFSWU stragglers and had taken over the old SFSWU role in leading thirty-two left-wing unions. In May 1959, the SGEU had 3,000 members, but after Lim Chin Siong came in as advisor after his release in June, by May 1960 it had 22,000. Moreover, following the passage by the new PAP government of a Trade Union Bill the same month to expedite the unification of the union movement, the old Trade Union Congress (TUC), a Labour Front vehicle under Lim Yew Hock's control, was infiltrated by leftists and renamed the Singapore Trade Union Congress (STUC). What came to be known as the so-called "Big Six" union leaders: Lim, Fong Swee Suan, Dominic Puthucheary,[146] S. Woodhull, Jamit Singh and S.T. Bani, were all part of the ten-man STUC Secretariat.[147] The highly resilient CUF roots, in other words, were evidently sprouting new *lallang* leaves.

By his own admission, the new prime minister of self-governing Singapore, Lee Kuan Yew, only thirty-five years of age when he assumed office in June 1959, "had no experience of administration" and felt "uneasy about taking power", especially knowing full well the myriad complex, interlocking economic, political and security problems he and the new administration had to face.[148] Within a few days of assuming power in June 1959, moreover, Lee realized that the previous Labour Front regime had been spendthrift with the reserves — using up $200 million — and a budget deficit of $14 million for 1959 was projected. Hence there "was absolutely no way to finance development schemes over and above what had already been allowed for, and even those would have to be ruthlessly pruned".[149] The most efficient way to balance the budget, Finance Minister Goh Keng Swee reckoned, was cutting expenditure on manpower, which meant salaries. With ministers taking the lead, the salaries in the public sector were significantly cut, with predictably deleterious morale consequences for scores of public servants who found themselves having to make drastic adjustments to their lifestyles. In fact such was the resulting exodus that by the end of the following year, there were concerns in official circles of the "dearth of professional staff, division one officers, engineers, architects and medical officers".[150] The "precipitate acts in the first few months of Government", Lord Selkirk, the new U.K. Commissioner in Singapore observed in May 1960, did considerable "damage" and resulted in "deterioration in the administration of Government and the running of public utilities". While this trend had been somewhat checked by the middle of 1960, the new government's relative inexperience and single-minded zeal for reform meant that there remained "an air of suspicion and stifling of ideas", with the result that "constructive achievement and the prospect of solid progress both in the social and economic fields at the end of their first year of office" remained "problematical".[151]

Selkirk worried especially that, despite "some re-organisation in the field of social services, particularly in education", the PAP government on the whole had "achieved so little in the way of bringing" the ordinary public "material benefit", as there was up to that time scant evidence "that improvement in the appalling conditions of the slums" or in "the conditions of the kampongs, is even likely". Worse, while "industrial development" appeared to be lagging, the "housing programme is almost at a standstill".[152] As it so happened, in May 1960, the PAP minister in charge of housing was one Ong Eng Guan, the Minister for National Development, whose personal ambition and political opportunism was to ultimately set in train a series of events leading to the final break-up of the uneasy marriage of convenience between the pro-Communist and non-Communist camps within the PAP — thus helping set in motion the events leading up to Coldstore.

By 1959, Ong was a high-flyer within the PAP. An Australian-educated accountant by background and effectively trilingual in English, Chinese and

Malay, he was made party treasurer at the time of the PAP's inauguration in November 1954. His strong anti-Communist leanings furthermore helped consolidate his position at that stage as one of the Big Three — the others at the time being PAP Chairman Dr Toh Chin Chye and Lee Kuan Yew — in the non-Communist faction within the party. Significantly, when Ong was ousted in the attempted August 1957 leftist capture of the PAP CEC, Lee admitted it was like "having one of his arms chopped off". Ong truly came to national attention, however, in the wake of the PAP victory in local elections held in December 1957 for a new City Council to handle public utilities and social services in downtown Singapore. He was picked by the elected PAP councillors to be the Council's first mayor and served from 1957 to 1959. Ong proved he could rouse the Chinese-speaking masses of coolies, trishaw riders and *samsui* women construction workers with his down-to-earth, populist and fiery anti-colonial Hokkien speeches. Ong became especially famous for symbolically wielding, in October 1958, a giant broom in leading 2,000 volunteers from the City Hall staff on an anti-litter drive. He shocked the British, moreover, by goading the non-Asian City Council staff to discard their jackets and join him in sweeping the streets. Making every effort to "show Singapore's white colonial masters that their days were numbered", he pointedly dispensed with colonial protocol and allowed City Council meetings to be observed by the often raucous *hoi polloi*, and ensured that the proceedings were translated from English into Malay, Chinese and Tamil, and vice versa. A Public Complaints Bureau was set up to provide a direct channel for ordinary people to bring their grouses over anything ranging from difficulties in getting access to public utilities, to low-level corruption. Neither local nor expatriate staff escaped his sharp tongue and calculated public scoldings aimed at keeping them on their toes. While he had his detractors within the PAP Old Guard, many observers also believed that Ong's energetic if highly controversial stint as PAP mayor of the Singapore City Council helped the PAP win the June 1959 elections.[153]

Ong was thus apparently disgruntled when he was not given a higher profile portfolio when the first PAP cabinet was announced, and some commentators suggest he even eyed the premiership itself. This did not escape Lee's notice, with the consequence that by March 1960, the two men "were unable to tolerate each other any longer".[154] Exacerbating matters was the fact that a month earlier, Lee and Goh Keng Swee — fed up with Ong's financially unsound plans for a housing programme — had installed their trusted friend Lim Kim San as chairman of a newly constituted Housing and Development Board (HDB), implying that Ong's own ministerial portfolio was being downgraded in influence.[155] Subsequently in June 1960 at a party conference held to review the performance of the government in the past year, Ong, also the chairman of the PAP branch in his home constituency of Hong Lim, tabled a set of sixteen resolutions for adoption, implicitly attacking Lee and the government for, *inter alia,* not working harder on releasing the remaining political detainees still incarcerated since the previous Lim Yew Hock administration; and being slow to seek fresh talks in London as the present constitution was not adequate to meet public aspirations for complete independence. It was clear that in tabling these resolutions, Ong was trying to reach out to the pro-Communist faction within the party to forge a coalition to oust Lee. Apparently two months earlier Ong had visited Lim Chin Siong at his home, but the latter was not in. In fact on the very day the PAP cabinet was sworn in — 5 June 1959 — Ong had tried to meet Lim to discuss "an alliance to check Lee" but was rebuffed.[156] Lim and the pro-Communists, to be sure, did not trust Ong, regarding him as an opportunist. The net result was that Ong was expelled from the party in July 1960 and lost his ministerial portfolio. After a few months attacking Lee as an Independent in the Legislative Assembly, he resigned and challenged the PAP to a fight in his Hong Lim constituency. Ong was a "hero" in Hong Lim, a Chinatown district, where "his fluency in the Hokkien dialect and his popularity with hawkers, shopkeepers, and tenement dwellers counted for much".[157] Ong's responsiveness as mayor between 1957 and 1959, moreover, in which he had overseen the "rapid delivery of standpipes, street lamps and other public amenities; his liberal issuance of hawker licences", and "severe crackdown on rude and inefficient civil servants" were still remembered with gratitude by the Hokkien-speaking and semi-literate "hawkers, petty traders, bumboat men, riverside workers, taxi drivers and the jobless" who comprised the bulk of the Hong Lim constituents.[158] He would not be easy to defeat.

Little wonder that CUF elements in the PAP saw an opportunity at this juncture to leverage on Ong Eng Guan to pressure Lee into making some concessions. During the by-election campaigning from 11 March to 29 April 1961, therefore, Lim Chin Siong approached Lee Kuan Yew and asked that the ISC — an institutional mechanism that both men knew was squarely aimed at the Communists — be abolished and that at the next constitutional talks due in 1963, Singapore be granted independence. Lee rebuffed Lim on both counts. The latter then "quietly passed the word around in Hong Lim not to support the PAP".[159] Still, as Ong was seen as untrustworthy by the pro-Communists, they were equally wary about giving him too strong a helping hand just in case he turned against them later. The real challenge was thus to empower Ong just enough to get Lee's attention, but not so much that the former himself became a big political threat to the PAP pro-Communists down the road.[160] Despite intensive door-to-door campaigning by the PAP in Hong Lim, as well as a publicity campaign aimed at exposing Ong Eng Guan as not merely an opportunist, but a "liar" and a "bigamist" as well, because he had apparently taken an oath as a bachelor and married a woman in Hong Kong while still being married with three children, it was to no avail. Ong defeated the PAP's Jek Yuen Thong in the 29 April 1961 election, winning a thumping 73 per cent of the vote.[161] The Hong Lim result shocked Lee and the PAP. Lee had calculated that the pro-Communists did not trust Ong and would never throw their lot in with him; after all, after Ong had tabled his sixteen resolutions at the party conference in June 1960, Fang Chuang Pi (the Plen) had written to Lee to disassociate the CPMSTC from Ong and his resolutions, and reiterated that it was keen to support Lee.[162]

The Hong Lim loss thus opened up the possibility that the pro-Communists could well have decided to switch allegiances. Lee accordingly offered his resignation to PAP Chairman Toh Chin Chye, but this was rebuffed. Lee's close PAP aide S. Rajaratnam reckoned later that this was a ruse by Lee to cause anxiety amongst the pro-Communists who knew that if the PAP quit, either the British or a caretaker right-wing government would take over, and would "probably swipe them again" — as had been the case under the Labour Front in 1956 and 1957.[163] As it turned out, moreover, Lee's resignation threat had another more profound effect: it drove home to the anxiously watching Malayan Prime Minister Tunku Abdul Rahman the uncomfortable fact that Lee's resignation would leave a vacuum in Singapore that could well be filled by a "left-wing group", making Singapore "a greater security threat to Malaya".[164] This edged Tunku closer to the idea of a political merger between the two territories. It was the issue of merger that was to cause the final acrimonious split between the PAP and the CUF — and brought the protagonists a fateful step closer to Operation Coldstore.

Merger was by no means a new issue: from its inception the PAP always sought to one day achieve reunification with the Federation. In a 1957 Legislative Assembly debate, Lee had famously commented that the idea of an independent Singapore was a "political, economic and geographical absurdity".[165] Since the PAP victory in the June 1959 elections, moreover, Lee had raised the merger issue with Tunku but had consistently been given the cold shoulder.[166] There were two reasons for Tunku's wariness. Incorporating Singapore — with its large Chinese population — would upset the delicate Malay-dominated demographic equilibrium in the peninsula. Worse, to Tunku's mind, the Singapore Chinese possessed visceral pro-Communist leanings. Bringing Singapore in was hence the last thing he wanted as the twelve-year-long Emergency on the peninsula was winding up by the end of the 1950s.[167] Lee remained unmoved. To mollify Tunku's concerns, he sought to "Malayanize" the Singapore population in various ways by adopting Malay as the official national language and promoting Malayan culture. Following Lee's very public spat with Ong Eng Guan from June 1960 onwards, moreover, the former ramped up public discussion on "Merger", which was gradually reframed as a broader political union encompassing not just the peninsula and Singapore, but the largely Malay British Borneo territories as well. This was proposed to nullify the numerical impact of Singapore's Chinese majority within an expanded Federation — and thereby resolve a key Tunku concern.[168] In fact, an expanded Federation was something the cheered British certainly had no objections to. On the contrary, since the early 1940s they had calculated that from the wider geopolitical standpoint, their security and economic interests were best served in a "grand design to bring all their charges in Southeast Asia under one roof in the care of an independent Malaya".[169]

In January 1961, therefore, when the British Secretary of State for Commonwealth Relations, Duncan Sandys, visited Singapore and Malaya to brief both governments on London's move to join the Common Market, he separately discussed the possibility of merger with the Tunku and Lee. Subsequently, on his return to London, Sandys raised the issue with British Prime Minister Harold Macmillan as well. When the Tunku was in London the following month, Macmillan took the opportunity to urge him to reconsider his stance on merger.[170] Still, back in Kuala Lumpur, on 18 April, the Tunku told High Commissioner Geofroy Tory that while he appreciated that "Lee was genuinely doing his best to Malayanise his Chinese", he would "never succeed", and that the Chinese in Singapore "will never be Malaya's friends in a thousand years".[171] Nevertheless, by late April just before the Hong Lim result, Lee could sense that the Tunku, apparently influenced by his deputy Tun Abdul Razak, "for the first time" showed "some idea of the possible dangers to the Federation of an independent Singapore". While Lee was appropriately cautious, he told Singapore's British Deputy Commissioner Philip Moore that he was cheered nonetheless at the Tunku's suggestion that he "should prepare a paper on the subject" of "the Grand Design and merger". Noting that "Tunku was clearly interested in the possibility of the Federation acting as the leader in a wider confederation of states", Moore suggested that such an entity be called "The Pan Malayan Union". Lee however, proposed "the United States" — of "Malaysia".[172]

The CPMSTC, meanwhile, was beginning to get edgy. Because the PAP was "full of CPM members", Lee Ting Hui reminds us, "there was no way of completely preventing the leadership of the CPM finding out what was afoot in the PAP." In March 1961, an anxious Fang Chuang Pi thus sought a meeting with Lee to "clarify matters".[173] They met secretly for the last time on 11 May, after the shock PAP reversal at Hong Lim. Fang pointedly asked Lee if merger was on the cards, to which Lee replied — pretty much factually at the time as the Tunku was still mulling over the issue — that it was thus far unlikely. The Plen reiterated the stock CUF position that Lee should work towards getting the ISC abolished at the next constitutional talks with the British, scheduled for 1963. Moreover, any discussion of independence for Singapore, whether via "merger with Malaya or by itself", should be deferred. Fang also advised Lee to grant citizenship to persons prominent in the anti-colonial fight — a euphemism for leading Communist activists; allow unions to form large federations; implement a more liberal immigration regime as well as free up book imports from China. Lee listened but committed to nothing. No less significantly, Fang queried Lee about reported speculation that he and his entire cabinet might quit following the Hong Lim result. Lee deliberately did not rule this out, a stance that "worried the Plen".[174] Accordingly, as insurance, CUF elements within the party began discreetly approaching and sounding out non-Communist PAP assemblymen who were not part of Lee's inner circle, to see if they would be willing to work with the pro-Communists should Lee's faction step down. The most important non-Communist PAP assemblyman who agreed to the idea was Dr Lee Siew Choh, who had been inducted into the PAP to stand for election in May 1959.[175]

Then two weeks later, on 27 May, came a bombshell, catching the Plen, the British and Lee on the back foot in equal measure. Speaking at a luncheon in Singapore organized by the Foreign Correspondents Association of Southeast Asia, the Tunku remarked that there was a need for a "closer understanding" between the peoples of Malaya, Singapore, North Borneo, Brunei and Sarawak. He remarked that it was "inevitable that we should look ahead to this objective and think of a plan whereby these territories could be brought closer together in political and economic cooperation". Lee's immediate reaction was that the Plen was surely going to think that he had been lied to when Lee had told him only two weeks earlier that merger was not likely in the near future.[176] Lee's intuition that the die had been cast was spot on. Fang reportedly called an urgent meeting with CUF elements in the PAP at a location along Upper Thomson Road. He was unequivocal: he told them to "oppose Malaysia at all costs even to the extent of splitting the PAP".[177] PAP branch official Koo Young[178] also separately received a similar instruction from his CPMSTC superior Chan Hock Wah, a subordinate of the Plen within the CPMSTC apparatus in Singapore. That the Plen was calling the shots in the CPMSTC's anti-merger campaign in Singapore at the time was attested to by his superior ECY, who in 1993, confirmed that the Plen was after all "the man on-the-ground" at that crucial time.[179] The instruction to oppose merger and Malaysia was also pretty much in line with the decision made by the CPM leaders in Beijing. Chin Peng later disclosed that he, together with Siao Chang and ECY, came to the conclusion that it would be in the best interests of the CPM if they worked to "sabotage" or substantially delay merger. They "interpreted Lee Kuan Yew's keenness for the Malaysia concept as due in part to his perception of the advantages it provided him in moving against the CPM".[180]

As such, on 2 June, not long after the Tunku's historic speech, the pro-Communist Big Six union leaders — Lim, Fong, Bani, Woodhull, Jamit Singh and Dominic Puthucheary — issued a joint public statement reiterating the gist of the Plen's line that he had taken with Lee during the secret 11 May meeting. The Big Six called on the government to seek genuinely full self-government for Singapore, together with full control of internal security via the abolition of the ISC at the constitutional talks in 1963. The Big Six added that abolition of the ISC was more important than merger itself and indicated that the unions would only give support to a genuinely left-wing anti-colonial PAP in the coming Anson by-election due for 15 July 1961.[181] A week later on 9 June, Deputy Prime Minister Toh Chin Chye affirmed the government's support for the Tunku's new, open position on merger, and a few days later the Big Six issued another, this time harder-edged statement, insisting on the immediate release of all political detainees; greater freedoms of press, speech and association; the unification of the unions and citizenship for those loyal to the anti-colonial struggle. Hence both public statements in June 1961 by the Big Six echoed the gist of the Plen's private communication to Lee on 11 May.[182]

The Anson by-election had been occasioned by the sudden death of a PAP assemblyman Baharuddin bin Mohamed Ariff on 20 April, even before the Hong Lim electoral stand-off nine days later. Former Chief Minister David Marshall, representing the Workers' Party he himself had formed in 1957, decided to stand in Anson — a working class ward "teeming with Indian and Chinese harbor workers" — against the PAP candidate, Mahmud Awang, a veteran unionist who was then TUC president and head of the Singapore Traction Company Employees' Union (STCEU). If the CUF was somewhat ambivalent about supporting Ong Eng Guan at Hong Lim a few months earlier, it was much less discreet in its anti-Lee stand now. Hence Mahmud Awang found to his consternation that six of his own TUC and PAP compatriots, the Big Six, had come out against him in early June. Worse was to come: on 13 July — just two days before the election — eight PAP Assemblymen led by Lee Siew Choh, recently cultivated by the pro-Communists, issued a statement backing the demands of the Big Six, and complained of a "lack of democracy" within the party. Soon after this, forty-two unions issued a statement backing the Big Six as well. It was a further sign to Anson workers to shift support to Marshall. An incensed Lee hit back, calling on Lim, Fong and Woodhull to resign as political secretaries and charging the trio and the eight rogue assemblymen led by Lee Siew Choh with coercion and "going to any lengths — even to destroy the party" to stop merger. In the event, Marshall won Anson on 15 July by 546 votes, quite explicitly with the help of the CUF elements within the PAP.[183]

The Plen was in no mood to let up. The day after Anson, he called for a secret meeting with three CUF elements within the PAP at an attap hut along Thomson Road that lasted for several hours, according to Special Branch surveillance. The latter believed that the Plen and his compatriots discussed how to topple the PAP government and form a new party to step up the anti-merger and anti-Malaysia struggle. One of the men the Plen met was apparently Lim Chin Siong.[184] Then on 18 July — just two days after the secret Plen meeting — Lim, Fong, James Puthucheary and Woodhull, sought an urgent audience with U.K. Commissioner Selkirk at his Eden Hall residence. Puthucheary had called Selkirk at noon that day and Selkirk wanted a meeting two days later. However Puthucheary — evincing the perceived urgency of the situation — insisted on an earlier meeting, so Selkirk agreed to one that very afternoon. Lim's group wanted to obtain an assurance that the British would not suspend the Constitution and resort to direct rule should Lee Kuan Yew be ousted and the Lim faction assumed control of the PAP. Selkirk apparently played it straight, telling them that his job was to maintain the stability Singapore needed to solve its economic problems and survive. Hence as long as the actions of the PAP leftists were within the law, there would be no question of British intervention. At some point Selkirk pointedly asked Lim and Fong if they were Communists, and they seemed "to be embarrassed by this question and failed to give a clear reply".[185] Most readers would wonder — legitimately — if Lim and Fong were wary of revealing their true status to Selkirk. The Alternates though, approach the exchange in unusual ways. Thum Ping Tjin completely fails to mention this extraordinarily significant exchange.[186] Hong Lysa for her part, in responding to the current writer's mention of the exchange,[187] produced this mystifying riposte:

> What is one to make of the statement that the British High Commissioner
> Lord Selkirk recorded that Lim and Fong had "seemed embarrassed" and
> "failed to give a clear reply" when he asked whether they were communists.
> Was it Lim Chin Siong or Lord Selkirk who was being "disingenuous"? Is
> the author so prone to repose uncritical belief in the superior intelligence of
> the British colonial rulers, or regard Lim Chin Siong as an imbecile, caught
> out by such a penetrating question? Or perhaps it is his readers' intelligence
> that the author is insulting.[188]

Recalling British historian Richard Evans' warning about the temptations
accosting postmodernist-inclined, partisan historians,[189] readers may well
wonder if in the current example the Eden Hall "facts" are being "mined
to prove a case", "inconvenient" evidence is being "ignored", and sources
"misconstrued or misinterpreted". In essence, readers may consider asking why
is attention being seemingly diverted from the blindingly obvious: perhaps
Lim and Fong appeared to be "to be embarrassed" by Selkirk's blunt question
"and failed to give a clear reply" because they did not want to publicly confirm
before the senior British official in Singapore that they were indeed the two
leading CUF elements.

At any rate, following the Anson defeat, it was pretty clear that the PAP's
hold on power had become very tenuous indeed. Selkirk observed that Lee
and Goh appeared edgy and broken men. Again, Lee offered to resign. After
an all-night CEC debate, Party Chairman Toh Chin Chye again rejected Lee's
offer, reminding the latter that that was precisely what the pro-Communists
were after and more to the point, merger was after all the key objective of the
PAP since its formation and from which "we cannot deviate".[190] As things stood,
there was no way for the PAP-CUF marriage of convenience to continue. On
20 July, therefore, Lee took the plunge, lifted the party whip and called for a
vote of confidence in the Legislative Assembly. Following more than thirteen
hours of debate, a vote was finally called: twenty-six PAP members and one
Independent voted for the government, while thirteen other PAP members,
including Lee Siew Choh's original eight who had opposed Lee in the run-
up to Anson, abstained, along with Ong Eng Guan and his two followers.
Seven persons from the Singapore People's Alliance led by Lim Yew Hock and
David Marshall from the Workers' Party voted against the motion. The pro-
Communists had lost. Lee moved quickly to expel the thirteen assemblymen
who had abstained as well as all persons associated with them from the party.
Lim Chin Siong, Fong Swee Suan, and S. Woodhull were sacked, along with
five parliamentary secretaries and three political secretaries. The Plen moved
equally quickly in response, giving instructions that a "new proxy political
party be formed". More PAP members then quit, including nineteen out

of twenty-three organizing secretaries in various branches. The police later estimated that a massive 60–70 per cent of the PAP membership quit.[191]

Led by Lim Chin Siong, the dissidents rapidly coalesced into a new party, the Barisan Sosialis Singapura (BSS — Singapore Socialist Front), on 30 July, purportedly pursuing exactly the same PAP objectives: "a democratic, independent, socialist, non-Communist Malaya, comprising the Federation and Singapore". The BSS was launched at a mass rally on 13 August at Happy World Stadium before a crowd of 10,000 and was officially inaugurated on 17 September 1961 with Lee Siew Choh as Chairman and Lim Chin Siong as Secretary-General. All the thirteen dissident former PAP and now BSS assemblymen retained their seats in the legislature as Opposition parliamentarians.[192] The Big Split between the non-Communist Lee and the pro-Communist Lim factions in the PAP was mirrored in the unions as well: the TUC also sundered, with most of the unions, including non-Communist ones, coming under the BSS-linked Singapore Association of Trade Unions (SATU), while the remainder flocked towards the PAP-backed National Trades Union Congress (NTUC).[193] The July 1961 Big Split within the PAP represented the failure of the CPM's strategy since 1957 to capture and manipulate the PAP as its preferred open-front vehicle to seize power through constitutional means in Singapore. Now the pro-Communists were flushed out into the open, no longer having recourse to the political cover previously afforded by Lee's non-Communists within the PAP and the labour movement. An intense battle — as we shall see shortly — soon ensued between July 1961 and February 1963, one that would have major consequences for Singapore's future political evolution. In the raw struggle for domination between the PAP and BSS — the latest public face of the ever-morphing, deeply resilient Communist United Front — there could be only one victor. As it turned out, the ultimate political fortunes of the BSS were inextricably linked with those of its charismatic and enigmatic Secretary-General: Lim Chin Siong.

Notes

1. Thum, "*The Fundamental Issue Is Anti-Colonialism, Not Merger*", p. 5.
2. Harper, "Lim Chin Siong", in Tan and Jomo, eds., *Comet in Our Sky*, p. 12.
3. Ibid., p. 13.
4. Michael Fernandez and Loh Kah Seng, "The Left-Wing Trade Unions in Singapore, 1945–1970", in Barr and Trocki, eds., *Paths Not Taken*, p. 212.
5. Cited in Sonny Yap, Richard Lim and Leong Weng Kam, *Men in White: The Untold Story of Singapore's Ruling Political Party* (Singapore: Straits Times Press, 2010), p. 320.

6. Harper, "Lim Chin Siong", in Tan and Jomo, eds., *Comet in Our Sky*, p. 13.
7. Barr and Trocki, "Introduction", in Barr and Trocki, eds., *Paths Not Taken*, p. 8.
8. Chin Peng, with Ian Ward and Norma Miraflor, *Alias Chin Peng: My Side of History* (Singapore: Media Masters, 2003).
9. Fong Chong Pik, *Fong Chong Pik: The Memoirs of a Malayan Communist Revolutionary* (Petaling Jaya: SIRDC, 2008). "Fang Chuang Pi" is also at times rendered in the historiography as "Fong Chong Pik".
10. R.N. Carew Hunt, *The Theory and Practice of Communism: An Introduction, with a Preface by Leonard Schapiro* (Aylesbury: Pelican, 1977), pp. 25–26.
11. Ibid., pp. 26–27.
12. Lee, *The Open United Front*, p. 1.
13. Carew Hunt, *Theory and Practice of Communism*, pp. 193–96.
14. Ibid., p. 194.
15. Cited in Aloysius Chin, *The Communist Party of Malaya: The Inside Story* (Kuala Lumpur: Vinpress, 1995), p. 72.
16. Lee, *The Open United Front*, p. 22; Chin, *Communist Party of Malaya*, pp. 22–23.
17. Kumar Ramakrishna, *Freedom News: The Untold Story of the Communist Underground Publication* (Singapore: S. Rajaratnam School of International Studies, 2008), p. 6.
18. Lee, *The Open United Front*, pp. 5–7.
19. Ibid., p. 6.
20. Cheah Boon Kheng, "The Communist Insurgency in Malaysia, 1948–1989: Was it Due to the Cold War?", in *Cold War in Southeast Asia*, edited by Malcolm H. Murfett (Singapore: Marshall Cavendish International, 2012), p. 40.
21. Chin Peng, *Alias Chin Peng*, p. 410.
22. Lee, *The Open United Front*, p. 7.
23. Ibid., pp. 6–7.
24. Ibid., p. 8.
25. Ibid., p. 19; Ramakrishna, *Freedom News*, p. 7.
26. Cited in Chin, *Communist Party of Malaya*, p. 72.
27. Lee, *The Open United Front*, pp. 8, 18–19.
28. Ibid., p. 21.
29. Chin, *Communist Party of Malaya*, pp. 72–73.
30. Ibid., p. 122.
31. Lee, *The Open United Front*, p. 21.
32. Chin, *Communist Party of Malaya*, pp. 88–89.
33. Ramakrishna, *Freedom News*, p. 7.
34. Chin Peng, *Alias Chin Peng*, p. 409.
35. Ramakrishna, *Freedom News*, pp. 7, 10.
36. The teenage Lim Chin Siong was to join the NDYL, to be discussed below.
37. Lee, *The Open United Front*, pp. 25–26.

38. Chin Peng, *Alias Chin Peng*, p. 193.

39. One of the major debates in the historiography is the extent to which the CPM launched the insurrection in response to international Communist instructions, or acted on its own. For discussion on the origins of the conflict, see A.J. Stockwell, "'A Widespread and Long-Concocted Plot to Overthrow the Government in Malaya?' The Origins of the Malayan Emergency", *Journal of Imperial and Commonwealth History* 21, no. 3 (September 1993): 66–88.

40. C.C. Chin, "The United Front Strategy of the Malayan Communist Party in Singapore, 1950s–1960s", in Barr and Trocki, eds., *Paths Not Taken*, pp. 60–61.

41. Ramakrishna, *Freedom News*, p. 10.

42. Chin, "The United Front Strategy", in Barr and Trocki, eds., *Paths Not Taken*, p. 75.

43. Harper, "Lim Chin Siong", in Tan and Jomo, eds., *Comet in Our Sky*, p. 22.

44. Ramakrishna, *Freedom News*, p. 10.

45. "Top Secret" paper on "Lim Chin Siong", 27 February 2014, Internal Security Department Heritage Centre. Hereafter ISDHC.

46. "Lim Chin Siong" paper. Zhou Guang, "First Anti-British League Group in Singapore Chinese High School", *Mainstays of the Anti-Colonial Movement: The Legendary Figures of the Singapore People's Anti-British League* (Hong Kong: Footprints Publishing Company, 2013), pp. 29–33.

47. Chin, "The United Front Strategy", in Barr and Trocki, eds., *Paths Not Taken*, p. 75.

48. Zhou Guang, "First Anti-British League Group in Singapore Chinese High School", p. 41.

49. Ramakrishna, *Freedom News*, p. 10; Chin Peng, *Alias Chin Peng*, p. 436; Lim Cheng Leng, *Story of a Psywarrior: Tan Sri Dr C.C. Too* (Selangor Darul Ehsan: 2000), pp. 196–97.

50. Zhong Hua, "A Preliminary Study on the History of Singapore People's Anti-British League", *Mainstays of the Anti-Colonial Movement: The Legendary Figures of the Singapore People's Anti-British League* (Hong Kong: Footprints Publishing Company, 2013), pp. 5–28.

51. "Lim Chin Siong" paper.

52. Bloodworth, *Tiger and the Trojan Horse*, p. 34.

53. Ramakrishna, *Freedom News*, p. 11; "Lim Chin Siong" paper.

54. Chin Peng, *Alias Chin Peng*, p. 238.

55. *Dialogues with Chin Peng: New Light on the Malayan Communist Party*, edited by C.C. Chin and Karl Hack (Singapore: Singapore University Press, 2004), p. 192.

56. Chin Peng, *Alias Chin Peng*, p. 193.

57. Ramakrishna, *Freedom News*, pp. 10–11.

58. Ibid., pp. 12–14.

59. Bloodworth, *Tiger and the Trojan Horse*, p. 37.

60. Ibid., p. 72; Chin Peng, *Alias Chin Peng*, p. 279; Lee, *The Open United Front*,

pp. 36, 134; Chin, "The United Front Strategy", in Barr and Trocki, eds., *Paths Not Taken*, pp. 64, 67; "Communist Party of Malaya Organisation from 1960–1968", 29 March 1969, ISDHC. ECY subsequently set up another CPMSTC organ, the Malayan National Liberation League (MNLL), with the aid of the Indonesian Communist Party (PKI) in Jakarta. Lim, *Story of a Psywarrior*, p. 197.

61. Chin, *Communist Party of Malaya*, p. 119.
62. Ibid., p. 122.
63. Ibid., p. 67; "Lim Chin Siong" paper.
64. Bloodworth, *Tiger and the Trojan Horse*, p. 130.
65. Ramakrishna, *Freedom News*, p. 16.
66. "The Communist Threat in Singapore", Cmd. 33 of 1957, 23 August 1957, p. 2, TNA, PRO: FCO 141/14774; Lee Kuan Yew, *Singapore Story*, pp. 160–61.
67. Lee, *The Open United Front*, p. 17.
68. Bloodworth, *Tiger and the Trojan Horse*, p. 70.
69. Lee, *The Open United Front*, p. 134.
70. "Lim Chin Siong" paper; Ramakrishna, *Freedom News*, p. 18.
71. Lim Hock Koon was a CPM district committee member and subordinate of the Plen (see below) at the time of his detention in 1971. He revealed to ISD his leading role in orchestrating the May 1954 anti-NS campaign as directed by his immediate superior Comrade R. He is the elder brother of Coldstore detainee Dr Lim Hock Siew. "Lim Chin Siong" paper.
72. Lim Kim Chuan was a student activist at Chung Cheng High School in the 1950s and a subordinate of the Plen. He was amongst CPM members who surfaced after the December 1989 CPM Peace Agreements with Malaysia and Thailand. He wrote the novel *The Mighty Wave*, about the anti-colonial movement in Singapore in the 1950s and mentioned the 13 May 1954 anti-NS incident involving the Chinese middle school students. This book was incidentally translated by two ex-political detainees, Tan Jing Quee and Low Miaw Gong, as well as Alternate historian Hong Lysa, and launched in May 2011 in Singapore, together with another book, *The May 13th Generation*. The latter book, edited by Tan Jing Quee, Hong Lysa and Tan Kok Chiang, contains recollections by activists of Chinese middle school student movements and Singapore politics in the 1950s, as well as academic contributions. "Lim Chin Siong" paper.
73. Woo Chong Poh @ Comrade R was the superior of Lim Hock Koon and Lim Kim Chuan. Woo himself reported to Wee Choo Leong @ Fong Chow, leader of the Chung Cheng High School Branch Committee of the CPMSTC's Students' Committee, led by Comrade D. Woo previously belonged to the CPM's militant 'E' Branch in Singapore, led by Wong Fook Kwong @ Tit Fung @ Iron Spearhead. Woo was detained under the Preservation of Public Security Ordinance (PPSO) from February 1959 to February 1960. "Lim Chin Siong" paper.

74. Chiam Chong Chian @ Gao Lao was recruited into the CPM by Comrade D during his student days at Chinese High School. Chiam was later amongst thirty CPM members who withdrew to Indonesia in 1963/4 to escape arrest. "Lim Chin Siong" paper.

75. Ibid.

76. Ibid.

77. Robert Soon Loh Boon @ Soon Tiong San played a prominent role in the May 1954 anti-NS student agitation. As the SCMSSU chairman from October 1955, he organized so-called *hsueh hsih* or self-study campaigns to indoctrinate students with Communist doctrine and encouraged them to prepare for armed struggle after he attended the Afro-Asian Student Conference in Bandung in 1956. Special Branch however could not detect any concrete evidence of CPM links after his 1956 arrest. However, one source, CPM member Choo Yeong Wah implicated Soon in 1964 as one of the CPM's three contacts in the SCMSSU. The other two were Chia Nam Wee and Yeong Kwok Sun, who were both CPM members. Soon was detained from 1956 to 1964. He was released on a suspension order in June 1964 after publicly renouncing his former activities in a television interview and public statement — which attracted criticisms from leftists who branded him a "traitor" to the cause. "Lim Chin Siong" paper.

78. *Riding the Tiger: The Chronicle of a Nation's Battle Against Communism* [dvd] (Singapore: Ministry of Information and the Arts, 2001).

79. Zhong Hua, "A Preliminary Study of the History of Singapore People's Anti-British League".

80. Ramakrishna, *Freedom News*, p. 18.

81. Revelation by Lim Chin Siong's ABL subordinate. "Lim Chin Siong" paper.

82. Lee, *The Open United Front*, p. 52.

83. Ibid., pp. 51–52, 93; Ramakrishna, *Freedom News*, p. 19.

84. Chin, "The United Front Strategy", in Barr and Trocki, eds., *Paths Not Taken*, p. 63.

85. Lee, *The Open United Front*, p. 84.

86. Ibid., pp. 84–89.

87. Bloodworth, *Tiger and the Trojan Horse*, pp. 76–77; "The Communist Threat in Singapore", Cmd. 33 of 1957, 23 August 1957, p. 2, TNA, PRO: FCO 141/14774.

88. Barr and Trocki, "Introduction", in *Paths Not Taken*, edited by Barr and Trocki, p. 8.

89. "Statement of Seet Chay Tuan", 19 December 1955, ISDHC. Seet was an ABL subordinate of Lim Chin Siong, who was expelled from Chinese High School in 1951 and arrested under the PPSO in December 1955 during which large quantities of CPM documents were seized from him by Special Branch. He was released in April 1956 and went to the UK for study.

90. Fong was a pro-Communist trade union leader and politician in the 1950s and 1960s. He orchestrated many labour and student disturbances, together with Lim

Chin Siong and others. Fong was detained on three separate occasions: June–July 1955; October 1956–June 1959; and following Coldstore, from February 1963 to August 1967. He was banned from Singapore between October 1966 and November 1990. He was allowed to return to Singapore in the 1990s and from 2006 he was given permanent residency. Fong only admitted to his CPM involvement as an ABL member together with Lim Chin Siong during their Chinese High School days in 2007. "Lim Chin Siong" paper.

91. Drysdale, *Struggle for Success*, p. 108.
92. Lee, *The Open United Front*, pp. 80–84; "Lim Chin Siong" paper.
93. Lee, *The Open United Front*, p. 83; "Lim Chin Siong" paper.
94. Thum, "Limitations of a Monolingual History", in Tarling, ed., *Studying Singapore's Past*, pp. 102–103.
95. Chin, "The United Front Strategy", in Barr and Trocki, eds., *Paths Not Taken*, p. 64.
96. Lee, *The Open United Front*, pp. 113–14, n. 15.
97. Chin, "The United Front Strategy", in Barr and Trocki, eds., *Paths Not Taken*, p. 64.
98. *Freedom News*, Issue no. 61, May 1955, reproduced in Ramakrishna, *Freedom News*, p. 209.
99. Zhang Taiyong, "Our Cohort's Commander — Lu Yexun", in *Mainstays of the Anti-Colonial Movement: The Legendary Figures of the Singapore People's Anti-British League* (Hong Kong: Footprints Publishing Company, 2013), pp. 60–73.
100. "Lim Chin Siong" paper; Lee, *The Open United Front*, pp. 92–93.
101. Lee, *The Open United Front*, pp. 86–87.
102. Ibid., p. 97.
103. "Lim Chin Siong" paper.
104. Marshall had actually allowed the registration of the SCMSSU on condition that it steered clear of politics and industrial disputes. However, most observers felt that that it was unlikely the "hot-headed Mao-inspired youngsters" would "live up to their pledge". Yap, Lim, and Leong, *Men in White*, p. 86.
105. Lee, *The Open United Front*, pp. 92–93; Yap, Lim and Leong, *Men in White*, pp. 86–87.
106. Lee, *The Open United Front*, p. 87.
107. Chia Ee Tian @ Chia Ek Tian was a subordinate of Lim Chin Siong in the ABL, Paid Secretary of the SFSWU in 1955, and a PAP Central Executive Committee member in 1956. He was detained under the PPSO from 1956 to 1957, then released on suspension orders to Johore. "Lim Chin Siong" paper.
108. Yap, Lim and Leong, *Men in White*, p. 90; "Lim Chin Siong" paper.
109. Lee, *The Singapore Story*, p. 249.
110. "Lim Chin Siong" paper.
111. Yap, Lim and Leong, *Men in White*, p. 91; "Lim Chin Siong" paper.
112. Yap, Lim and Leong, *Men in White*, pp. 91–92; Ramakrishna, *Freedom News*, pp. 22–23, 26, n. 111.

113. Lee, *The Open United Front*, p. 135.

114. Ibid., p. 137.

115. "The Communist Threat in Singapore", Cmd. 33 of 1957, 23 August 1957, p. 4, TNA, PRO: FCO 141/14774.

116. Chin Peng, *Alias Chin Peng*, p. 409.

117. Lee, *The Open United Front*, pp. 134–35; Fong, *Memoirs of a Malayan Communist Revolutionary*, p.126.

118. Fong, *Memoirs of a Malayan Communist Revolutionary*, p. 166.

119. Ibid., p. 167.

120. Lee, *The Open United Front*, p. 135.

121. "The Security Threat to Singapore (Communism and Nationalism)", 24 July 1959, ISDHC; Chin, "The United Front Strategy", in Barr and Trocki, eds., *Paths Not Taken*, pp. 65–66.

122. Lee, *Singapore Story*, p. 173.

123. Ibid., pp. 177–79.

124. Yap, Lim and Leong, *Men in White*, p. 75.

125. Ibid., p. 82.

126. Yeo Kim Wah and Albert Lau, "From Colonialism to Independence, 1945–65", in Ernest C.T. Chew and Edwin Lee, eds., *A History of Singapore* (Singapore: Oxford University Press, 1991), pp. 134–35.

127. Sandrasegaran (Sydney) Woodhull was an influential pro-Communist trade unionist in the 1950s and 1960s, and a founder member of the PAP. He was detained by Lim Yew Hock in October 1956 for pro-Communist activities and released following the PAP election victory in 1959. As advisor to several pro-Communist unions, Woodhull set them on the course of industrial unrest against the Singapore government. In 1961, Woodhull and others dissident PAP members formed the Barisan Sosialis Singapura. Detained in Coldstore in February 1963, Woodhull was released in November the same year and left for the U.K. to study law. On graduation in 1966 he returned to Malaysia to start his own law firm. "Lim Chin Siong" paper.

128. Yap, Lim and Leong, *Men in White*, pp. 82–83.

129. Ramakrishna, *Emergency Propaganda*, pp. 195–96; Chin, *Communist Party of Malaya*, pp. 47–48.

130. Chin, *Communist Party of Malaya*, pp. 47, 50.

131. Goh Boon Toh @ Ng Mau Tau was involved in various pro-Communist unions, such as the Singapore Cycle and Motor Workers' Union, in the 1950s. He was a member of the PAP CEC in 1956 and Vice-President of the PAP Central Education and Cultural Committee in 1957. He was detained in 1957 and banished to China the following year. Goh has been allowed to visit Singapore since 1991. "Lim Chin Siong" paper.

132. *Riding the Tiger*; Yap, Lim and Leong, *Men in White*, pp. 106–108.

133. Yap, Lim and Leong, *Men in White*, p. 108.

134. "Lim Chin Siong" paper; Yap, Lim and Leong, *Men in White*, pp. 103–106; Lee, *Singapore Story*, p. 287.

135. Chin, "The United Front Strategy", in Barr and Trocki, eds., *Paths Not Taken*, p. 67.
136. Lee, *Singapore Story*, pp. 280–83; "Lim Chin Siong" paper.
137. "Lim Chin Siong" paper; Lee, *The Open United Front*, pp. 144, 149.
138. Edwin Lee, *Singapore: The Unexpected Nation* (Singapore: Institute of Southeast Asian Studies, 2008), p. 143.
139. James Puthucheary was an ABL member of the English-speaking branch who was first detained in 1951. On release, he played an active part in the formation of the University of Malaya Socialist Club (UMSC) and served on the editorial board of the UMSC organ *Fajar*. After graduating in 1954, Puthucheary actively engaged in CUF work in pro-Communist unions and was also a founding PAP member. He was detained a second time in 1956 following the 1956 riots. He was released in 1959 and returned to the PAP fold, but was among the pro-Communists who split off in July 1961 to form the BSS, to whom he acted as advisor. Because of his skill as a "Marxist theoretician" he was one of Lim Chin Siong's closest advisors. He was arrested a third time under Coldstore in February 1963 and rusticated back to Malaya. He was released in November after pledging to quit politics. "Lim Chin Siong" paper.
140. "Lim Chin Siong" paper; Yap, Lim and Leong, *Men in White*, pp. 158–61.
141. Lee, *The Open United Front*, p. 189.
142. CJ W-L Wee, "The Vanquished: Lim Chin Siong and a Progressive National Narrative", in Lam and Tan, eds., *Lee's Lieutenants*, p. 181.
143. Lee, *The Open United Front*, p. 191.
144. Bogaars would later become Director of the Singapore Special Branch.
145. Cited in Lee, *The Open United Front*, p. 214, n. 21.
146. Dominic Puthucheary, brother of James Puthucheary, was dismissed from his teaching post in 1956 for an anti-British remark in his speech while welcoming back the Malayan delegation to the Afro-Asia Conference. He later became a paid Secretary of the pro-Communist Singapore General Employees' Union (SGEU) and close associate of CUF leaders like Lim Chin Siong and Fong Swee Suan. He joined the BSS and was elected into its CEC. He was arrested during Operation Coldstore on 2 February 1963 and later rusticated to the Federation, but released in December that year. His son Janil was elected as a PAP Member of Parliament in the May 2011 general elections. "Lim Chin Siong" paper.
147. "Lim Chin Siong" paper; Lee, *The Open United Front*, pp. 207–209.
148. Lee, *Singapore Story*, pp. 306, 328.
149. Ibid., p. 317.
150. Yap, Lim and Leong, *Men in White*, pp. 172–74.
151. Lord Selkirk to Iain Macleod, 20 May 1960, TNA, PRO: CO 1030/1148.
152. Ibid.
153. Yap, Lim and Leong, *Men in White*, pp. 57, 97, 108, 138–43; Clement Mesenas, *Dissident Voices: Personalities in Singapore's Political History* (Singapore: Marshall Cavendish International, 2014), pp. 12–19.

154. Yap, Lim and Leong, *Men in White*, p. 187; Lee, *Singapore: The Unexpected Nation*, p. 163; Lee, *The Open United Front*, p. 195.

155. Yap, Lim and Leong, *Men in White*, pp. 188–89; Lee, *The Open United Front*, p. 215, n. 39.

156. Lee, *The Open United Front*, p. 217, n. 41; Yap, Lim and Leong, *Men in White*, p. 197.

157. Lee, *Singapore: The Unexpected Nation*, p. 163.

158. Yap, Lim and Leong, *Men in White*, p. 192.

159. Lee, *Singapore: The Unexpected Nation*, p. 164.

160. Yap, Lim and Leong, *Men in White*, pp. 194–96.

161. Ibid., p. 192.

162. Lee, *The Open United Front*, p. 197.

163. Ibid., p. 198; Yap, Lim and Leong, *Men in White*, p. 196.

164. Lee, *The Open United Front*, p. 200.

165. Raymond Lim, Minister for Transport and Second Minister for Foreign Affairs, "Staying Relevant in the Midst of Globalisation", 26 July 2006 <http://www.mfa.gov.sg/content/mfa/media_centre/special_events/pedrabranca/press_room/sp_tr/2006/200607/press_200607_1.html> (accessed 18 August 2014).

166. Lee, *Singapore: The Unexpected Nation*, p. 177.

167. Lee, *The Open United Front*, p. 190.

168. Ibid., p. 199.

169. Lee, *Singapore: The Unexpected Nation*, p. 178; Tan Tai Yong, *Creating Greater Malaysia: Decolonization and the Politics of Merger* (Singapore: Institute of Southeast Asian Studies, 2008), pp. 15–21; Matthew Jones, *Conflict and Confrontation in Southeast Asia: 1961–1965* (Cambridge: Cambridge University Press, 2002), p. 61.

170. Lee, *Singapore: The Unexpected Nation*, p. 179.

171. Geofroy Tory to Neil Pritchard, Commonwealth Relations Office, 18 April 1961, TAN, PRO: DO 169/10.

172. Record of Conversation between the Prime Minister, Mr Lee Kuan Yew, and Mr P.B.C. Moore, United Kingdom Commission, 28 April 1961, TNA, PRO: DO 169/25.

173. Lee, *The Open United Front*, pp. 200, 218, n. 76.

174. Ibid., pp. 201–202; Lee, *Singapore: The Unexpected Nation*, p. 180.

175. Lee, *The Open United Front*, p. 201.

176. Lee, *Singapore Story*, p. 365.

177. Bloodworth, *Tiger and the Trojan Horse*, p. 331.

178. Koo Young was a CPM member directed by Chan Hock Wah, a former Chinese High School student and CPM district committee member under the direction of the Plen since 1958. Koo had joined the PAP in 1959 and was concurrently active in the CPMSTC-controlled Singapore Chinese School Teachers' Union between 1960 and 1962. In July 1961, Koo was amongst the CUF elements who left the PAP to form the BSS. In 1963 he was amongst thirteen BSS

members elected to Parliament as the MP for Thomson. He was arrested in 1967 but released in January 1968. "Lim Chin Siong" paper.

179. Ibid.
180. Chin Peng, *Alias Chin Peng*, p. 437.
181. Ibid.; Lee, *The Open United Front*, pp. 202–203.
182. "Secret: The Security Situation in Singapore as on the 1st August, 1961", paper by the Singapore Representative, Internal Security Council, 10 August 1961, TNA, PRO: CO 1030/1162; Lee, *The Open United Front*, p. 203.
183. "Lim Chin Siong" paper; Bloodworth, *Tiger and the Trojan Horse*, p. 231; Drysdale, *Struggle for Success*, p. 265; Lee, *Singapore Story*, p. 371; Yap, Lim and Leong, *Men in White*, pp. 203–205.
184. "Surveillance Report", 18 July 1961, ISDHC; "Lim Chin Siong" paper.
185. "Lim Chin Siong" paper; "Note of a Meeting Held at Eden Hall, at 4.30 p.m. on Tuesday, 18 July 1961", 31 July 1961, TNA, PRO: FCO 141/17161. Woodhull though categorically denied being a Communist.
186. See Thum, "The Fundamental Issue is Anti-Colonialism, Not Merger", p. 12; idem, " 'Flesh and Bone Reunite as One Body': Singapore's Chinese-Speaking and their Perspectives on Merger", in Poh, Tan and Hong, eds., *The 1963 Operation Coldstore*, p. 99.
187. Ramakrishna, "Lim Chin Siong and that Beauty World Speech: A Closer Look".
188. Hong, "What is History; A Glance at 'Lim Chin Siong and that Beauty World Speech: A Closer Look' ".
189. Evans, *In Defence of History*, p. 219.
190. Yap, Lim and Leong, *Men in White*, p. 205; Lee, *Singapore: The Unexpected Nation*, p. 182.
191. "Lim Chin Siong" paper; Lee, *The Open United Front*, p. 205; Bloodworth, *Tiger and the Trojan Horse*, pp. 239–40.
192. "Lim Chin Siong" paper.
193. Lee, *Singapore: The Unexpected Nation*, p. 185.

3

THE CURIOUS CASE OF
LIM CHIN SIONG

THE ALTERNATE HISTORY OF LIM CHIN SIONG

To recapitulate, the titular leader of the BSS and the central figure in the ambitious Alternate attempt to construct a New Singapore History — with Coldstore as its point of departure — has been the enigmatic Lim Chin Siong. It is worth reiterating how Lim has become almost a mythical symbol amongst the Alternate community. One former Coldstore detainee, Dr Lim Hock Siew, on the occasion of Lim's passing on 5 February 1996, declared:

> His ability to communicate with the common man, his ability to explain complex political issues in simple layman's language, his complete identification with the oppressed and downtrodden — these were the hallmarks of Chin Siong's political leadership — a leader whose ability, sincerity and dedication aroused the people to free themselves from colonial domination.[1]

Lim's long-time friend and comrade Fong Swee Suan recalled that people who listened to the former's speeches likened his performance to "watching a classic drama", while the PAP's Toh Chin Chye marvelled at how "huge crowds" used to greet him at PAP rallies.[2] Even Lee Kuan Yew admitted that Lim's speeches had a "hypnotic effect".[3] Lim Chin Siong's personal charisma always seemed to make an impression. When the Australian journalist Peter Hastings interviewed him in September 1961, he made the following observation:

> Lim is youthful, firm and good-looking. His manners are quiet. He is polite but his essential toughness shows through. He has a sense of humour and

laughs quite readily although sometimes out of politeness. His English is rapid, fluent and at times hard to follow ...[4]

To be sure, a great deal has been made of one major Path Not Taken by Singaporeans: having Lim Chin Siong instead of Lee Kuan Yew as independent Singapore's first Prime Minister. The following anecdote related by David Marshall when he was Chief Minister in the mid-1950s has been well trodden in accounts sympathetic to the Alternate perspective:

> Chin Siong was introduced to me by Lee Kuan Yew [LKY]. Kuan Yew came to visit me in my little office underneath the stairs and said, "Meet the future Prime Minister of Singapore!" I looked at Lim Chin Siong and I laughed. LKY said, "Don't laugh! He is the finest Chinese orator in Singapore and he will be our next Prime Minister!"[5]

The Alternates are in particular most eager to promote the idea that Lim's detention in Coldstore was utterly unjustified. The claim is that the "latest research" suggests that the "status of Lim Chin Siong — the most prominent pro-communist operative in post-war Singapore — was not clear to either the British or to the Singapore Special Branch, and remains a point of debate among academics".[6] Certainly, as early as September 1961, when Hastings challenged Lim to declare if it was true that he was a Communist, the latter replied: "It is not true. I am not a Communist. I have even stated in print that I am not a Communist."[7] Soon after the Big Split within the PAP in July that same year, Lim had charged his great rival Lee Kuan Yew with "crying 'Communism' to cover a multitude of sins" and reiterated: "Let me make it clear once and for all that I am not a Communist or a Communist front-man, or, for that matter, anybody's front-man." He castigated the alleged tactic of his non-Communist opponents of "repeating the fiction that I am a Communist front-man" in the "hope that it would stick in the minds of some".[8] As late as 1995, a year before he passed away, Lim assured historian Melanie Chew that he had never been a Communist.[9] For our purposes in this work, there are only really two related questions worth pursuing: First, was he a Communist? And second and perhaps more importantly: was his arrest under Coldstore warranted?

LIM CHIN SIONG'S CPM BACKGROUND

In early 1948, when Lim Chin Siong was a fifteen-year-old student in Pontian, Johore, the CPMSTC front organizations were all still operating openly. Lim joined the New Democratic Youth League (NDYL), which had at the time fifteen branches throughout Malaya and Singapore and a membership of about 800. The NDYL, which had branches in Johor Bahru, Segamat, Batu Pahat, Muar, Kluang, Mersing, Pontian, Senai-Kulai, Paloh, Yong Peng and Tangkak, was ostensibly committed to unite the youth of Malaya, raise the standard of living of the war-weary country and agitate for world peace. These were all issues of great appeal to the idealistic young man Lim, whose own "political consciousness" had been awakened by his "progressive" older brother Chin Kiat as well as his own experiences at school where he encountered "pro-KMT scoundrels". The NDYL institutional entity was the incubator for Lim's political and ideological beliefs; it was there that he was immersed in the stock mechanisms of Maoist indoctrination: concert parties, picnics, processions, mass rallies — many of which he was to use with great effect in Singapore a few years later. In 1949 — following the declaration of the Emergency and the CPMSTC being forced to go underground — Lim crossed the Causeway to further his studies in Singapore. He spent a term at Catholic High School before transferring to Chinese High, where as seen, the CPMSTC had set up underground ABL cells. To be sure, Chinese High had had open CPM elements before the Emergency was declared and now these all disappeared from public view. Once underground, a three-man Chinese High School Student Branch Committee was set up under the auspices of the CPMSTC, and commenced recruiting students for ABL work. Lim was to become part of that milieu.[10] While years later he told historian Melanie Chew that although technically the ABL was an "illegal organization", it was also anti-colonial and anti-British and thus "something legitimate". He claimed he "did not know it was communist", and only found out later from "western anti-communist books and works by historians like Yeo Kim Wah".[11]

To be candid, Lim was being rather disingenuous. That the illegal CPMSTC was behind the no less illegal ABL would have been hard to ignore for those who were involved at the time. In December 2012, a book was published in Hong Kong,[12] written by six former ABL members who finally came out and admitted to their previous ABL affiliations and that they had been based in Chinese High School at the time Lim was a student there. It was confirmed that the first ABL cell in the school was established in 1949, by CPM member Lu Jian Wen. Lu recruited his classmates Ng Meng Keong (the future Comrade D), Zeng Ai Mei and Lim Shee Ping into the cell. It was reiterated in the book that the ABL was explicitly "an underground peripheral arm led by the Singapore Town Committee of the Communist Party of Malaya",[13] and ABL members were tasked with carrying out "illegal activities and violence" before being assessed as suitable for absorption into the CPM proper. Special Branch records identify

Lim as among eleven Chinese High students involved in the ABL — not merely engaged in anti-colonial activism — but more precisely, directed by the Chinese High Branch Committee of the Students' Committee of the CPMSTC. Lim Chin Siong even had an ABL/CPM superior to whom he reported: a former Chinese High student named Loo Yeh Shing, who was a member of the Chinese High School Students' Committee headed by CPM member Wong Mau Choong until the latter's arrest in January 1954. Loo subsequently took guidance from Comrade D, until his own arrest in 1956 and banishment to China the following year.[14]

Lim Chin Siong himself was in fact arrested on 31 August 1951 under the Emergency Regulations following a police crackdown on ABL activities. He was released a few days later, on 3 September, because it could not be proven he was an ABL member; he denied owning the pro-Communist, banned books that happened to be found in his residence at the time. In October, Lim was expelled from Chinese High, along with Fong Swee Suan and Chen Say Jame, after leading a boycott against new Junior Middle Three examinations that many of his cohort had found meaningless, since the pathway to higher education in China had closed after the fall of that country to Mao's forces. Lim was likely following the guidance of his ABL superior Loo Yeh Shing who was also involved in organizing the boycott and subsequently expelled as well.[15]

Lim resumed studies at Eastaff English School from 1952 to May 1954 and of no small significance, because of his by-now apparent "zeal" and "efficiency in indoctrination" he was authorized by the Party to set up his own ABL cell. As ABL leader, he supervised the activities of Seet Chay Tuan, Kok Thong Eng,[16] Chia Ee Tian and Lim Woon Kiat.[17] Interrogations of these four men following their arrests in 1955 and 1956 provided more information on Lim's clandestine Communist work: he had adopted the party name Wang Ming and conducted *hsueh hsih* classes with his charges using Marxist, Leninist and CPM material including *Freedom News*. Chia Ee Tian recalled that when he joined the ABL, he had to swear an oath of allegiance in the presence of Lim before a picture of Stalin. Lim told Chia to go out and get more recruits to the cause, while also collecting monthly subscriptions of between fifty cents to two dollars from him. Further evidence that Lim was a CPM asset was found when his ABL subordinate Seet was arrested under the PPSO in 1955. Seet was caught with notes in Lim's own handwriting, signed off by Lim using the moniker Wang Ming and dated 28 March 1954. The notes were an attempt to guide his charges in reading the CPM journal *Hsueh* (*Study*). Additional notes on a talk by Lim on the implications of the death of Soviet leader Joseph Stalin in 1953 were also found, as well as some jottings by Lim involving "self-criticism" — a standard Communist practice to ensure personal ideological hygiene — of his party work. The internal Special Branch analysis noted that Lim clearly had a "high degree of understanding of Communist theory" and was able to "interpret CPM documents" accurately. Moreover, he showed "understanding and support of international communist policies", as well as "admiration for Communist revolutionary tactics". The conclusion was that Lim was likely "a Party member of some standing".[18] Incidentally, following the Big Split within the PAP in July 1961, between 13 September and 9 October, Lee Kuan Yew gave a series of twelve radio talks that were later compiled into a booklet published in January 1962, called *The Battle for Merger*. In Appendix 1 of the booklet Lee exposed the evidence of Lim's CPM connections just discussed.[19]

Further confirmation of Lim Chin Siong's actual identity, status and CPM involvement has come from former Communists close to him and even leading CPM figures themselves. According to Aloysius Chin, a retired Senior Assistant Commissioner of Police (Malaysian Special Branch — MSB) who closely monitored CPM activity in Malaya for many years, CPM leaders Siu Cheong and Ah Hoi cited Lim as an example of CPM members who were deployed in open front activities in political parties: "Lim Chin Siong was chosen because he was considered a very important CPM member, who had excellent qualities as a Communist United Front cadre, namely, dedication, trustworthiness and moreover, he had been involved in CPM activities since his schooldays."[20] Despite Lim's constant public denials, the Malayan and Singapore authorities were convinced of his Communist inclinations. Even British officials in Singapore — whom as we shall see tended to be relatively more cautious about classifying individuals as CPM members — were quite certain that Lim was a CPM member. In September 1959 one official observed that for "tactical reasons, the Communist Party is in favour of legal activity through the extreme left-wing of the PAP led by Lim [Chin Siong]", who the official pointedly noted, "is almost certainly a secret party member".[21] By July 1962, moreover, the Deputy U.K. Commissioner for Singapore, Philip Moore, adopted an even stronger line, asserting that "we accept that Lim Chin Siong is a communist".[22]

Furthermore, the CPM directing figure in Singapore, Fang Chuang Pi @ the Plen, later revealed his close association with Lim Chin Siong. In his memoirs Fang admitted — somewhat idiosyncratically — that "Lim Chin Siong and I did have a 'definitely not normal' association" and that "Lim Chin Siong was the left-wing's most important person." Fang added that Lim was "a person with whom I have had a special acquaintance" and that they had shared "a relationship as fellow workers".[23] Furthermore, when the

Plen's subordinate Lim Hock Koon asked about the future open activities of the BSS, he was advised that activities could be carried out "in accordance with the views expressed by Lim Chin Siong" which tellingly, "would not be incompatible with the stand of the Party".[24] More recently, former CPM member Zhang Taiyong revealed that Lim Chin Siong was transferred from underground activities in the ABL to open front activities in the mid-1950s. He confirmed that Lim, after being expelled from Chinese High School for his role in an examination boycott, "continued his studies at an English-stream school but later accepted the organisation's decision and devoted himself to trade union movement and constitutional struggle". Zhang recalled that while Lim accepted the new assignment with some apprehension, he later excelled and became a "shining star in the history of independence, democratic and trade union movements in Singapore".[25] Moreover when historian Lee Ting Hui showed his *Open United Front* manuscript to Lim Chin Siong himself, the latter did not challenge Lee's description of his CPM membership or role. Lim merely informed Lee that he had "read the book with benefit".[26]

LIM CHIN SIONG ON VIOLENCE

Of particular relevance was Lim's stance on violence. The Alternates spill much ink insisting that Lim was a Progressive Leftist committed to achieving power by peaceful, constitutional means.[27] To be fair, a secret Special Branch assessment in June 1963 conceded that "to a certain degree" Lim believed that a "socialist revolution" could be successful through "peaceful constitutional struggle" and that he was doubtful about the effectiveness of the use of arms and violence by the CPM. In public speeches on 13 September 1962, 10 October and 31 December 1962 he claimed that he recognized the difficulties inherent in constitutional struggle but stressed that such a mode of agitation was certainly "worthy of consideration".[28] Hence, in January 1961, following the assassination of Patrice Lumumba, the first Prime Minister of the Democratic Republic of Congo, at the hands of secessionist rebels backed by the departing Belgians and the U.S. Central Intelligence Agency (CIA), the PAP leftists led by Lim and Fong Swee Suan orchestrated mass protests in Singapore in a show of anti-colonial solidarity with the Congolese. The climax of the activities was a rally held at Happy World Stadium in February, attended by an estimated 12,000 people, mainly from the unions and rural associations. When a group of 4,000 later marched from Happy World to the U.S. Embassy on Cecil Street, chanting "Long Live Lumumba" and "I Love Malaya", things threatened to get out of hand — but Lim reportedly prevented the crowd from stoning the embassy.[29]

This did not mean, however, that Lim Chin Siong was against violence as a matter of principle. *He was fully alive to the use of violence — but under the right conditions and at the right time.* In fact one could trace an evolution in his thinking on the issue from 1954 onwards. During the anti-NS registration agitation in May 1954 for instance, Lim appeared to adopt a pretty militant stance, instructing his ABL subordinate Seet Chay Tuan that the students should stand their ground even if their representatives were arrested and to "take preventive measures" should the police attack them with batons or tear gas. He urged that the students should even recongregate should they be forced to disperse. After a barricade in Chung Cheng High, formed by 3,000 students from eight middle schools, was dispersed by the police the same month, Lim criticized the student leaders for not staying put and launching a hunger strike.[30] Furthermore, Lim later told his ABL charges that while the riots arising from the 13 May incident did not scuttle the NS Bill, it was still a success because it exposed the "intrigues of the British Colonial Master" and persuaded the student masses of the importance of "unity".[31] The following year, in the wake of the Hock Lee disturbances, moreover, Lim called together the executive committee of the SFSWU and declared that the incident "has clearly told us that bloodshed is necessary for the betterment of the livelihood of all the workers in the Colony".[32] Lim's then-fellow PAP left-wing comrade, Devan Nair, later recalled that the Hock Lee dispute could have in fact been ironed out much earlier but Lim had deliberately stalled, because in his calculation "the anger of the workers must first be allowed to explode".[33]

LIM CHIN SIONG, *"PAH MATA"* AND *THAT* OCTOBER 1956 BEAUTY WORLD SPEECH

On 25 October 1956, moreover, at the height of the stand-off with Lim Yew Hock, Lim delivered his notorious speech at Beauty World Park that was said to be inflammatory, seditious and inflamed the passions of the crowd. It is worth carefully analysing this incident in some detail, if only because in May 2014, the Alternate historian Thum Ping Tjin claimed on *The Online Citizen* website that the Labour Front government's subsequent arrest of Lim, for allegedly inciting the Beauty World crowd to *"pah mata"* or "beat the police" and hence engage in violence, was totally unwarranted. Thum attached a copy of the actual Special Branch report of Lim's 25 October Beauty World speech, and highlighted that Lim did not tell the crowd to *"pah mata"*. What Lim actually said was as follows:

With regard to police … they are all wage-earners and they are all here
to attend this meeting to oppose Lim Yew Hock. (Loudest cheers of the
meeting so far) We gladly welcome them, and the more of them that attend
will make us even stronger. (crowd cheers wildly) A lot of people don't want
to shout Merdeka! They want to shout *"pah mata"*. This is wrong. We
want to ask them to cooperate with us because they are also wage-earners
and so that in the time of crisis they will take their guns and run away.
(Laughter and cheers).

In short, Thum argued that "the government deliberately misrepresented
Lim Chin Siong's speech", and that the "Special Branch files show that Lim
was framed".[34] It has to be said though that Thum views the *"pah mata"*
comment of Lim Chin Siong *in vacuo*. One has to view the episode in wider
context and read the whole speech — not just the snippet Thum reproduces
— to get a clearer sense of what Lim was trying to achieve that evening.
A fuller reading of the entire speech as it turns out was indeed — as observers
recounted — inflammatory and aimed to stoke anti-government resentment
toward the Lim Yew Hock government. The basic message was that Lim
Yew Hock was a stooge of the British, utterly reliant on them to maintain
power. Lim Yew Hock did nothing for the people, and was more interested
in buying a new car for himself. He was never going to change. Lim Chin
Siong moreover warned that "tonight" Lim Yew Hock "may beat the students",
and "use force to oppress the innocent students". Tellingly, Lim added that
"we warn him if he uses force against the students, we the people of Singapore
will not tolerate it"; that "tonight there is the possibility that something big
will happen" and that "we must take *certain action* to retaliate against their
oppressive action" (emphasis mine).

   Anyone having a basic understanding of social psychology would recognize
a skilled demagogue's classic construction of a victimized, morally superior
in-group — the workers and students — and a morally evil, materially more
powerful out-group — Lim Yew Hock and the British.[35] In addition, by the
use of dehumanizing language — "Lim Yew Hock has clearly shown today
he has become a running dog of the British (*ang moh lang*)"; "the British in
Malaya today are like dogs"; "look at the British and spit, filthy spit" — Lim
not only succeeded in whipping the crowd up to a wild frenzy (as the Special
Branch note-taker clearly records) he consigned the out-group members to
a state of what Orlando Patterson calls a state of social death. When that
happens, out-group violence is not too far off.[36] As we know, following Lim's
speech, violence did ensue. It does not matter therefore that Lim Chin Siong
did not literally tell the crowd to *"pah mata"*. Perhaps he was trying to drive

a wedge between the police and the government they were representing. Or maybe he was being sarcastic, and the crowd knew it and lapped it up, as the record hints at. In the final accounting, Lim Chin Siong's October 1956 Beauty World speech as a whole would today be regarded as a good example of non-violent extremism. Non-violent extremist leaders do not actually tell their followers to go out and attack specific targets. They merely focus on creating a psychological climate in which out-group violence in general is morally legitimized — which prompts some of their followers to go out and take action of their own volition.[37] As Lim said in his speech: "we must take certain action to retaliate against oppressive action" — and he shrewdly left it to his followers to figure out what that "certain action" meant. Hence the ensuing violence was not — as Thum weakly and unconvincingly suggests — because "public anger was too strong". Violence broke out because Lim had skilfully fostered an emotionally combustible climate in which any small skirmish with police was bound to spark a full-fledged riot. If all this sounds familiar, there are good reasons for it: "I am only a craftsman making knives," a well-known violent Islamist extremist leader in Indonesia asserted famously not so long ago, "so how am I responsible for how those knives are used?" Notwithstanding the differences in ideology, time and space, such words might as well been uttered by Lim Chin Siong on the evening of 25 October 1956.[38] In the profoundest of ironies, moreover, Thum's assertion that Lim Chin Siong's October 1956 arrest had been unjustified was repudiated by the latter himself in February 1963. While Lim unsurprisingly challenged the grounds of his latest detention under Coldstore, he conceded that "there was justification in my arrest in 1956 because there were riots."[39]

The bottom line is that Lim was not opposed to violence on principle; rather he possessed a thoroughly instrumental view of its utility, completely in line with CUF precepts. Hence on 13 September 1956, following the failure of David Marshall's London constitutional mission in April, he made the following telling remark to his CUF comrades:

> After the failure of the April Talks, it can be said that the people's movement met with a temporary setback. Since it was decided that the central point of struggle in Singapore should be achieved by constitutional means, the struggle becomes necessarily a long and difficult one. The work of organising the masses is a decisive factor. *It was because the masses were not well organised that we could not resort to armed struggle after the failure of the talks* (my emphasis).[40]

Historian Lee Ting Hui drives home the point, emphasizing that the "reason for the Communists adopting a conservative attitude" was not because of high principle; it was simply that "they were not really in a position to be violent" and could "by no means match the British in strength".[41] The ensuing October Revolution of 1956 only confirmed that left-wing adventurism had to be avoided at all costs if the CUF was to be able to preserve itself for future activism. Little wonder then that following his release from detention in June 1959, Lim's "speeches then and after" were those of a "more serious, reflective, analytical speaker, quite different from the flaming raw eloquence which had endeared him to the crowds in earlier years". It was at this time that Lim cultivated most strongly the image of an anti-colonial leader of the Progressive Left, committed to constitutional struggle — the very persona some of the Alternates seem most enthralled by today.[42] The Alternates however fail to appreciate that this persona was cultivated solely for self-preservation after the October Revolution and the massive government crackdown on Communist violence through arrests, deportations and deregistration of CUF front organizations. In short, it is hard to escape the conclusion that Lim Chin Siong was indeed a Communist who was not at all opposed to violence in principle. As to whether his arrest under Coldstore was warranted, this is best evaluated in the next chapter.

Notes

1. Lim Hock Siew, "Tribute to Lim Chin Siong", in Tan and Jomo, eds., *Comet in Our Sky*, p. 128.
2. Yap, Lim and Leong, *Men in White*, p. 71.
3. Lee, *Singapore Story*, p. 186.
4. "Conversation with Lim Chin Siong on Tuesday, 19th September, 1961", TNA, PRO: FCO 141/17161.
5. Cited in "History of PAP (Part IV) — Lim Chin Siong — The Man Who Almost Became Prime Minister", 6 July 2006 <http://singaporegovt.blogspot.sg/2006/07/history-of-pap-part-iv-lim-chin-siong_06.html> (accessed 20 August 2014); "How Lee Kuan Yew Stole Democracy from Lim Chin Siong and the People of Singapore", 18 November 2013 <http://therealsingapore.com/content/how-lee-kuan-yew-stole-democracy-lim-chin-siong-and-people-singapore> (accessed 20 August 2014);
6. Michael Fernandez and Loh Kah Seng, "The Left-Wing Trade Unions in Singapore, 1945–1970", in Barr and Trocki, eds., *Paths Not Taken*, p. 207.
7. Ibid.
8. Letter to *Straits Times*, 31 July 1961, TNA, PRO: FCO 141/17161.
9. Melanie Chew, *Leaders of Singapore* (Singapore: Resource Press, 1996), pp. 113–18.
10. "Lim Chin Siong" paper.

11. Chew, *Leaders of Singapore*, p. 113.
12. *Mainstays of the Anti-Colonial Movement: The Legendary Figures of the Singapore People's Anti-British League* (2013). The six contributors to the book were Zhang Taiyong @ Cheung Tai Wing; Zhou Guang @ Comrade D; Chen Binbin; Hong Wende; Fu Yongcheng and Zhong Hua.
13. Ibid.
14. Ibid. "Lim Chin Siong" paper.
15. "Lim Chin Siong" paper; Tan Jing Quee, "Lim Chin Siong: A Political Life", in Tan and Jomo, eds., *Comet in Our Sky*, p. 61.
16. Kok Thong Eng was an ABL subordinate of Lim Chin Siong, and an official of the SCMSSU prior to his arrest under the PPSO from September 1956 to January 1957. "Lim Chin Siong" paper.
17. Lim Woon Kiat, a former Chinese High student and member of the SCMSSU, was arrested in March 1956 for illegal ABL activities. He was released in April 1958 and enrolled in Nanyang University where he engaged in pro-Communist activities. He escaped the Coldstore dragnet in February 1963 but later gave himself up in May 1965. He was released in May 1967. His brother Lim Oon Chai and sister-in-law Leow Wai Cheng, former ABL/CPM members, were detained under Coldstore. "Lim Chin Siong" paper.
18. "Lim Chin Siong" paper.
19. Lee Kuan Yew, *The Battle for Merger* (Singapore: Government Printing Office, 1962). *The Battle for Merger* was reissued to the general public in October 2014.
20. Chin, *Communist Party of Malaya*, p. 67.
21. Note by Humphrys, "The Outlook in Singapore up to the end of 1960", 22 September 1959, Appendix 9, TNA, PRO: CO 1030/656.
22. Moore to Wallace, Tel. 363, 18 July 1962, TNA, PRO: CO 1030/1160.
23. Fong, *Memoirs of a Malayan Communist Revolutionary*, pp. 170, 176–77.
24. Lim Hock Koon statement, "Lim Chin Siong" paper.
25. Zhang Taiyong, "Our cohort's commander — Lu Yexun", in *Mainstays of the Anti-Colonial Movement: The Legendary Figures of the Singapore People's Anti-British League* (Hong Kong: Footprints Publishing Company, 2013).
26. Lee, *Open United Front*, p. vi.
27. Thum, "*The Fundamental Issue is Anti-Colonialism, Not Merger*", pp. 18–19.
28. Translation of a comment on Lim Chin Siong's statement, 8 June 1963, ISDHC; "Lim Chin Siong" paper.
29. "Lim Chin Siong" paper; Sunil S. Amrith, "Internationalism and Political Pluralism in Singapore, 1950–1963", in Barr and Trocki, eds., *Paths Not Taken*, pp. 44–45.
30. "Statement of Seet Chay Tuan", 19 December 1955, ISDHC.
31. "Statement of Koh Thong Eng", 1 October 1956, ISDHC.
32. "Lim Chin Siong" paper.
33. Cited in Wee, "The Vanquished", in Lam and Tan, eds., *Lee's Lieutenants*, p. 177.

34. Thum Ping Tjin, "Lim Chin Siong was Wrongfully Detained", *TOC*, 8 May 2014 <http://www.theonlinecitizen.com/2014/05/lim-chin-siong-was-wrongfully-detained/#> (accessed 23 August 2014).

35. For a good discussion of the social psychological dynamics underlying the in-group/out-group divide that is a key factor in inter-group violence, see James Waller, *Becoming Evil: How Ordinary People Commit Genocide and Mass Killing* (New York: Oxford University Press), pp. 239–42.

36. Ibid., pp. 236–37. Albert Bandura has an excellent discussion on the potentially dangerous effects, under conflict conditions, of dehumanizing members of the out-group. See his "Mechanisms of Moral Disengagement", in W. Reich, ed., *Origins of Terrorism: Psychologies, Ideologies, Theologies, States of Mind* (Washington D.C: Woodrow Wilson Center Press, 1998), pp. 161–91.

37. For a discussion, see Alex P. Schmid, *Violent and Non-Violent Extremism: Two Sides of the Same Coin?* The Hague: International Center for Counterterrorism (ICCT) Research Paper, 2014.

38. Ramakrishna, "Lim Chin Siong and that Beauty World Speech: A Closer Look". Alternate historian Hong Lysa later attempted a somewhat shrill if unconvincing defence of Thum in her "What is History; A Glance at 'Lim Chin Siong and that Beauty World Speech: A Closer Look' ".

39. "Report of Lim Chin Siong Interview", 5 February 1963, ISDHC.

40. Lee, *The Open United Front*, p. 122, n. 176.

41. Ibid.

42. Tan Jing Quee, "Lim Chin Siong", in Tan and Jomo, eds., *Comet in Our Sky*, p. 81.

4

WHY "WAS OPERATION COLDSTORE DRIVEN BY POLITICAL AND NOT SECURITY GROUNDS?" IS THE WRONG QUESTION

THE ALTERNATES' "POLITICS-AND-NOT-SECURITY" ARGUMENT

To recapitulate, the Alternate claim is that Coldstore was an exercise that could not be justified on standard security grounds, for several reasons. First, the threat was exaggerated: while there certainly was an anti-colonial Progressive Left movement in Singapore in the 1950s to early 1960s, and it at times turned violent as in the Hock Lee incident of mid-1955 for example, this was not necessarily a movement that was closely manipulated by the CPM behind the scenes. In short, it was not a Communist United Front (CUF) in the traditional sense of the term. As the former leftist Dominic Puthucheary put it, there was "a movement with a wide range of political views from extreme left to social democratic right which attempted to create an alternative to a colonially-designed society, an embryo for creating a new Malaya".[1] The Alternates make great capital of a contemporary analysis in April 1962 by the Security Liaison Officer (the MI5 representative) in Singapore, Maurice L.B. Williams, who was sceptical of a Singapore Special Branch analysis of the threat:

> It is far more likely (as was envisaged by the Party themselves in the October Resolutions of 1951) that the "United Front" represents an amalgam of

different and conflicting interests, individual ambitions, industrial grievances, Chinese nationalism, housing problems of the peasant population and educational frustration of the students. At present they are united only in their dissatisfactions with the P.A.P. Government, and they cannot be considered to form a monolithic Communist edifice under strict Party management...[2]

Related to this perspective is the view that the CPM as a whole was by 1963 heavily weakened due to arrests and hence its "influence on the radical politics of Singapore in the late 1950s and early 1960s was, if anything, weaker than it had been between 1945 and 1951".[3]

Second, the British felt constrained by the fact that they could only agree to any arrest programme if there was clear evidence that Lim Chin Siong and company were about to depart from the constitutional path to embark on violent action. In his April 1962 threat assessment, SLO Maurice Williams had dismissed any notion of evidence of such a Communist conspiracy.[4] In late June moreover British officials in Kuala Lumpur cautioned that the evidence that "the leading Barisan figures, Lim Chin Siong and Fong Swee Suan", were Communists was "very stale" and there "has been no recent proof of Communist activity or allegiance on their part".[5] Four months later, Selkirk reiterated that "satisfactory evidence has not yet been produced to show that the persons concerned have been involved in any unlawful activity since they were released from detention in 1959". He added that "to arrest politicians who have kept within constitutional limits" would be politically indefensible for the British "in the House of Commons and in the United Nations".[6] For his part, the Deputy British Commissioner in Singapore Philip Moore,[7] in July 1962 had warned that it would be "plain foolishness to decide upon repressive action in Singapore"; that Lim Chin Siong was "working very much on his own", and that his "primary objective is not the communist millennium but to obtain control of the constitutional Government of Singapore". Moore added that "Nothing could provide a more effective rallying point for the chauvinistic and moderate elements against merger and Malaysia than to arrest leading members of the main Opposition party without adequate cause."[8] Third, the Alternates focus attention on contemporaneous British and Malayan concerns about Lee Kuan Yew's own personal drive for power. The Alternates emphasize that after the Hong Lim and Anson by-election defeats in 1961, the PAP was teetering on the political ropes. Moreover the PAP non-Communist leadership led by Lee had by then alienated opinion within the party itself, the civil service and the public as well.[9] Both the British and Tunku had also to contend with Lee's constant attempts during ISC discussions — in order to protect his own political standing with the

Chinese public in Singapore — to shift responsibility for the arrests of pro-Communists away from himself and towards the ISC.[10] Selkirk meanwhile opined that Lee was "probably very much attracted by the idea of destroying his political opponents".[11] Moore on his part noted how much Lee "greatly feared" Lim Chin Siong's "popularity with the masses".[12]

The Alternates' New Singapore History in short frames the catalytic events of 1959 to 1963 through the prism of the supposedly duplicitous, power-hungry nature of Lee. In this light, Lee's failure, following the release of Lim Chin Siong, Fong Swee Suan and the other key PAP leftists in June 1959, to follow up with serious representations to the ISC to release the remaining detainees — and to cynically seek instead ISC agreement to accept public blame for the situation — is unsurprising. It was a "deliberate misrepresentation of responsibility for continuing detentions in order to help the PAP government remain in power".[13] Furthermore, that the Referendum on Merger of 1 September 1962 became a "Hobson's choice" in which "the Barisan could not plausibly back any of the alternatives on offer" should have similarly raised no eyebrows. Little wonder then that following the thumping PAP victory in the Referendum with 71.1 per cent of voters choosing Lee's preferred Alternative A, Lim Chin Siong accused the PAP of — predictably, in the Alternate view — "cheating", declaring that the "referendum result did not indicate the real public opinion".[14] Last but not least, another way the Alternates have drawn attention to Lee's inherently crafty nature is his allegedly opportunistic seizure of the outbreak of the Brunei Revolt on 8 December 1962 to persuade the Tunku and the British that the timing was just right for finally mounting the Coldstore operation. The uprising was led by one A.M. Azahari, leader of the Partai Rakyat Brunei (PRB), who was opposed to Brunei joining the expanded Malaysian Federation and who wanted a separate federation of the Borneo states instead. Exploiting the fact that the BSS had issued a statement of support for the anti-colonial PRB comrades and Lim Chin Siong's fateful meeting in Singapore with Azahari himself, Lee is reported to have declared that these developments constituted "a Heaven-sent opportunity of justifying action" against Lim and his BSS colleagues.[15]

DECONSTRUCTING THE ALTERNATES' POSITION ON COLDSTORE

As we have painstakingly shown in the earlier part of this study, in contrast to the protestations of the Alternate historians and their supporters that the CUF was more imagined than anything else, we have carefully demonstrated instead that this was not the case. Constructed over many years, in line with the tenets of the established Communist theory that was well known to the CPM leadership, the CUF was all too real an entity in Singapore from the 1940s to the 1960s, orchestrated by the CPM's continually battered, but stubbornly resilient and continually evolving Singapore Town Committee. The Alternate viewpoint that Communist control of the disturbances was consistently disrupted due to security force action throughout the 1950s would never have been news to the elusive CPMSTC leaders themselves: they acknowledged that their ability to exert direct tactical control of disturbances such as the Anti-NS registration violence of May 1954, the Hock Lee riot of a year later and the October Revolution of 1956 was always going to be challenging and likely limited. The strategic intent rather was to foster a climate of collapse and make political capital of the situation afterwards, though this often generated blowback in the form of government repression — hence the complaint by *Freedom News* of the sin of "left-wing adventurism". The CUF at any rate was never static but mutated at different points in its development in tandem with environmental pressures.

Hence while the CUF found full expression in the AMCJA-PUTERA coalition in the relatively peaceful, constitutional open and legal phase from 1945 to 1948, it went into hiatus somewhat with the onset of the Emergency between 1948 and 1954, with continued arrests and disruptions of the CPMSTC in this period; however from 1954 to 1957, with the decision by the CPM to shift the strategic focus to Singapore following the failure of the shooting war in the Malayan jungles, the worker-based SFSWU and the student-based SCMSSU emerged in this period as key CUF vehicles. Finally, following the failure of the Baling talks at the end of 1955 and the disastrous October Revolution a year later, the CUF strategy refocused on capturing key left-wing political parties — above all the PAP — from 1957 to 1961. As seen, the Big Split in the PAP occurred in July 1961, producing the BSS, which was from then till Coldstore, the "main CUF vehicle" in Singapore.[16] The BSS was thus by no means a natural and spontaneous outgrowth of the so-called Progressive Left. It was to all intents and purposes the "business end" of the CUF in its final phase of effective existence, from July 1961 to February 1963. Finally, in his 2003 memoirs, although noticeably cautious in what he was willing to reveal, CPM Secretary-General Chin Peng himself did publicly concede the existence of the very CPM-led "underground network" at the time of Coldstore that the Alternates insist was more imagined than real.[17]

Certainly, British officials, particularly the men on the spot in Singapore, Selkirk and his deputy Philip Moore, have been consistently painted in the New Singapore History as fighting, by the second half of 1962, a desperately heroic rearguard action to stop the ostensibly nefarious schemes of Lee Kuan

Yew and the Tunku to ravish the practically politically virginal and hapless Progressive Left opposition before Malaysia Day. Scrutiny of the records, however, reveal a different story: Selkirk and Moore in fact fully conceded that rather than some inchoate and spontaneous left-wing Chinese-educated political ferment, they were indeed faced with Communist elements seeking power via "constitutional United Front tactics".[18] Moreover, by then these officials displayed little doubt about Lim Chin Siong's actual status as well. Moore, referring to the aforementioned interview of Lim by the Australian journalist Peter Hastings, observed confidentially to his Australian counterpart G.A. Jockel that Hastings "does not seem to have had much experience of a really clever United Front Communist operator!"[19] Moore unequivocally told the Colonial Office in July 1962 moreover that "we accept that Lim Chin Siong is a Communist".[20] The British position as noted was that in order for their assent to be granted for Coldstore, they had to be persuaded not so much that the CUF existed or that its titular leader was Lim, but rather that they were about to engage in violence to capture power. But this was precisely what Lim and the CUF would not do, because as seen, since April 1957, the CUF had been instructed to keep a low profile and stick to constitutional action, so as to gradually rebuild its decimated ranks following the disastrous October Revolution of 1956. Hence going back to the very same April 1962 threat assessment by SLO Maurice Williams cited by some Alternates, it is clear that a complete reading of the document reveals that the former himself alluded to the intelligence difficulty of detecting weak signals of activity in the new low-signature CUF climate after April 1957:

> Ever since [the October 1951 Directives], and particularly after the executive action of 1956, it has become increasingly difficult to identify the key Communist Party members directing the United Front … *The very tightness of Communist Party discipline and extreme security of Party contacts and activity* is a source of weakness in this situation (my emphasis).[21]

Note that Williams did not say that there was no Communist threat, but more accurately, that it was simply hard to detect signs of the threat after Communist security measures imposed, especially after April 1957. These are quite separate issues. To reiterate, CUF elements keeping a low profile "took the greatest care to conceal their connections with the CPM" and "being trained communists they did not require frequent direction from the Party". They were fully capable of interpreting events, and "any published statements that might be made by the Party, in the correct Party manner", and hence there was no need for them to have any contact for long periods with their superiors in the Party", to reduce the chances of exposure.[22] Philip Moore hence admitted by mid-July 1962 that the "lack of evidence" of Communist direction to the United Front was due to Communist tradecraft and secrecy precautions.[23] The absence of evidence, therefore, was not necessarily evidence of absence.[24] Exacerbating matters further, to reiterate, was that after April 1957 the CPMSTC under Fang Chuang Pi was not inclined to give the PAP government any excuse to crack down on them. The Plen's key operative, Lim Chin Siong, equally emphasized that in order to preserve strength, any move against the PAP must be made within the ambit of the law, and tellingly, he cautioned against "counter-attacking" the PAP even if the PAP attacked — referring to arrests — to avoid "repeating the mistakes of 1956" when mass detentions by Lim Yew Hock in the wake of the October riots had decimated the CUF.[25] Such a deceptively low-signature CUF threat had significant implications from a security perspective, as will be made explicit shortly.

The upshot of all this was that despite the undoubtedly weakened nature of the CPM threat by the early 1960s, as long as the "roots" of the CPMSTC — comprising the experienced CPM and ABL activists — remained intact, the possibility of regeneration of the CUF to a once–again dangerous level remained a strong possibility. As seen, as early as August 1957, the painful process of "recovery" of the CPMSTC had already become "significant" and new CUF elements were being created. For example, former Singapore Farmers' Association (SFA) members had regrouped to start the Singapore Country People's Association (SCPA), while in place of the SCMSSU, "the focus of open Communist activities in the student field shifted from the secondary schools to Nanyang University", a Chinese-medium university set up in March 1956 to cater to the further education needs of the Chinese middle school graduates.[26] Little wonder then, that in a 1957 meeting in Indonesia, despite the reverses of the previous year, the Plen learned from ECY that "the CPM Central Committee took a positive view of the widespread development of the open mass movement in Singapore and sent its praises".[27] These were not the sentiments of a fatally weakened movement, as the Alternates would have us believe; these were the sentiments of one willing to patiently take the long view.

REFRAMING THE POLICY QUESTION AND THE ENSUING NEW INSIGHTS

Basically, the Alternates ask the wrong question. The *real* national security policy question after the July 1961 Big Split within the PAP was: how to neutralize a resilient, clandestine subversive organization, whose leaders' ideological beliefs legitimated the full employment of "all sorts of stratagems, manoeuvres, illegal methods, evasions and subterfuges in order to achieve their end", while simultaneously not alienating the Chinese-educated mass base within which this entity had embedded itself — as well as a largely anti-colonial international opinion.[28] Reframing the issue in this way provides really the best response to the stock Alternate position that Coldstore was driven by crass political and not legitimate security concerns.

In this regard, part of the problem at the time from the governance perspective was arguably the relative newness of the British men-on-spot in Singapore. Selkirk — despite his genuinely impressive credentials[29] — was no seasoned Malaya hand, having been appointed as the U.K. Commissioner in Singapore only in December 1959, while his deputy Philip Moore arrived later, serving first as Counsellor then from 1961 onward, as Deputy Commissioner. SLO Maurice Williams had arrived even later, in March 1962[30] — which suggests that his report of just one month later should be reassessed with this in mind. Hence it is unlikely that from the get-go Selkirk, Moore and Williams were as *au fait* with the nature of the CPM and the CUF as perhaps Geofroy Tory in Kuala Lumpur, who had been in place since 1957,[31] but more so senior Singapore Special Branch officers, such as Richard Corridon who had first arrived as part of the British Military Administration in late 1945,[32] and former Singapore Governor William Goode, who had served in the Malayan Civil Service since the 1930s.[33] Tory, and especially Corridon and Goode, had had more time to develop a deeper understanding of the CPM's wiles. There were other factors to consider as well: Selkirk and Moore were keenly aware that international events such as the infamous Hola Camp massacre in Kenya in 1959 had damaged London's image in the highly charged anti-colonial atmosphere of the late 1950s, and were anxious to avoid doing anything in Singapore to sully British international standing further. Furthermore, both men soon recognized that preserving Chinese majority support in Singapore was equally important, and Selkirk was wary of "repressive action against the leaders of a party" — the BSS — "which draws its support very largely from the Chinese speaking people — who are some 60% of the electorate".[34]

The British officials hence approached the whole issue of arresting alleged CUF elements with utmost caution and emphasized in Internal Security Council (ISC) discussions that above all the rule of law must be observed. The 26th ISC meeting on 8 September 1962 was instructive in this sense. Selkirk — who chaired the meeting — emphasized to the Singapore Commissioner of Police that any arrests cannot simply be based on a "link with the general conspiracy"; citing PPSO guidelines, Selkirk insisted that to be detained an individual must be explicitly shown to have engaged in action "prejudicial to the security of Malaya or the maintenance of public order therein or the maintenance therein of essential services"[35] — as noted not at all a straightforward task given that the CUF was at the time deliberately keeping a low profile precisely to avoid provoking government to take action! The Federation Director of Police Affairs chimed in to support his Singapore police colleague, clarifying that "the idea was to show that those detained were aiding and abetting a local Communist conspiracy", and added for good measure that individuals "shown to be Communists would almost certainly be a threat to long-term security and it was only sensible to deal with them before they got too strong". He reminded the meeting that "Communist writings showed that they tried to achieve their aims by underground as well as constitutional means."[36] It soon became clear, however, that Selkirk and Moore were taking a very narrow, minimalist view of what a "security threat" meant: explicit evidence that an individual or group was about to embark on violent action to attain power. Those who knew the Communists for far longer recognized immediately that this was a profound mistake. Goh Keng Swee urged Selkirk to take a broader view of the CPM threat:

> In reply to the Chairman [Goh] agreed that *there was no immediate security threat in Singapore in the sense that the Communists could now overthrow the state by violent action. The real nature of the threat was that they could be in a position to take over the state in a future general election. This no longer becomes a political issue in the sense of competition between democratic political parties.* The materialization of the Communist threat in this respect would lead to calamitous results not only in Singapore but also in the Federation. Communist strength in Singapore was based on Chinese working class support while the Federation Government derived its main support from the Malay peasantry. Unless the Communists were conscribed, the end result could be open conflict on racial lines, a tragedy that must be avoided at all costs (my emphasis).

The Federation representative on the ISC, Malayan Deputy Prime Minister, Abdul Razak, "agreed that this was a fair assessment".[37] In other words, the Singaporean and Malayan ISC representatives considered the *capture of political power by the CPM in Singapore itself as "prejudicial to the security of Malaya"* — a *maximalist understanding* compared to Selkirk's minimalist interpretation of the PPSO guidelines as implying the employment of violence against public order. In fact, earlier, on 29 September 1961, Lee Kuan Yew, during one of his *Battle for Merger* radio broadcasts, had similarly warned that if the BSS — "just a front for the Communists" — captured power and formed the Government, they would use Singapore as a base to "extend massive aid to the Communists in the Federation to bring the Federation down from within" and hence spark "conflict and hostility between the two governments". Hence the maximalist conception of a security threat: a CPM capture of power in Singapore itself — even if through constitutional means — had been in the minds of the non-Communist PAP leaders for quite a while.[38]

However, even after Goh's intervention, Moore reiterated Selkirk's minimalist definition of "security threat", arguing that "[o]f course the Communists in Singapore, as in any country, were aiming to achieve power; the point was that they did not constitute a significant threat to security and until such time as it could be demonstrated that they did, arbitrary action against them would only make matters worse". Razak at this point — in a hint of exasperation — countered that the "Communists in Singapore could not be separated from the Communists in Malaya — the people of Singapore knew about the Communists in Malaya and it should be simple to show them why arrests were needed in Singapore." However, Toh Chin Chye, Acting Singapore Prime Minister and sitting in for Prime Minister Lee Kuan Yew at this meeting, inadvertently encouraged Selkirk and Moore to disagree with Razak that the operation would be a politically simple exercise and to defend the minimalist definition of "security threat". Toh insisted throughout the meeting that the Chinese ground — which he felt did not as yet fully see the BSS as a CUF entity — had to be carefully prepared before any arrest programme, to "deny the Communists a rallying point" and prevent the PAP government from suffering the same widespread odium Lim Yew Hock had faced from that constituency following his crackdowns of late 1956 and 1957.[39] Perhaps it was no surprise then that at the very next ISC meeting on 9 October, Selkirk repeated the view that "it was basically not a threat of violence but a political problem that was presented in Singapore"; to which Razak "interjected" that "this was true in the short term but in the long term there would be a threat of violence". Selkirk however tenaciously persisted with the minimalist line, arguing that "there was no immediate threat to law and order". He reiterated that the "long term threat was political and required a political approach" rather than "police action", and since the "united front were [sic] playing the game constitutionally" he insisted that the "Singapore Government should if possible endeavor to meet them on the constitutional front".[40] Lee Kuan Yew, back in the ISC, unsurprisingly "disagreed with the Chairman's assessment of the nature of the threat" and countered that it "was not just a question of a constitutional political challenge". Reminding the meeting that the "Communist threat of violence and the overthrow of public order was real", Lee warned that "if they achieved power they intended to keep it and suppress all opposition". Moreover, he added that "[p]eople fear the M.C.P. which had a history of retribution against those who stood in its way."[41]

The basic problem really was that Selkirk and Moore had not been present during the violent years of 1954 to 1956, as seen engineered if not entirely controlled at ground level by the CUF, led principally by Lim Chin Siong and Fong Swee Suan, under CPMSTC instructions. By the time these British officials had arrived in Singapore at the end of the 1950s, the CUF was already functioning in its tactical low-profile phase to avoid generating precisely the kind of violent, unlawful signature that would have given the ISC ample reason to crack down on them. This is probably why a bemused Goh Keng Swee, at the 26th ISC meeting in September, pointedly asked Selkirk "if, after nearly three years' Chairmanship of the Security Council, he really doubted the reality of the Communist conspiracy in Singapore." Selkirk, displaying his stubborn inability to conceive of the broader, maximalist interpretation of "security threat" that the subterranean CUF challenge at that stage fully warranted — replied that "in a sense every political opposition could be said to constitute a 'threat' to the government, and the opposition could be said to 'conspire' to remove the government: the question was, what was the exact nature of the threat and who were the people involved in the conspiracy." One can almost imagine the resigned sigh of Goh as the note-taker recorded that the Singapore "Finance Minister stated he was glad to know" that at least "there was no disagreement as to the existence of the conspiracy".[42] One begins to understand moreover why Lee himself — while certainly appreciating other aspects of the cultured Selkirk's personality — did not consider him a "heavyweight" possessed of "a powerful mind", prompting Moore to periodically remind him that Selkirk had enjoyed Cabinet rank and had "direct access" to the British Prime Minister.[43] The Singapore and Malayan representatives on the ISC were not the only ones to have concerns about the attitude of the British officials in Singapore towards the CUF either. Geofroy Tory, the British High Commissioner in Kuala Lumpur, had since August 1961 warned that playing by Queensbury Rules[44] with the Singapore Communists would be utter folly.[45] Meanwhile the Federation Inspector-General of Police Claude Fenner, an old Malaya hand, also regarded the Singapore British officials as "pusillanimous", warning that failing to move decisively against the CUF would be a tragic repeat of June 1948, when the then-High Commissioner "Sir Edward Gent had failed to nip the Emergency in the bud by arresting Chinese trade union leaders."[46]

While Selkirk and Moore appeared most eager to play — and be seen to be playing — by Queensbury Rules, Lee and the non-Communist leaders in the PAP had long since regarded such notions as naïve. The great shortcoming of the Alternates' attempts to analyse PAP Government decision-making in regard to Coldstore is their near-total lack of appreciation of how the abortive attempt in August 1957 by PAP leftists to capture power of the CEC — as noted via fraudulent means — left an enduring mark on the psyche of Lee and his colleagues. To aver that the effect had been profound would be an understatement. Rajaratnam captured the epiphany of the moment:

> You don't play according to Queensbury Rules with these chaps. First time we learnt how naïve we were playing even the constitutional game with the communists. They knew all the tricks. It was quite clear that they had fixed the whole damn thing.[47]

When the British Labour Party Leader Hugh Gaitskell visited Singapore four months later in December, he reported a "very frank" discussion with Lee, who told him "that he now realized that he himself would have to take a stand against the Communists, a reversal of his previous policy of endeavoring to work with their support".[48] Dominic Puthucheary reckoned years later that the leftists' near-capture of the CEC was a defining moment because Lee "never trusted the left again and PAP was never [the] same again". Moreover, "it taught the English-educated leaders the lessons of a lifetime" that despite the very best of intentions, "you can't always play by the rules and you've got to fix them as you go along and that if you don't demolish your opponents, they will demolish you."[49]

In any case, during his three-month incognito hiatus in Singapore from June to August 1962 to advise Lee on the Merger Referendum, the legendary Malaysian CPM and psychological warfare expert C.C. Too was, according to authoritative sources, a member of a top-level ad hoc internal security committee chaired by Lee himself and including Minister for Home Affairs Ong Pang Boon, Director of Special Branch George Bogaars and Lee's personal advisor and Director of the Singapore Political Training Centre, George Thompson. During this time Too intently studied the case files of the subversive elements compiled by Singapore Special Branch, recently strengthened by seconded officers from Kuala Lumpur. Too's former colleague, biographer and retired senior Malaysian Special Branch official Lee Cheng Leng captured the basic dilemma facing Lee and his ISC colleagues up to that time — a CUF that was lying low, rebuilding its strength and biding its time:

> *C.C. Too came to the conclusion that no solid [technical] legal case could be made against the urban guerrillas and subversive elements.* There was little doubt, however, about their individual and collective intentions to use illegal and even militant means to overthrow the PAP Government, and there was ample evidence for such intentions from their speeches and publications.

But these intentions had not been translated into actions, and it was extremely difficult, if not impossible, to have them arrested and indicted in a court of law with the evidence only hanging on the strength of their apparent and implied intentions (my emphasis).[50]

ENDGAME: 1 SEPTEMBER 1962 TO 2 FEBRUARY 1963

Events gathered momentum after the 1 September 1962 Referendum on Merger though. The massive public endorsement of the PAP government's Alternative A appeared proof to Lee that perhaps the calculated risk he had taken in his *Battle for Merger* radio talks between September and October the previous year had had impact and the ground had slowly begun to shift against the BSS following his disclosures about the Communist credentials and tactics of Lim Chin Siong, Fong Swee Suan and their colleagues. Certainly following the publication of the radio talks in a booklet in early 1962, James Puthucheary himself apparently paid a visit to Lee's City Hall office and "tacitly admitted" that what the Prime Minister had disclosed about "the Plen and the communists had sunk home". Lee also interpreted the "real anger and hatred" displayed by Chinese-speaking groups already committed to the CPM cause whenever he passed their "union or society premises", as well as the "sullen and sour faces" of Chinese press reporters covering his press conferences, as "evidence of the effectiveness of my disclosures". He began to feel "more confident that we could paint" the Communists "into a corner and prepare the ground for later action against them".[51] While Toh Chin Chye had warned at the September ISC meeting that it was important to ensure that police action did not create a rallying point for the Communists, Lee himself knew he had to tread a fine line between the David Marshall and Lim Yew Hock approaches to dealing with the CUF:

> Marshall had taught me how not to be soft and weak when dealing with the communists. Lim Yew Hock taught me how not to be tough and flat-footed. It was not enough to use administrative and legal powers to confine and cripple them. Lim did not understand that the communist game was to make him lose support of the masses, the Chinese-speaking people, to destroy his credibility as a leader who was acting in their interests. They were thus able to portray him as an opportunist and a puppet acting at the behest of the "colonialist imperialists". *Of the two, the more valuable lesson was Lim Yew Hock's — how not to let the communists exact a heavy price for putting them down* (my emphasis).[52]

Lee's sentiments were spot on. By September 1962 in fact, clandestine Special Branch surveillance of discussions within the BSS found that CPM elements were similarly arguing that government "oppression is beneficial and not harmful to us" because "in the long run it increased our 'mass following' ".[53] At any rate, historian Edwin Lee records that when the Referendum results were announced Lee apparently wept tears of joy, overwhelmed with emotion. He felt the results showed that the people were gradually "overcoming their fear of the communists"; hence after the PAP had had little choice but to "work with them, argue with them, free them, break with them, and tolerate them", it seemed suddenly possible that the PAP could now "defeat them in the political arena with popular backing".[54] This was a complete turnaround from the bleak situation just a year earlier in the wake of the Hong Lim and Anson by-election defeats. Furthermore, Lee interpreted the Referendum victory as proof that Philip Moore's repeated dark warnings to drop the whole Referendum idea had been indeed incorrect: "Lee believed that he understood the mind of the electorate better", and he could "rely on the people's sense of realism and understanding that, to fight the communists, it was not possible to use purely democratic tactics as Moore would have liked".[55]

As noted, in September and October 1962, Selkirk and Moore had stubbornly adopted a minimalist understanding on what a security threat constituted at the 26th and 27th ISC meetings respectively. But their positions soon shifted. On 7 December, Moore rushed off a "Top Secret and Personal" note to Ian Wallace at the Colonial Office, enclosing the aforementioned Special Branch surveillance reports of BSS meetings on 23 and 30 September that provided "conclusive evidence than we have had hitherto for the belief that Barisan Sosialis are Communist controlled" and therefore had "a clear bearing on the attitude to be taken to the Federation's request for repressive action". Moore admitted that while previously, apart from Lee's *Battle for Merger* disclosures, "there was nothing very definite to go on apart from circumstantial evidence and stale security records", the new reports now confirmed that the BSS was indeed heavily Communist controlled, from CEC to Branch Committee level and that "the Communists seem to be sufficiently entrenched to control policy and action". Moreover — and importantly as far as the future Coldstore dragnet was concerned — while the reports did not imply that all BSS committee members were Communists, it would be "difficult to acquit many of the leading members as unwitting dupes". Equally crucial, Moore observed that "although the Communists in the Barisan Sosialis value the armed struggle highly in theory, they see no other practical course for them at present but to pursue their aims by constitutional means".[56] In other words, here finally was official British recognition of the posture of the BSS — "the principal instrument" of the CPM "on the political front" — that any opposition to violence within its ranks in favour of constitutional agitation was always tactical rather than based on high principle. This was in line with the consistent refrain in internal CPM propaganda to avoid left-wing adventurism that would prompt a massive security crackdown as during the Lim Yew Hock years. If the situation warranted it, CUF elements would certainly have switched to violence if it was assessed to be the best way to advance their interests.[57]

That the BSS — the leading edge of the CUF at the time of Coldstore — was open to depart from constitutional methods if the prevailing circumstances changed, was certainly clear. The question of resorting to armed struggle had in fact been discussed at length at a BSS internal meeting attended by about forty Exco and Branch representatives on 23 September 1962, after the BSS lost the Merger Referendum. BSS CEC member Chok Kok Thong (who was also a CPM element) summed up the views expressed at the gathering, asserting *inter alia* that party members must analyse the situation to decide on the appropriate form of struggle; "basically armed struggle is the highest form of struggle" but whether it should be adopted or not would depend on "the entire international situation". Chok elaborated:

> no one could say that the revolution was complete if it took the form of an armed struggle or incomplete if the peaceful and constitutional method were used. ... Experience elsewhere showed that there was no country in the world which had "attained a thorough success in revolution through constitutional processes", and that throughout South East Asia, including Malaya, the "ruling classes would not lightly hand over political power to the leftists". Nevertheless everyone disliked bloodshed and the use of arms and the question of whether it would be necessary to resort to them would depend not on the people, but on the reactionary Government of the bourgeoisie.[58]

While this highly significant meeting saw no other practical course for the BSS at that time but to pursue its aims via the constitutional route, the discussions clearly indicated that CUF controlling elements in the BSS did not rule out resorting to armed struggle depending on the circumstances or if an opportunity presented itself. BSS Secretary-General Lim Chin Siong himself had said in a speech eleven days earlier at a gathering for referendum workers that the struggle would continue using constitutional means but only as long as that option remained available to them. It is now known that in April 1964 Lim himself conceded that within the BSS there was a faction that felt that its political objectives could not be met via constitutional means and thus more drastic measures such as armed struggle should be considered.[59] The Alternates' sanitized view of the BSS as constituting a legitimate Progressive

Left political option to the PAP that was committed to principled peaceful and lawful constitutional struggle is thus — it has to be reiterated — not only inaccurate but well off the mark.

The "Heaven-sent opportunity of justifying action" against Lim Chin Siong and his BSS colleagues offered by the outbreak of the Brunei revolt the day after Moore dispatched his telegram to Wallace, therefore, should be seen in this light.[60] That the BSS issued a statement of support for A.M. Azahari and his PRB rebels — and Lim Chin Siong's meeting in Singapore with Azahari himself in early December — could no longer be ignored from a security perspective. Even before the BSS had lost the Merger Referendum, Lim and his colleagues had begun more seriously exploring if the support of "external forces" could be secured in the struggle against the Malaysia Plan. In this respect, the increasing influence of the Indonesian Communist Party (PKI) on President Sukarno seemed worthy of closer monitoring, while Sukarno himself had publicly opposed Malaysia because of his own vested interests in the Borneo Territories. In fact it was reported that in April 1962 Lim had been quoted in the Indonesian newspaper *Bintang Timur* that given a choice, he would much prefer merger with Indonesia than the Federation, though he later denied saying this. Six months later, Lim's close associate Said Zahari, editor of the BSS Malay organ *Rakyat,* went to Brunei to meet Azahari and reportedly became privy to the latter's plans.[61] Then a few days before the revolt, Azahari had his well-known meeting with Lim in Singapore, though the purpose of the meeting, according to a 2008 account by Edwin Lee, was "unclear".[62] In fact, we now have access to still-classified Special Branch reports of what apparently transpired. Central to the meeting was Said Zahari, who apparently served as a broker of the meeting between Azahari and Lim in Singapore. Zahari apparently also persuaded the pro-Communist Partai Rakyat Singapura (PRS) to hold a rally in support of Azahari's rebels.[63]

Fong Swee Suan later dismissed accusations that Lim and Azahari had conspired to mount simultaneous uprisings in Brunei and Singapore, saying that the only thing both men had in common was anti-colonial sentiments.[64] However, according to an interview with Singapore SLO Maurice Williams on 28 April 1963, Lim revealed that during the fateful Singapore meeting on 3 December the previous year, he and Azahari had spoken about armed struggle in general and the latter even sought Lim's cooperation and assistance in sourcing arms. Lim claimed however that he had not agreed with Azahari's stance on armed struggle and that the latter did not mention his plans to start a revolt in Brunei either. When Williams asked the entirely reasonable question of why Azahari had believed Lim "might have armaments available", Lim appeared "unable to answer".[65] At this interview though, Lim, while "cordial and polite", also appeared "evasive and non-committal" in his responses.[66] Some observers believe that Azahari, while seeking to ride on Lim's reputation to garner support from left-wing groups for his own plans, had offered arms to the BSS Secretary-General if he wished to mount a similar operation in Singapore. They suggest that Lim was certainly privy to plans for the Brunei revolt as well.[67]

When the revolt broke out on 8 December 1962, while PKI leader D.N. Aidit called on the Indonesian government to give Azahari "concrete assistance to make the revolution a success",[68] Sukarno himself declared his support, arguing that this conflict was proof of his anti-colonial ideological concept of the "New Emerging Forces" and that Indonesians should "take the side of the people who are struggling".[69] While the Brunei uprising was put down within forty-eight hours by British forces hastily airlifted from Singapore, the BSS — "foolishly", in Lee Kuan Yew's openly candid view — issued a public statement in support of it, "hailing it as a popular uprising against colonialism that merited the backing of all genuine anti-colonialists, and declaring that that the Singapore and Federation governments would stand condemned if they did not oppose the British".[70] On 11 December, Lim and Fong Swee Suan discussed a plan — in response to Azahari's earlier request for help — to generate local left-wing support for the Brunei rebels. At a meeting attended by Lim, it was decided that the BSS Malay Section would collaborate with Malay PRS members to recruit local volunteers to fight alongside the Brunei rebels — although the Special Branch report makes it plain that Lim's "exact stand" on this decision was "not documented". The same meeting decided that if the Singapore government stopped recruitment of the Brunei volunteers, the BSS Malay Section and Malay PRS members would stage a protest against the dispatch of British forces and Malayan police to Brunei.[71] On 15 December, furthermore, Lim evidently directed BSS activists putting up pro-Azahari posters in public places to adopt "guerrilla tactics" to avoid arrest. He even suggested deploying Malay BSS members for the task as he calculated the government would not risk offending the Malay public by arresting these individuals.[72] By the time the BSS held a mass rally on 23 December in support of Azahari, during which Lim spoke out in support of the Brunei revolt as an "anti-colonial struggle deserving of support" and rejected the Malaysia Plan as a "new form of colonialism",[73] it really did seem to most observers that he and the BSS were clearly "trying to line up with dangerous and powerful external forces to help fight its anti-merger battle within Singapore".[74]

There were other factors contributing to the rapidly gathering official momentum for security action against the BSS and other CUF entities in Singapore. In mid-1962, Lim had a lengthy discussion with his CUF colleagues on united front strategies and tactics to be adopted in anticipation of a "major clash with the PAP". Lim lamented that the CPM's "fatal mistake" was not to have initiated the armed struggle in 1945 when the British had just returned, because by 1948 "circumstances no longer favored the CPM". He remarked that the Central Committee — again, tacitly admitting to his association with them — also shared this view and believed that they could have "replicated the Vietnamese success" against the French had they launched earlier.[75] Interestingly, CPM Secretary-General Chin Peng later echoed this exact view, recalling that the CPM leadership had committed historical errors, one of which was failing to seize political power immediately after the Japanese surrender when the CPM was at that juncture clearly "the most effective and most organized political party in Malaya".[76] In any case Lim Chin Siong also had plans to divide the CUF "clandestine network" engaged in "both legal and extra-legal methods" of struggle into three categories: the first group, comprising "expendable" individuals were to be cultivated and used in clashes with the PAP government — their ensuing arrests could be accepted. The second group, the committed "open workers" like Lim himself, should be prepared for arrest. The third most important group, whom Lim referred to as "the others" — the aforementioned "roots" that produced the lallang leaves — should go into hiding upon commencement of any police action, and re-emerge when the situation had calmed down. Lim opined that this third group of experienced cadres could possibly be made available for the Communist struggle elsewhere should the situation in Singapore be untenable.[77] The need for the roots of the *lallang* leaves — the CUF vanguard — to be thoroughly shielded from security action by layers of less important, dispensable personnel reinforces the old Comintern adage that for revolutionary success, it would always be necessary to "reinforce the Communist vanguard" by a "still larger expendable army" of "useful idiots". No surprise then that the Coldstore dragnet brought in such a large number of persons.[78]

Given the confluence of such ominous external and internal trends, when Tunku called for an emergency ISC meeting on 13 December to initiate discussions for a comprehensive arrest programme against the CUF, there were no objections from the British — whose "residual obstructionism" had "evaporated"[79] — and quite obviously the Singapore representatives.[80]

The whole idea behind a specific programme of arrests had in truth been in concerted gestation within official circles since the spring of 1962, when the Malayan and Singapore Special Branches formulated its first outlines.[81] The impetus for this was likely a pointed comment in July 1961, when Tunku made clear to the British that no left-wing socialist government would ever be allowed to come to power in the Federation as the "Malay elite would use its control of the administration and security forces to install a dictatorship". Hence as Harper correctly observes, it became "clear to all sides that a further, comprehensive sweep of arrests in Singapore would be, for the Tunku, an essential precondition for Merger".[82] Lee had initially treaded cautiously in regard to an arrest programme because he himself did not want to be accused by the Chinese-speaking public of cynically using such a tactic to secure a positive vote at the Merger Referendum. After March 1962, however, he began to accept the "necessity for action", but only after the Referendum.[83] Following discussions in late July with senior British officials in London, moreover, it was agreed that "the three governments were to work together for an agreement on the arrests after the Singapore referendum on Merger".[84] As observed earlier, however, the British officials in Singapore, Selkirk and Moore, maintained a minimalist posture, insisting "that they could not detain Barisan members just because they were politically inconvenient; the ISC would need to see firm evidence that individuals presented a real security threat".[85]

In any case, between the 13 December ISC meeting and in ongoing discussions leading up to the planned operation, called Coldstore,[86] three days hence, Lee made a few key points: BSS Chairman Dr Lee Siew Choh, because he did not "play the communist game", should be given a second chance; pro-Communist unions should not be banned after their leaders were arrested, to avoid giving the unhelpful impression that Singapore had no "real autonomy" in the labour field; the PRS should not be banned either so that "the remaining communists would gravitate towards it rather than to Ong Eng Guan's United People's Party (UPP), which would take a Chinese chauvinist line"; detainees of Malayan birth would be rusticated back to Malaya; and finally, just before the operation, Lee requested that two key "subversive" left-wing figures in the Federal Parliament, Ahmad Boestamam, leader of the Partai Rakyat in Malaya, and Lim Kean Siew, Secretary of the Malayan Labour Party, be arrested as a *quid pro quo* for nine pro-Communist BSS assemblymen who would be detained in Singapore as well.[87] It was decided that about 180 persons would be arrested by Singapore Special Branch with the cooperation of its Federation counterparts. The planned security sweep planned for 0200 hours on 16 December did not occur, however, because the Tunku, after apparently initially agreeing to the incarceration of his two parliamentarians, backpedalled on advice from his professional security advisors that there was insufficient justification for their proposed detentions. He further exacerbated matters by refusing to see Selkirk and Lee — who had flown up to Kuala Lumpur for the operation. Frenzied British attempts to mediate between an upset Lee and the Malayans could not prevent the acrimonious collapse of the Singapore operation, with the Federation representative pulling out from the ISC.[88]

By the end of December 1962 Selkirk was feeling the heat. The Malayans had made it amply clear that without the arrests of the CUF in Singapore, merger would be off and that the political opportunity to strike afforded by the Brunei Revolt — a view shared by London — was fast fading. Selkirk by now was also genuinely uncomfortable with having CUF elements free and "continuing to work in Singapore in the light of the Indonesian activities in Borneo" and wanted arrests of communists in Singapore as soon as possible.[89] He accepted that while there was a chance that an arrest programme at this stage may be portrayed by the Indonesians and by some quarters in the U.K. as "further evidence that Malaysia is being imposed by the British", he judged that a far worse outcome would be if the Tunku dropped merger completely. The latter nagging possibility was occupying Lee's thoughts at this time as well, prompting him to explore the possibility of the British securing a written undertaking from the Tunku that he would not go back on his word — an idea that was quickly rebuffed.[90] Eventually, following a mid-January visit by Lee to Kuala Lumpur, progress towards a remounting of the arrest programme by a reunified ISC appeared to have been made, and the next meeting of the Council was scheduled on 1 February 1963.[91]

An issue that cropped up during the final run-up to Coldstore was Lee's proposal to arrest three UPP members. Lee told Moore on 23 January 1963 that he "fears Ong Eng Guan may attempt to make political capital" out of the planned arrests, and wished "to make it clear that if Ong Eng Guan were to cause serious trouble, action would have to be taken against him". Moore replied that the British could "give no undertaking at this stage" and in accord with the minimalist line both he and Selkirk had consistently taken — iterated that "it would depend entirely upon what Ong Eng Guan did" and "there would have to be a very strong case to take any action against him."[92] Five days later, the Tripartite Working Party of the ISC agreed on a list of 172 names comprising 100 in category A (hard-core organizers of the Communist conspiracy); 51 in category B (leading collaborators), and 21 in category C (collaborators). However, the Singapore representatives added into category C "three members of Ong Eng Guan's United Peoples' Party whom the Federation and U.K. representatives did not agree warranted inclusion".

Two of them had been detained following the October 1956 riots.[93] Lee was concerned that "Ong Eng Guan would be a rallying point after the operation and that these three arrests were necessary to show that the UPP would not be allowed to play the communist game". Lee's maximalist view of a "threat to public order" encompassed the possibility of the CUF regrouping behind the ever-opportunistic Ong and the UPP, should the BSS be decimated by the arrest programme.[94]

The issue of protecting the PAP government's flank against Ong's potential opportunism following an arrest programme was not outlandish. While Ong was anti-Communist he did certainly try — as shown earlier — to reach out to Lim Chin Siong to forge a tactical alliance against Lee, a move which Lim had pointedly ignored, as the Communists did not trust him either. Neither was Lee having a sudden afterthought. Deputy Prime Minister Toh Chin Chye had earlier raised the Ong Eng Guan/UPP issue at the 26th ISC meeting on 8 September 1962, arguing then that even "if action were taken to shut down the Barisan Sosialis", and "however many people were arrested it would not be possible to stop a whispering campaign against the PAP for having taken the action" — with the result that "the left-wing vote would simply be transferred to the United People's Party and this was exactly what Ong Eng Guan was hoping for".[95] After much deliberative to-ing and fro-ing between the various parties, the British, including the Colonial Office, and the Tunku ultimately accepted Lee's proposal, partly to save the merger plan and partly because of the increasingly tense regional security environment and friction between the Federation and Indonesia, which had declared a policy of *Konfrontasi* on 20 January 1963.[96]

Thus Coldstore was finally mounted on 2 February 1963 at 0215 hours, organized around a finalized arrest list of 169 names. Police arrest parties that had been assembled 30 miles inside Johore to avoid alerting CUF elements in Singapore rushed quickly across the Causeway at 0315 hours, and about six hours later, 97 people had been arrested. By the end of the round-up on 28 February, 130 were in detention, including Lim Chin Siong and 30 others from the political sphere, "40 trade union leaders, 18 from the education sphere, 11 from cultural circles, seven members of rural communities or hawkers, nine people only identified as members of the CPM and 14 others".[97] All of the "best known Communist leaders in the Barisan Sosialis were located and detained without difficulty", while, as the ISC stipulated, "those born in the Federation" were sent back across the Causeway to be detained there.[98] While the Alternate historian Geoff Wade quotes Lee Ting Hui's Coldstore arrest statistics, at the same time he totally omits Lee's important assessment in the very same place that one should not be misled that "only" nine CPM members were arrested and the rest of those detained were *ergo* guiltless. It is worth quoting Lee here:

> These statistics show that nine persons from the CPM were arrested. *The actual figure, however, was much larger than this.* The point was that these nine operated only underground and not in any of the open front organisations. It was because of this that they got classified by the police as members of the CPM itself. *Among those who were detained in the political, trade union and other fields were many members of the CPM who functioned in the open and were classified under the other categories.* The police at that time made divisions only on the grounds of operational convenience…*Thus the damage suffered by the CPM as such was actually much more serious* (my emphasis).[99]

Lee Kuan Yew recalled that following Coldstore, he "watched anxiously in the days that followed" to see whether the CPMSTC would order replacements from its underground reserves to emerge from the shadows and "fill the vacancies" in the open-front organizations. This did not happen. The implication was that Coldstore had not only snipped off the *lallang* leaves of the CUF, it had also practically ripped out the hidden roots themselves. CPM Secretary-General Chin Peng himself confirmed this years later, admitting that Coldstore "shattered our underground network throughout the island", and that those "who escaped the police net went into hiding", and many "fled to Indonesia".[100]

Intriguingly, moreover, as far as Lim Chin Siong was concerned, following his arrest, he received a note from Lee Kuan Yew offering him the opportunity to go into exile and "not return".[101] Lee had actually broached this idea in mid-January, explaining that it was in line with "Chinese custom towards old friends who become vanquished enemies".[102] This idea was something that the Tunku and his Malayan colleagues had initially found disturbing, prompting Internal Security Minister Dr Ismail Abdul Rahman to send a frosty note to Geofroy Tory on 29 January expressing that they "do not like or understand proposal Lim should go to Indonesia" and insisting on an undertaking from Lee that "Lim will not be allowed to slip away beforehand".[103] That Kuala Lumpur was genuinely concerned about Lim being allowed to slip away, particularly to Indonesia, given the tense relations with that country at the time, was evinced by the fact that Ismail even threatened to cancel the operation a second time and even consider pulling out of the merger.[104] However by the eve of the operation, 1 February, both the British and Malayan ISC members had accepted Lee's slightly amended proposal to arrest Lim first and then provide "an offer of passage to any country, to be taken up within 24 hours".[105] In the event, after his arrest, Lim rejected the offer.[106] While

Philip Moore felt that Lee had wanted to get Lim out of Singapore so as to prevent the latter from becoming a "political martyr and serving as a focus of Chinese-speaking agitation and political opposition",[107] Lee himself offered a candid explanation on his own motivations years later. In his memoirs, he asserted that the letter to Lim — that was released to the press — had served his "political purpose" of being seen as even-handed toward his political foes and "former united front comrades in the anti-colonial movement". More to the point, Lee was hoping that the Plen, who after all ran "elimination squads", would appreciate the gesture and "behave likewise". Lee expressed no surprise that Lim had rejected the offer; he did not want to be seen to be deserting his CUF comrades.[108]

ASSESSMENT

Alternate historians of Coldstore as seen have long painted a picture of highly principled Singapore-based British officials Selkirk and Moore, and in Kuala Lumpur, Tunku and Dr Ismail, as being politically outflanked by the highly Machiavellian and cynical antics of the authoritarian Lee Kuan Yew-led PAP government. They suggest that Lee acted outside the law in securing the agreement of the British and Tunku in going ahead with the Coldstore detentions without any hard evidence that Lim Chin Siong and his CUF colleagues were going to engage in violence to capture power. To reiterate, however, the policy challenge after the July 1961 Big Split in the PAP was how to neutralize a resilient, clandestine subversive CUF organization, whose leaders' ideological beliefs legitimated the full employment of "all sorts of stratagems, manoeuvres, illegal methods, evasions and subterfuges in order to achieve their end", while simultaneously not alienating the Chinese-educated mass base within which this entity had embedded itself — as well as a largely anti-colonial international opinion. As noted, Selkirk and Moore — motivated by their desire not to do anything that might sully further London's already battered international image, stubbornly insisted that the CUF must actually engage in violent actions prejudicial to public order, before security action would be taken.

This was the problem. Lim Chin Siong and company, over and above the usual Communist operational tradecraft to avoid detection — following the CPMSTC's April 1957 directive to lay low and quietly rebuild strength — were even more so, never going to engage in the kind of action Selkirk and Moore were looking for. It bears reiterating that the absence of evidence was never at any time evidence of absence. This is precisely why Lee and Goh Keng Swee — and to some extent Razak — during ISC discussions from the third quarter of 1962 onwards, insisted on a maximalist interpretation of "security threat": the prospect of the deeply Communist-penetrated BSS capturing power through a skilfully executed constitutional strategy based on cynical, purely tactical considerations rather than high principle, as the Alternates would have us believe. Such an outcome, both Singapore and Malayan ISC officials agreed, could have severely destabilized relations between Chinese-majority Singapore and Malay-majority Malaya. This was incidentally not just a view of the Singapore and Malayan officials. Lim Chin Siong's long-time confidante and keen Marxist theoretician James Puthucheary, following much soul-searching whilst in detention following the Lim Yew Hock purges of October 1956, wrote to Lee Kuan Yew a long, confidential missive in September 1957 and came to very much the same conclusions:

> The continuation of a struggle between a government supported by almost the entire Malay population and a group whose support comes entirely from a section of the Chinese has *catastrophic potentialities*. The risk involved is the sparking off of a communal struggle which can do incalculable harm to the country. *No utopia is worth that price. If the price is paid no utopia will be possible* (my emphasis).[109]

Another of Lim Chin Siong's one-time ideological bedfellows, Devan Nair, echoed similar concerns. "If you develop as a multiracial party", Nair observed, "and all the issues you rake up are Chinese education, Chinese language, Chinese culture, it becomes very upsetting for all the other communities."[110] The bloody race riots in both territories in 1964 and 1969 remain concrete proof that such "maximalist" security concerns were never at any time exaggerated.

Alternates like to remind readers that when Lee was an opposition assemblyman debating with David Marshall in October 1956, the former had argued against overly strong government crackdowns, asserting that repression "is a habit that grows" and that it is akin to "making love", as "it is always easier the second time!"[111] Hence the suggestion is that Lee proved himself disingenuous, hypocritical and cynical in his entire approach to the Merger Referendum and ultimately the Coldstore arrests. The Alternate constituency however seems to ignore the plain fact that Lee himself has never pretended that he adopted Queensbury Rules in his duel with the CUF. Instead he has come out publicly to assert the very opposite, flatly asserting that:

> You don't argue with [Communist] killer squads.... *I have not claimed that we have beaten the communists fighting Queensberry rules and they using Siamese boxing.* We have put curbs on them. And as a result they have not been able to expand and grow (my emphasis).[112]

The Alternates have basically freeze-framed Lee in two-dimensional terms, failing to recognize that Lee the idealistic young opposition politician debating David Marshall on the dangers of government crackdowns in October 1956 — thanks to harsh learning experiences, in particular the attempted leftist capture of the PAP CEC in August 1957 — was a somewhat different creature from the older, worldly-wise and politically embattled Prime Minister of Singapore in February 1963. Seven years could be a long time in politics, especially during that era. By the time of Coldstore, the scales had long fallen from Lee's eyes as to the true nature of the Communists — that they would use any means fair or foul to win power. Hence, the Queensbury rules-gripped minimalist interpretation of security threat by the likes of Selkirk, who had not done battle with the Communists in the mid-1950s like more seasoned Malaya hands such as William Goode, would have seemed utterly foolhardy to Lee and his senior non-Communist PAP colleagues at the time. It is also noteworthy that relatively more experienced contemporary British observers such as Geofroy Tory in Kuala Lumpur basically agreed with Lee's approach, arguing that playing by "Queensbury rules" with the Communists would have been folly;[113] while one veteran former Singaporean Malay journalist, recalling the Byzantine moves and counter-moves played out between Lee's non-Communists and the CUF during the critical period highlighted by the Merger Referendum and the Coldstore arrests, said it all:

> To me, the way Lee outmanoeuvred the communists over the merger proposals, showed him at his most brilliant. It was political poker at its best. Of course, if you want to be unkind you can describe it as Lee at his most cunning. *I saluted him and the conclusion I drew then: If you are on firm moral ground, cast aside the Queensberry rules. Do whatever is necessary to win, within the bounds of human decency* (my emphasis).[114]

This is not to say that Lee took a cavalier attitude to the rule of law. On the contrary, he saw the rule of law as utterly integral to the successful political and economic development of Singapore. However — and this is again another piece of the Lee Kuan Yew worldview that the Alternates always fall well short of grasping — Lee's view of the rule of law was one that was instrumental and subordinate to Singapore's needs and not vice versa; he rejected an un-contextualized absolutist, abstract, liberal conception of the law. In particular, the experiences of fighting the Communists and later the communalists engendered in Lee the conviction that order must always precede and establish the basis for legal frameworks. In a generally under-appreciated speech to the University of Singapore Law Society on 18 January 1962 — about a year before the Coldstore arrests — Lee had already formulated the opinion that in "a settled and established society, law appears to be a precursor of order", but "without order, the operation of law is impossible":

> And when a state of increasing disorder and defiance of authority cannot be checked by the rules then existing, new and sometimes drastic rules have to be forged to maintain order so that the law can continue to govern human relations. *The alternative is to surrender order for chaos and anarchy.* So it is that we have to allow the use of extraordinary powers of detention, first in the case of political offenders under the PPSO and next in the case of secret society gangsters under the Criminal Law (Temporary Provisions) Ordinance (my emphasis).

Lee added that the "realities of the sociological and political milieu in Malaya and of the world of 1962 are that if you allow these shibboleths of 'law and order' to be uttered out of context" and without reference to "the actual social and political conditions we are in", disaster may strike, simply because in "the last analysis if the state disintegrates then the rules of all laws must vanish".[115] Far from being capricious and unprincipled in his attitude towards the law, therefore, in the run-up to Coldstore, Lee had formed and was being guided by a conception of the law that privileged order and stability as the overriding criterion, rather than the abstract liberal principles Selkirk and Moore and their latter-day Alternate supporters were obviously wedded to, seemingly at all costs. This is precisely why Lee and his non-Communist PAP colleagues sought a maximalist interpretation of security threat as opposed to the minimalist idea championed by Selkirk and Moore. Hence, rather than waiting in vain for the by-then left-wing adventurism-averse CUF elements to engage in violence and then act, Lee and Goh Keng Swee in particular understood that an intact CUF — whether coalesced around the BSS or even the UPP of the ever-opportunistic Ong Eng Guan — posed a dangerous latent threat to the political order and stability of Singapore and for that matter Malaya — waiting to be actualized through any concatenation of inclement external and internal developments. The entirely reasonable foundational premise, therefore, of the maximalist interpretation of security threat preferred by Lee and his colleagues, was always that laws could only function optimally within a strong framework of order.

This is not to say either that Lee was not Machiavellian in his manoeuvrings with Lim Chin Siong, Ong Eng Guan and even to some extent his titular allies the British and Tunku. He knew what his endgame was: the destruction of the CUF in Singapore, and he pursued this with energy, skill, determination and well, yes, cunning. The last point is not unimportant, as sometimes the Alternates themselves acknowledge in a backhanded sort of way. M.K. Rajakumar, for instance, in a candid moment, admitted that David Marshall — one of Lee's closest political rivals, "was an honest man in politics, and that alone would have made him unfit for survival", as despite the fact that he "communicated beautifully in English" he "lacked the low cunning that is the key to success in politics".[116] Marshall himself poignantly and magnanimously admitted in an interview many years later that Lee "had more iron in his soul than I had" and was thus better equipped to employ political "cover as control" over the Communists.[117] Even more telling, Communist elements themselves within the Barisan itself — whom seasoned observers such as C.C. Too considered to be possessed of "animal cunning"[118] — at a key internal meeting on 30 September 1962, conceded that out-foxing Lee's PAP would not be an altogether easy task since "in methods of political chicanery the PAP was quite different from the Progressive Party and the LIM yew-hock clique."[119] Tough-minded British interlocutors like Commonwealth Relations Secretary Duncan Sandys therefore, while on the one hand complaining that in the negotiations over the Coldstore arrest programme Lee would "bluff, bully, and blackmail up to the eleventh hour" and did not shy away from exposing the Tunku as "feeble and wooly-minded", nevertheless conceded that Lee was a "worthy personal opponent".[120]

Perhaps the Alternates — who as a whole appear to tut-tut at Lee's admittedly abrasive personality — may be tempted to draw attention to the fact that Selkirk personally found Lee "arrogant";[121] the Tunku felt he was "too clever by half";[122] and *Life* magazine, quoting an unnamed "British high official in Singapore", even went so far as to call Lee "the most brilliant man around, albeit just a bit of a thug".[123] Denis Healey, a Labour Party Minister in British Prime Minister Harold Wilson's cabinet of the late 1960s, knew Lee well, considered him "an intellectual through and through" and liked him personally. Still Healey did notice that Lee's "combative nature often made him unnecessary enemies; he could indulge in sarcasm no less wounding because it was so elegantly expressed".[124] To be brutally candid, though, that Lee was never quite the saint is utterly irrelevant. On 22 September 1963, seven months after Coldstore, and a day after the PAP victory at the post-Merger general elections — most significantly, won on the back of gradual material improvements in Singaporeans' quality of life[125] and without CUF support as had been the case in 1959 — the ever-so-correct Philip Moore composed a note to his colleagues in Kuala Lumpur. He conceded that given the "ruthless, fast-moving, and mendacious" nature of decolonization politics in Singapore at the time, "Lee Kuan Yew" — warts and all, really, was "the only man who can run this city".[126] Hence while some historians complain that the "standard historiography tends to portray" the period leading up to Coldstore "as one in which Lim Chin Siong and the left were outmanoeuvred by a tactically more astute Lee Kuan Yew, a 'Lee well astride the Tiger' ",[127] the conclusion of this study seems to be, that, well, yes, that does seem to be pretty much what happened. Whether the "riding the tiger" phrase is "hackneyed",[128] is beside the point.

In sum, in this chapter we have shown that the stock Alternate argument that Operation Coldstore was driven by crass political and not security grounds is both naïve and simplistic. Coldstore was indeed driven on security grounds — maximalist ones, to be precise: the major concern was preventing the BSS from winning the next general election via a constitutional strategy based on cynical tactical considerations rather than high principle, an outcome that both Singapore and Malayan officials agreed could have severely destabilized relations between Chinese-majority Singapore and Malay-majority Malaya. To reiterate the maximalist security concern: a Communist-manipulated BSS government in Singapore, employing inflammatory communal appeals to radicalize the large Chinese minority in the Federation, would have likely precipitated severe intra- and inter-state conflict. A closely related concern was stopping the highly resilient, hydra-like CUF from reconstituting itself around a new locus of allegiance such as the UPP, in the event of the decimation of the BSS. That the CUF was stubbornly resilient and hydra-headed is something that bears reiterating. Pamela Hickley, Personal Assistant to Singapore Governor William Goode, acknowledged in an interview that Lee and his colleagues had a "daunting" challenge on this score, because "the Communists were very flexible people and were very capable of resurging into different forms."[129]

To be sure, Queensbury Rules were decidedly not followed by Lee and the PAP government in dealing with Lim Chin Siong and the BSS, because the CUF strategy of ideologically legitimated cheating and prevarication were by then well known to the non-Communists. It would have been simply ludicrous to have been expected to fight with one hand tied behind one's back because of insufficient positivist legal powers, while the other side felt totally morally unshackled by such pristine and abstract scruples and in fact, like doctrinaire Leninists, cynically depended on this posture to attain their goals. This dilemma, by the way, of operating under a legal regime plainly unsuited to cope with extraordinary existential threats is not at all unknown to jurists. Some scholars have long argued for recognition of a legal concept sometimes called a "state of exception", in which it is held that "it is neither possible nor desirable to control executive action in times of emergency using standard accountability mechanisms" and that "legal space must instead be opened for untrammeled state action" to neutralize the existential threat, including measures "transgressing individual rights".[130] In other words, sometimes, during emergencies and in order to restore public order, one may have no choice but to violate certain individual rights in order to save the overall legal edifice of a society.[131]

Finally, some elements of the Alternate constituency, in their apparent desire to portray the Old Guard PAP government leaders as two-dimensionally unscrupulous and power-hungry, do them a grave disservice. The record shows that the decision to put their former comrades in the party behind bars under the PPSO in February 1963 was anything but easy for the PAP government at the time. Ong Pang Boon, then the Minister for Home Affairs, recalled that "signing detention orders against people you know" was "an unpleasant task" but "it was in the national interest", and a "collective responsibility" of both the "Cabinet" and the "Internal Security Council".[132] For his part, Devan Nair recalled that as "PM [Lee] once said, you can't afford to be sentimental when you are fighting for the life of a community"; and that the "outcome was crucial not only for ourselves but also for the ideals we were fighting for...we had to grow what is known as calluses".[133] As a last word, the complex and difficult moral calculus underlying Lee's thinking on Coldstore was revealed in part during a series of February 1969 interviews with the New Zealand political scientist Raj Vasil that really deserve wider re-reading. Lee recounted how in 1955, not long after the April elections won by David Marshall's Labour Front, he had been personally present at a tea-party in a Hakka school in Cairnhill, when a CPM "elimination squad came, summoned a man downstairs and shot him through the head". Just like that. Over the next few years, working closely with the CUF in the PAP and elsewhere, and gradually seeing at first hand the "streak of the ruthless and the inhuman in them", and how they "were caught in a machine" that utterly obliterated any iota of individual autonomy, whilst terrorizing potential defectors with "that awful fear of elimination", Lee told Vasil he began to ask himself, given that the CPM obviously did not "bother about arguments" to justify their behaviour: "why should the communists have this advantage over me?" He thus explained his thinking on internal security dragnets like Coldstore:

> *I do not feel apologetic [for security action taken against the Communists] because I believe they ought to be grateful that we are sufficiently liberal in our instincts not to use their methods against them. If we were to do that, they would not be alive ... This is the dilemma. If we were communists or we adopted communist standards to deal with communists we have negated something on our side ...*
> I have to face the awkwardness, both internally and internationally, of

having a hardcore communist leader under detention without trial. But my political and personal sense of decency has not been compromised. *These are the facts of a hard situation. They have to be faced.* If we do not face them, we will be dead. And Singapore will be an awful mess (my emphasis).[134]

Notes

1. Yap, Lim and Leong, *Men in White*, p. 320.
2. Cited in "United Front Were no Communists: British Intelligence", 6 December 2013 <http://www.theonlinecitizen.com/2013/12/united-front-were-no-communists-british-intelligence/> (accessed 25 August 2014).
3. Harper, "Lim Chin Siong and the 'Singapore Story'", in Tan and Jomo, eds., *Comet in Our Sky*, p. 23.
4. Thum, "*The Fundamental Issue is Anti-Colonialism, Not Merger*", p. 16.
5. Matthew Jones, "Creating Malaysia: Singapore Security, the Borneo Territories, and the Contours of British Policy, 1961–63", *Journal of Imperial and Commonwealth History* 28, no. 2 (2000): 92. Jones, it might be worth noting, is not being regarded here as part of the broad "Alternate constituency" identified in this study, as his chief focus is not on Singapore political history.
6. Selkirk to Sandys, 5 October 1962, TNA, PRO: FCO 141/12682.
7. Moore was a most interesting character whom Lee Kuan Yew genuinely respected for his energy, vitality and "keen intelligence". An avid sportsman whilst at Oxford and excellent rugby player who had represented England in the sport, Moore during the war served in Royal Air Force Bomber Command as a navigator. In 1942 he was shot down over France and he was the only member of his aircrew to survive; miraculously, just after he had been blown out of the fuselage of his doomed Lancaster bomber, a parachute pack somehow fell into his grasp, and he deployed it to land safely. Following his capture by German troops, however, he spent three years as a prisoner-of-war in a camp run by the German Air Force (Luftwaffe) for enemy airmen. However, he then partook in the famous "wooden horse" escape plan, in which a vaulting horse was kept in constant use by British prisoners-of-war to mask the excavation of a tunnel under the barbed wire. He was later to develop on the whole, a good working relationship and friendship with Lee, with whom he was a regular golf partner. "Obituary of Lord Moore of Wolvercote", *Daily Telegraph*, 28 April 2009; Philip Purser, "Obituary: Lord Moore of Wolvercote", *The Guardian*, 5 May 2009; Lee, *Singapore Story*, p. 382.
8. Cited in Jones, "Creating Malaysia", pp. 96–97.
9. Thum, "*The Fundamental Issue is Anti-Colonialism, not Merger*", p. 8.
10. Ibid., pp. 43, 55.
11. Selkirk to Sandys, 5 October 1962, TNA, PRO: FCO 141/12682.
12. Cited in Wade, "Operation Coldstore", in Poh, Tan and Hong, eds., *The 1963 Operation Coldstore in Singapore*, p. 57.

13. Moore cited in Harper, "Lim Chin Siong and the 'Singapore Story'", in Tan and Jomo, eds., *Comet in Our Sky*, pp. 32–33.

14. As formulated by the PAP Government, the Referendum on 1 September 1962 provided for three Alternatives: Alternative A, which was the PAP vision of merger, called for Singapore to be absorbed into the Federation with internal security, defence and foreign affairs under central control, while the island retained control of education and labour. In addition, Singapore would have fifteen seats in the Federal Parliament as opposed to the twenty-five seats it was entitled to because of population size, while Singaporeans would become Malaysian nationals and not Malaysian citizens. This was amended prior to the Referendum so that Singaporeans would also become Malaysian citizens, but with the proviso that they would not be able to vote in the Malaysian elections, and vice versa. Alternative B was the BSS version for full and complete merger, with proportionate representation in the Federation Parliament and automatic Federation citizenship on identical terms with other Malaysian citizens — although it meant in practice half of Singapore's citizens becoming unable to meet the stricter standards of Malaysian citizenship. Alternative C was Lim Yew Hock's Singapore People's Alliance version, which called for merger on terms "no less favorable than those granted to the Borneo territories". Thum, *"The Fundamental Issue is Anti-Colonialism, not Merger"*, pp. 17–18; Lee, *The Open United Front*, pp. 231–38; Lee, *The Unexpected Nation*, pp. 202–12; Secret: P.B.C. Moore to Reginald Maudling, 12 July 1962, TNA, PRO: CO 1030/1150.

15. Wade, "Operation Coldstore", in Poh, Tan and Hong, eds., *The 1963 Operation Coldstore in Singapore*, p. 48.

16. "Lim Chin Siong" paper.

17. Chin Peng, *Alias Chin Peng*, p. 439.

18. Lord Selkirk to Duncan Sandys, 5 October 1962, TNA, PRO: FCO 141/12682.

19. Moore to Jockel, 27 September 1961, TNA, PRO: FCO 141/17161.

20. Moore to Wallace, 18 July 1962, TNA, PRO: CO 1030/1160.

21. "Security Situation in Singapore", 25 April 1962, TNA, PRO: CO 1030/1160.

22. Chin, *Communist Party of Malaya*, pp. 88–89.

23. Moore to Wallace, 18 July 1962, TNA, PRO: CO 1030/1160.

24. Attributed to the late American astronomer Carl Sagan, who was referring to the possibility of alien life beyond our planet. This pithy statement, though, has potential applications in other contexts as well.

25. "Lim Chin Siong" paper.

26. Lee, *The Open United Front*, p. 137.

27. Fong Chong Pik, p. 124

28. Chin, *The Communist Party of Malaya*, p. 72.

29. During World War II Selkirk had been first Chief Intelligence Officer of the Royal Air Force (RAF) Fighter Command and then Personal Assistant to Lord Hugh Dowding, Commander-in-Chief, Fighter Command. Later he was First

Lord of the Admiralty between 1957 and 1959. He was also invested as a Queen's Counsel in 1959.

30. M.L.B. Williams arrived in Singapore on 12 March 1962 as MI5 Security Liaison Officer (SLO) under the cover of First Secretary of the British High Commission. Soon after his arrival he composed the assessment "Security Situation in Singapore" dated 25 April 1962 (CO 1030/1160) which attacked the Special Branch paper "Security Situation since August 1961" dated 17 April 1962 for "lack of evidence in its assessment of extensive communist conspiracy in Singapore directed by the CPM and led in the open by the BSS". "Lim Chin Siong" paper.

31. "Sir Geofroy Tory", *The Telegraph*, 10 October 2012 <http://www.telegraph.co.uk/news/obituaries/politics-obituaries/9600062/Sir-Geofroy-Tory.html> (accessed 27 August 2014).

32. Leon Comber, *Malaya's Secret Police 1945–60: The Role of the Special Branch in the Malayan Emergency* (Singapore/Melbourne: Institute of Southeast Asian Studies/Monash University Press, 2008), p. 51, n. 40.

33. <http://www.bodley.ox.ac.uk/dept/scwmss/wmss/online/blcas/goode-wac.html> (accessed 27 August 2014).

34. Selkirk to Sandys, 5 October 1962, TNA, PRO: FCO 141/12682.

35. "Secret: Revised Minutes of the 26th Meeting held at Eden Hall, Singapore at 6 p.m. on Saturday, 8th September 1962", 10 September 1962, TNA, PRO: CO 1030/1164.

36. Ibid.

37. Ibid.

38. Lee Kuan Yew, *The Battle for Merger* (Singapore: National Archives of Singapore/Straits Times Press, 2014), pp. 49–50.

39. "Secret: Revised Minutes of the 26th Meeting held at Eden Hall, Singapore at 6 p.m. on Saturday, 8th September 1962", 10 September 1962, TNA, PRO: CO 1030/1164.

40. "Secret: Revised Minutes of the 27th Meeting held in Kuala Lumpur at 10.30 a.m. on Tuesday 9th October, 1962", TNA, PRO: CO 1030/1165.

41. Ibid.

42. "Secret: Revised Minutes of the 26th Meeting held at Eden Hall, Singapore at 6 p.m. on Saturday, 8th September 1962", 10 September 1962, TNA, PRO: CO 1030/1164.

43. Lee, *Singapore Story*, p. 363.

44. This refers to a gentleman's code of fair play in the sport of boxing. The concept is named after Sir John Sholto Douglas, the 8th Marquis of Queensbury and English boxing patron. The full list of the original twelve Queensbury Rules for boxing can be found at <http://iml.jou.ufl.edu/projects/spring03/bueneventura/rules.htm> (accessed 8 September 2014).

45. Tory to Pritchard, 14 August 1961, TNA, PRO: CO 1030/1149.

46. S.J. Ball, "Selkirk in Singapore", *Twentieth Century British History* 10, no. 2 (1999): 177.

47. Yap, Lim and Leong, *Men in White*, p. 108.
48. The Governor of Singapore to The Secretary of State for the Colonies, 23 December 1957, "Visit of Mr. Hugh Gaitskell", TNA, PRO: FCO 141/15306. Gaitskell was Leader of the Labour Party from 1955 to 1963.
49. Yap, Lim and Leong, *Men in White*, pp. 108–9.
50. Lim Cheng Leng, *The Story of a Psywarrior*, p. 207. For a shorter examination of the eventful career of this most interesting and colorful personality, who earned a well-deserved international reputation for his prowess in anti-Communist psychological warfare, see Kumar Ramakrishna, "The Making of a Malayan Propagandist: The Communists, the British and C.C. Too", *Journal of the Malaysian Branch of the Royal Asiatic Society* 73, no. 1 (278) (2000): 67–90.
51. Lee, *Singapore Story*, pp. 398–99.
52. Ibid., p. 251.
53. "Meeting at Barisan Sosialis Headquarters on 23rd September, 1962", TNA, PRO: CO 1030/1160.
54. Lee, *Singapore: The Unexpected Nation*, p. 212.
55. Ibid., p. 209.
56. P.B.C. Moore to W.I.J. Wallace, 7 Dec. 1962, TNA, PRO: CO 1030/1160.
57. Ibid.; Lee, *The Open United Front*, pp. 86–87; 122, n. 176.
58. Special Branch Source Report on BSS Meeting of 23 September 1962, TNA, PRO: CO 1030/1160.
59. "Report of Lim Chin Siong Interview", 1 April 1964, ISDHC.
60. Wade, "Operation Coldstore", in Poh, Tan and Hong, eds., *The 1963 Operation Coldstore in Singapore*, p. 48.
61. *Straits Times*, 6 February 1963.
62. Lee, *Singapore: The Unexpected Nation*, p. 220.
63. "Lim Chin Siong" paper.
64. Yap, Lim and Leong, *Men in White*, p. 248.
65. "Note on Interrogation of Lim Chin Siong at Changi Gaol, 28 April 1963, 0950–1150 hours", 10 May 1963, ISDHC.
66. Ibid.
67. Drysdale, *Singapore: The Struggle for Success*, pp. 315, 467.
68. Lee, *Singapore: The Unexpected Nation*, p. 220
69. Lee, *Singapore Story*, pp. 466–68.
70. Ibid., p. 467.
71. "Report on Barisan Sosialis: AM Azahari's 'Government'; Political Asylum; Protest Demonstration and Recruitment of Volunteers", 13 December 1962, ISDHC.
72. "Report on Barisan Sosialis: Pasting [sic] Up Posters", 11 February 1964, ISDHC.
73. "Lim Chin Siong" paper.
74. Lee, *Singapore: The Unexpected Nation*, p. 221.
75. "Lim Chin Siong" paper.
76. Chin, *Communist Party of Malaya*, p. 119.

77. "Lim Chin Siong" paper.

78. S. Rajaratnam, Senior Minister (Prime Minister's Office), "Is God a Liberation Theologian?", National University of Singapore Lecture Theatre 13, 14 August 1987.

79. Harper, "Lim Chin Siong and the 'Singapore Story'", in Tan and Jomo, eds., *Comet in Our Sky*, p. 42.

80. Lee, *Singapore: The Unexpected Nation*, p. 221.

81. Matthew Jones, *Conflict and Confrontation in South East Asia 1961–1965* (Cambridge: Cambridge University Press, 2002), p. 117; Jones, "Creating Malaysia", p. 92.

82. Harper, "Lim Chin Siong and the 'Singapore Story'", in Tan and Jomo, eds., *Comet in Our Sky*, pp. 36–37.

83. Ibid., p. 37; Jones, "Creating Malaysia", p. 92.

84. Harper, "Lim Chin Siong and the 'Singapore Story'", in Tan and Jomo, eds., *Comet in Our Sky*, p. 41.

85. Jones, "Creating Malaysia", p. 91.

86. Ironically, despite his reservations, SLO Maurice L.B. Williams came up with the name of the operation and helped with the planning too. "Lim Chin Siong" paper.

87. Lee, *Singapore: The Unexpected Nation*, p. 221; Lee, *Singapore Story*, pp. 470–71.

88. Lee, *Singapore Story*, p. 471; Wade, "Operation Coldstore", in Poh, Tan and Hong, eds., *The 1963 Operation Coldstore*, pp. 51–52.

89. Selkirk to SSC, Tel. 603, 28 December 1962, TNA, PRO: CO 1030/1160.

90. Wade, "Operation Coldstore", in Poh, Tan and Hong, eds., *The 1963 Operation Coldstore*, pp. 53–54; Jones, "Creating Malaysia", pp. 100–101; Moore to Secretary of State for the Colonies, 3 January 1963, TNA, PRO: FCO 141/15306.

91. Wade, "Operation Coldstore", in Poh, Tan and Hong, eds., *The 1963 Operation Coldstore*, p. 55; Jones, "Creating Malaysia", p. 101.

92. Moore to SSC, 23 January 1963, TNA, PRO: FCO 141/15306.

93. Selkirk to SSC, 28 January 1963, TNA, PRO: FCO 141/15306. The three UPP members were Yuen Puay Koon, the UPP Administrative Secretary, a "suspected communist sympathiser" who had between 1958 and 1959, held office in the CPM-penetrated Sembawang Branch of the Singapore Itinerant Hawkers and Stallholders Association. Yuen had taken the CPM line during the Merger Referendum campaign, denouncing the PAP merger proposals and calling on the public to cast blank votes. Another was Tay Thiam Meng, a known "Communist" who had been one of the principal Hock Lee riot agitators in 1955 and was responsible for spreading communist ideology amongst Singapore Traction Company workers, while also being active in the "communist-inspired riots of 1956 and was arrested in October, 1956". On his release in 1958 he "immediately reverted to his old trade union activities" and was now a committee member of the Aljunied branch of the UPP. The

third UPP member was Na Ho @ Wong Ho @ Wong Or, a taxi driver and "suspected communist sympathizer" who had been involved in the 1955 Hock Lee agitation and had been in fact an official of the SBWU Hock Lee branch. He had also supported the "Chinese school students campaign in defiance of authority and took an active part in the October 1956 riots", and was detained on 27 October 1956. He was released in March 1957 but the following year started a pro-Communist publication. He was now chairman of the UPP Tiong Bahru branch and an executive committee member of the party as well. See Selkirk to SSC, Immediate Top Secret No. 57, 29 January 1963, TNA, PRO: CO 1030/1576.

94. Selkirk to SSC, 28 January 1963, TNA, PRO: FCO 141/15306.
95. "Secret: Revised Minutes of the 26th Meeting held at Eden Hall, Singapore at 6 p.m. on Saturday, 8th September 1962", 10 September 1962, TNA, PRO: CO 1030/1164.
96. Kuala Lumpur to CRO, Top Secret No. 149, 31 January 1963, TNA, PRO: CO 1030/1577; Selkirk to SSC, Emergency Top Secret No. 71, 1 February 1963, TNA, PRO: CO 1030/1577; Selkirk to SSC, Emergency Top Secret No. 77, 2 February 1963, TNA, PRO: CO 1030/1577.
97. Top Secret No. 77, Selkirk to SSC, 2 February 1963, TNA, PRO: CO 1030/1577; Wade, "Operation Coldstore", in Poh, Tan and Hong, eds., *The 1963 Operation Coldstore*, pp. 61–62; Lee, *Open United Front*, p. 257.
98. Secret Annex to JIC (FE), "Review of Current Intelligence as at 8 February 1963", TNA, PRO: CO 1035/164.
99. Wade, "Operation Coldstore", in Poh, Tan and Hong, eds., *The 1963 Operation Coldstore*, pp. 61–62; Lee, *Open United Front*, p. 257.
100. Chin Peng, *Alias Chin Peng*, p. 439.
101. Secret Annex to JIC (FE), "Review of Current Intelligence as at 8 February 1963", TNA, PRO: CO 1035/164.
102. Wade, "Operation Coldstore", in Poh, Tan and Hong, eds., *The 1963 Operation Coldstore*, p. 57; Top Secret No. 53, Singapore to SSC, 28 January 1963, TNA, PRO: CO 1030/1576.
103. Top Secret No. 135, Kuala Lumpur to CRO, 29 January 1963, TNA, PRO: CO 1030/1576.
104. Ismail to Tory, 29 January 1963, TNA, PRO: CO 1030/1577.
105. Wade, "Operation Coldstore", in Poh, Tan and Hong, eds., *The 1963 Operation Coldstore*, p. 61.
106. Secret Annex to JIC (FE), "Review of Current Intelligence as at 8 February 1963", TNA, PRO: CO 1035/164.
107. Top Secret No. 51, from Singapore to SSC, 24 January 1963, TNA, PRO: CO 1030/1576.
108. Lee, *Singapore Story*, p. 473.
109. "Appendix 11: James Puthucheary's Statement of Political Belief", 2 September 1957, in Lee Kuan Yew, *The Battle for Merger*, p. 198.

110. Drysdale, *Struggle for Success*, pp. 181–82.

111. <http://leewatch.info/quotes/> (accessed 13 September 2014); see also Harper, "Lim Chin Siong and the 'Singapore Story'", in Tan and Jomo, eds., *Comet in Our Sky*, p. 27; Tan Kok Fang, Poh Soo Kai and Hong Lysa, "Introduction: Why Operation Coldstore Matters", in Tan, Poh and Hong, eds., *The 1963 Operation Coldstore in Singapore*, p. 10.

112. Cited in Loh, "Within the Singapore Story", p. 11.

113. Ramakrishna, "Revising the Revisionists".

114. The journalist is Ismail Kassim. See <http://nohardfeelingsmemoir.wordpress.com/category/1/page/2/> (accessed 13 September 2014).

115. Han Fook Kwang, Warren Fernandez, Sumiko Tan, eds., *Lee Kuan Yew: The Man and His Ideas* (Singapore: Times Editions, 1998), p. 411.

116. Rajakumar, "Lim Chin Siong's Place in Singapore History", p. 105.

117. *Riding the Tiger*.

118. Kumar Ramakrishna, *Emergency Propaganda: The Winning of Malayan Hearts and Minds 1948–1958* (Surrey: Curzon, 2002).

119. "Meeting at Barisan Sosialis Headquarters on 30 September, 1962", TNA, PRO: CO 1030/1160.

120. Ball, "Selkirk in Singapore", p. 185.

121. "Note of Conversation between Lord Selkirk and the Prime Minister, Mr. Lee Kuan Yew, on April 4, 1961", TNA, PRO: FO 1091/104.

122. Christopher S. Bond and Lewis M. Simons, *The Next Front: Southeast Asia and the Road to Global Peace with Islam* (New Jersey: John Wiley And Sons, 2009), p. 214.

123. "Brilliant, but a Bit of a Thug", *Life*, 16 July 1965, pp. 43–48.

124. Denis Healey, *The Time of My Life* (London: Penguin, 1990), p. 286.

125. Improvements by 1963 included expanded primary and secondary education, increased access of ordinary homes to electricity, gas, piped water and telephones. The PAP mantra at the time moreover was a "one new flat built every 45 minutes". Yap, Lim and Leong, *Men in White*, p. 260.

126. Ball, "Selkirk in Singapore", pp. 187–90.

127. Harper, "Lim Chin Siong and the 'Singapore Story'", in Tan and Jomo, eds., *Comet in our Sky*, p. 26.

128. Hong, "They Do Say the Darnest Things".

129. *Riding the Tiger*.

130. Stephen Humphreys, "Legalizing Lawlessness: On Giorgio Agamben's State of Exception", *European Journal of International Law* 17, no. 3 (2006): 677–79.

131. Opponents of the "state of exception" concept argue that leading advocates such as Carl Schmitt were to an extent indirectly responsible for the excesses of hideous regimes like those of the Nazis. More recently, the extraordinary legal and counter-terrorist measures undertaken by the U.S. following the 11 September 2001 Al Qaeda attacks, have also been blamed on the adoption within Bush Administration circles of a "state of exception" standpoint that

justified controversial measures such as internment of detainees at Guantanamo Bay, Cuba, extraordinary rendition, waterboarding, etc. See Kim Lane Scheppele, "Law in a Time of Emergency: States of Exception and the Temptations of 9/11", *University of Pennsylvania Journal of Constitutional Law* 6, no. 5 (2004): 1001–83. Nevertheless, proponents insist that "constitutional endorsement of the state of exception is a pragmatic recognition of limited constitutional dominion". They cite U.S. founding father Alexander Hamilton himself, who argued that the circumstances "that endanger the safety of nations are infinite", and thus "no constitutional shackles can wisely be imposed on the power to which the care of it is committed". Humphreys, "Legalizing Lawlessness", p. 678.

132. Sai and Huang, "The 'Chinese-educated' Political Vanguards", in Lam and Tan, eds., *Lee's Lieutenants*, p. 145.
133. Yap, Lim and Leong, *Men in White*, pp. 248–49.
134. Raj Vasil, *Governing Singapore: Interviews with the New Leaders*, rev. ed. (Singapore: Times Books International, 1988), pp. 228, 237–38.

CONCLUSION
The Enduring Need for a
Singapore Story 2.0

COMMUNISM — THE "GOD" THAT FAILED LIM CHIN SIONG

As seen, in an interview with historian Melanie Chew in 1995, Lim Chin Siong denied being a Communist. This was a prevarication. We now know that privately, on 14 December 1982, Lim had finally admitted to his CPM ties. That day, in an interview with ISD officers, Lim conceded that he had indeed met Fang Chuang Pi @ the Plen as alleged by Lee Kuan Yew in his *Battle for Merger* radio talks more than twenty years before.[1] Lim added at another meeting with the ISD on 11 January 1984 that he had met the Plen three times between the late 1950s and the early 1960s and these meetings had been initiated by the Plen through a third party.[2] In further interviews later that year, Lim revealed that in 1954, the CPM — through Lim's ABL superior Loo Yeh Shing — had instructed him to join the PAP and make contact with Lee Kuan Yew, "as the latter was planning to form a political party". This instruction was the genesis of Lim's involvement in politics.[3] Lim Chin Siong, therefore, quite unlike the portrait painted by the Alternates, was no mere left-wing anti-colonial activist who had spontaneously emerged from the teeming, energetic ranks of the anti-colonial Chinese-educated milieu of the tumultuous 1950s. Rather his career in the CUF "appeared to have been planned and charted from the start by the CPM".[4] Lim's admission of his CPM ties was certainly a long time coming. Following his detention in Coldstore in February 1963, to be sure, he had consistently resisted giving a full account of his past CPM involvement. Even from 1964 onwards, when he had even claimed to have lost faith in global Communism, he revealed nothing. The Special Branch and later ISD assessment was that his "own ideological struggle and his insistence on abiding by his principles, presumably borne out of his reluctance to implicate his comrades and associates", were reasons as to why he "agonized and vacillated whether to accept Government's terms for release, which included giving a full account of his activities". Sadly, this inner struggle, together with the breakdown of his standing with his fellow detainees in the late 1960s — due to complaints that he appeared to expect to be treated as *primus inter pares* amongst them and to have better privileges — "undoubtedly" contributed to his "mental breakdown" and ultimately, even "suicide attempts".[5] Finally, in July 1969, after a meeting with Prime Minister Lee Kuan Yew at Sri Temasek, the latter's official residence, Lim confirmed he would "give up politics for good" and expressed the desire to leave for London to further his studies, together with his girlfriend and fellow detainee, a former SFSWU activist in the 1950s. Lee accepted and Lim subsequently wrote to Dr Lee Siew Choh of the BSS to resign from all posts in the Barisan, declaring "I have completely lost faith in the international communist movement." Lee Siew Choh predictably denounced him as a "spineless and barefaced renegade traitor" and expelled him from the BSS.[6] For his part, CPM Secretary-General Chin Peng himself "expressed his indignation over the change in attitude of Lim Chin Siong since his arrest in 1963", noting that Lim had "gradually wavered in his support towards the communist cause" and admitted he had not expected Lim "to give in so easily in view of his Chinese educational background".[7]

Ironically, while Lim's erstwhile comrades were severely chastising him, the Singapore government — his putative foe — was genuinely trying to help him. He was released on 27 July 1969 and flew off to the United Kingdom immediately, accompanied by a psychiatrist and an ISD rehabilitation officer. In London the ISD arranged for Lim to meet Dr Denis Leigh, a psychiatrist at Maudsley Hospital, on 29 July 1969. Lim was found to be in a "heightened state of paranoia" and Leigh was not even confident that Lim could be cured.[8] At any rate, after several months of treatment in London, Lim began to slowly recover, enrolling himself in an English course in 1970. Meanwhile, as Lee had promised, Lim's fiancée, Wong Chui Wan, was released from detention in September 1969 and joined him in London, and they were married on 1 September 1970. Lim went on to secure both his GCE 'O' and 'A' Level certificates, but could not complete his undergraduate studies at the London School of Economics because he fell into depression while struggling to cope with his studies and uncertainty over the future. In

1977, he was warded for psychiatric treatment. The Singapore government paid for his initial psychiatric treatment, and even offered to cover his living expenses. Lim, however, declined to accept the offer of money, as he was well supported by his family "and he did not want to be seen to have 'sold out' to the Government". Lim thus supplemented his family income by working part-time at a grocer's store near Bayswater, not too far from where he lived. At any rate, Singapore Embassy staff based in London kept periodic contact with Lim and rendered assistance as and when needed, such as in 1973 when he tried to extend his stay in London and ran afoul of U.K. immigration.[9]

After a decade in the United Kingdom, Lim returned to Singapore with his wife and two young sons. He did not have an easy time, battling depression and finding it hard to hold down a regular job; he had to rely on his brother Chin Joo for support. He suffered a heart attack in 1981, requiring an artery bypass operation in Sydney the following year. While many of his former associates in Singapore and Malaysia kept contact with him, he noticed some of his former colleagues keeping a distance from him. This affected him deeply, prompting him at some point to consider migrating to Australia to forget the past and start afresh. However, he retained social ties with former associates like Said Zahari, Poh Soo Kai, Lim Hock Siew — and given the passage of time — even Dr Lee Siew Choh. He also remained in contact with ISD officers throughout the early 1980s; while the ISD occasionally sought Lim's help in talking to certain political detainees, Lim also sought the department's assistance in helping former CPM-linked activists return to Singapore or secure early release. The ISD actually managed to get Lim to talk to the long-serving political detainee Dr Lim Hock Siew in November/December 1981 to try to persuade him to settle his case with the government. This exercise however, did not appear to have borne much fruit. Lim was also asked by the ISD in January 1984 to try to talk to the longest-serving detainee, Chia Thye Poh, but Lim demurred, because he claimed he did not know Chia well enough, and hence was in no position to provide "an accurate assessment of Chia's character, ability, knowledge and ideology". Lim told his ISD interlocutors that "he was not responsible" for Chia "politically and individually" but admitted he was responsible for Poh Soo Kai and Lim Hock Siew as he had persuaded them to "join the BSS".[10]

The reasonably cordial working relationship Lim had developed with the ISD by 1984 was put to good use in August that year. He contacted the department, informing them that his younger sister, Lim Siew Hong, had left home the previous year to meet up with her boyfriend in China and had disappeared. While he did not go into much detail, he expressed concern that "his sister had been deceived into joining the CPM at the Thai-Malaysian border". Three months later, Lim disclosed that Siew Hong had written from a "neighbouring country" to reveal that she had been criticized by the CPM for being a "petty bourgeoisie" and had been separated and forbidden from marrying her boyfriend Lee Key Bak. Lee @ Lee Kee Mok, a Nanyang University graduate, had been a Singapore Rural Residents' Association (SRRA) activist as well as a CPM member who had evaded Coldstore. He was among the 1,091 CPM militants who would later lay down their arms and emerge from the jungles at the Thai-Malaysian border after the 1989 peace agreements between the CPM and the Thai and Malaysian governments. At any rate, Lim was extremely upset at his sister's predicament, believing that she had been "deceived into treading a path of death" and said that he would persuade her to leave the CPM if she fell into the hands of the authorities. He was frustrated that he could not even respond to his sister's letters as she had not provided any return address. In fact, during a meeting with ISD officers on 24 October 1984 to further discuss his sister's situation, Lim confided that he, together with his brothers Chin Joo and Chin Kiat, had assessed that the CPM had enticed their sister to join the party as a means of compelling the Lim brothers themselves to return to the fold as well. Lim — the one-time star of the powerful left-wing Chinese-educated anti-colonial movement in Singapore, the man at one time slated to be Singapore's first post-independence prime minister, now declared that he and his brothers had endured much suffering as a result of their involvement with the party and they had collectively resolved never to "tread that hopeless path of struggle again".[11] Lim and some of his family members in short now very much rued the faith they had once blindly reposed in the Communist "god" — tragically discovering that the "path they had taken" had led to dystopia and not the hoped-for utopia. Communism — as the British Labour politician Richard H.S. Crossman once said — had proven in a very personal and tragic way, to be the "god that failed".[12]

THE VIOLENT, FALSE GOD OF COMMUNISM

In truth, Lim Chin Siong's critical moment of epiphany thirty years ago now about the true nature of the false god he and his family and friends had worshipped, represented a microcosm of what was also proving true by the late 1980s at the global level: it is not for nothing that a well-known book on the history of global Communism by the American scholar-practitioner Zbigniew Brezezinski was called *The Grand Failure*.[13] Communism suffered from a basic internal contradiction. Its founder Karl Marx had envisaged it as a scientific, historically inevitable system for overcoming the dehumanizing impact of industrial capitalism in separating the working class from enjoyment of the fruits of its labour. Ironically, however, once in power Communist regimes — in line with Lee Kuan Yew's comments to Raj Vasil in 1969 — were even more dehumanizing, emphasizing class interests over individual happiness. "In spite of its glowing talk about the welfare of the masses", the American civil rights leader, Martin Luther King, Jr observed, "Communism's methods and philosophy strip man of his dignity and worth, leaving him little more than a depersonalized cog in the ever-turning wheel of the state." Such logic ultimately legitimized violence against putative class enemies.[14] While nowadays the world is appalled at the brutal atrocities of violent extremist Islamists such as the Islamic State in Iraq and Syria (ISIS), it is virtually forgotten how brutal and sadistic the CPM could be as well — a most egregious omission in the revisionist analyses of the Alternate constituency. In the Plentong District of Johore, for example, Communist Terrorists (CTs) shot dead a Chinese squatter and hacked his wife to death with a *parang* before setting alight their hut and throwing their terrified eight-year-old daughter into the flames. In Kampar, Perak, the CTs hammered a nail through the head of a Chinese girl. At Pantai Seremban, two young men were forced to their knees, had their arms strapped behind their backs, and were bludgeoned to death by CTs wielding *changkuls*. At Tapah, near Cameron Highlands, the CTs raided a *Sakai* (aboriginal) settlement, massacred the men in cold blood and took the women into the jungle. A police report prepared in late 1952 insisted that this "senseless cruelty" was not at all "isolated" but typical of "hundreds of similar incidents" throughout the country. Even captured CTs baulked at the CPM's methods, with one confessing that "tortures are too horrible for description".[15]

No surprise then that Lee Khoon Choy, a key Chinese-educated member of the PAP Old Guard, who said he had been influenced by Communist ideals at one point, ultimately recoiled in disgust when "he came to realise that communism was a destructive rather than a constructive force."[16] Lee remembered that just before the Big Split in the PAP in July 1961, the Communist elements had tried to intimidate him into defecting from the Lee Kuan Yew camp, and when he resisted, he received "a bullet with a letter" telling him to quit the Assembly. Worse, "hooligans appeared at my home in the early hours of the morning" and yelled "at the top of their voices, 'Come out KC, we want your body'."[17] Furthermore, Chan Chee Seng, another non-Communist PAP member, was even threatened by the pro-Communist PAP elements at the height of the debate on merger: "Chee Seng, how dare you challenge us? One day if we win, we will put you against the wall as a traitor and shoot you!"[18] To reiterate, to the CPM, non-violence was a tactical and never a principled stance; if they calculated they could achieve their aims by violence, they would have done so. Such a penchant for violence prompted C.J. W-L Wee to ask: how could "a doctrine of liberation" lead "to the atrocities that it did"?[19]

This is a good question: despite the high-flown rhetoric, Communist regimes only brought decades of suffering and misery to their populations; and were unsurprisingly overthrown in Eastern Europe and in the Soviet Union by 1989–91, signifying the end of the Cold War. Meanwhile massive reforms have been required in countries whose leaders had originally bought into the dreams of Communist utopias: hence the governments of China and Vietnam are now trying to restructure in a more capitalist direction. Other remaining hard-core Communist regimes like North Korea and Cuba meanwhile are seen as pariah states in the international community.[20] In short, if the heavily Communist-penetrated BSS and other CUF elements had not been disrupted by Coldstore — and a BSS government was formed in Singapore in September 1963 — the country would likely have embarked on a truly dangerous path. As seen, even Lim Chin Siong himself, the leading light of the BSS/CUF, eventually denounced and utterly vilified his one-time Communist faith in 1984.

This is why it is truly mystifying that an Alternate writer in September 2014, in criticizing former Communists Jek Yuen Thong and Devan Nair for courageously turning on their old comrades and joining Lee Kuan Yew's PAP faction, could insist that "the MCP deserves much better from its historians than to be credited for producing men" like Jek and Nair. Granted, for the sake of a fuller historical record, there is merit in her observation that CPM members should not be regarded by posterity as two-dimensional cardboard cut-outs and that "the lives of the ordinary footsoldiers" in the jungle as well as their "deep friendships, the disappointments, the daily struggles, the little triumphs of the spirit that the men and women lived through" deserve retelling.[21] This, however, at no time exculpates these individuals of guilt for choosing to remain part of an organization that had a well-deserved reputation for sadistic cruelty towards suspected "imperialist running dogs", as discussed above. David Marshall clashed with Chin Peng at the December 1955 Baling Talks precisely over this very question of CPM violence. Marshall charged that the use of "violence to secure public compliance with an ideology they did not want" was totally incompatible with Chin Peng's claim that he was fighting for the "dignity of man". Tellingly, Chin Peng refused to discuss the matter further, saying that they had "different outlooks".[22] The Alternates should thus take heed of social psychologist James Waller's apt reminder that individuals such as the CPM members retain "full moral and legal accountability" for their actions and are not mere "hapless victims of human nature or their social context".[23] It is perhaps possible that some Alternates have inadvertently gotten too close to their subjects of study, failing to preserve the emotional detachment needed for the necessary degree of objective analysis — a structural failing of postmodernist approaches that tend to slide too easily into agenda-driven adversarial political exercises. In the final analysis, Adrian Hayter's timeless warning deserves reiteration: as far as Singaporeans' attitude towards the CPM is concerned, while there may be many rational explanations for evil behaviour, there can be in the end no excuses for it.[24]

Nevertheless, some Singaporeans have apparently bought — hook line and sinker — into the dubious Alternate narrative that thanks to Coldstore, a potentially humane and egalitarian BSS-governed Singapore after 1963 was sadly, a path not taken. Such individuals justify their stance according to the following dubious logic:

> Just as with any choices we make in life, just cos [sic] you chose option A and it turned out well, does NOT mean option B would've been worse or a bad option. *We will never know* (my emphasis).[25]

"We will never know"? If anything, the upshot of the analysis in this study is most assuredly that had Coldstore not happened and the "option B" of a BSS-led government after 1963 had eventuated, this would have been a most ominous path taken for Singapore, given the patently apparent horrible track record of global Communism, something that even Lim Chin Siong himself came to experience in a most visceral way. Clearly, such distressing evidence of historical amnesia on the part of some elements of the general public, suggests that the attempt by the Alternate constituency to construct a deeply flawed New Singapore History needs to be more effectively countered. The Singapore Story, in short, needs buttressing.

FOUR STRATEGIES FOR BUTTRESSING THE SINGAPORE STORY

Systematic Pluralization of the Singapore Story around the Master Narrative

There are at least four options for strengthening the Singapore Story. First and foremost, it seems clear that the gradual broadening of the Story beyond the contributions of Lee Kuan Yew and his PAP Old Guard to include additional voices outside the political elite — and create say, a Singapore Story 2.0 — is a trend that needs to be further intensified. The Singaporean historian Tan Tai Yong in this regard has rightly argued for "pluralizing" history so that the Singapore Story goes "beyond the realm of politics" to encompass "accounts of social, cultural and community level histories, to add layers to the national narrative".[26] Journalist Chua Mui Hoong adopts a similar stance, arguing that "a lot of the story-telling has been from the point of view of the elite" and that we have heard "the Singapore Story from the politicians who led the country; from the mandarins; and some from the captains of industry". She wonders what "Singapore Stories might we tell, of our own lives, and the lives of our parents, and friends?"[27] Some scholarly works focusing on "history from below" or "people's history" in Singapore have in fact already appeared.[28] While systematically pluralizing the Singapore Story to create a version 2.0 is the right way to go, there are limits, though. Postmodernist commentators arguing from a strict relativist standpoint, pushing as seen for a "New Singapore History" and insisting that that there is no need for a "master narrative" underpinning the project, are quite wrong.[29] For relatively young, globalized nations like multi-cultural, multi-religious Singapore — by economic necessity open to flows of ideas, ideologies, technologies, and immigrants of diverse backgrounds — a master narrative is absolutely essential to provide overall structure and coherence to the ongoing nation-building project. This is nothing new, as mentioned previously. Dr Nicholas Tate, a former Chief Executive of the Qualifications and Assessment Authority in the United Kingdom in the 1990s, was "outspoken on the link between the teaching of history in schools and the strengthening of a national sense of identity" and that a "society which is not passionate about its past is in danger of losing its identity".[30] One of the reasons British and European governments, incidentally, are finding that their immigrant youth are today so attracted to the ISIS terror network in Iraq and Syria, is precisely because these countries never invested adequately in "civic education in the school system". As Jonathan Eyal explains:

> That meant that not only members of the Muslim minorities but also a large share of the broader population *were left to search for their own identity and sense of belonging*; multiculturalism was supposed to create "rainbow nations" but instead generated atomised societies. Unsurprisingly therefore, many young Muslims in Europe gravitated towards a pan-Islamic identity which, however distant or theoretical, was still more meaningful than *the identity void* which faced them at home (my emphasis).[31]

As is well known, scores of young Southeast Asians, including some Singaporeans, attracted by the appealing but virulent ISIS ideology, have already left for Syria and Iraq and the fears are that when they do return as radicalized violent Islamists, they would pose a major threat to their respective societies.[32] As the ancient saying goes, "Without a vision, the people perish"; hence the evolving Singapore Story should not be allowed to become a haphazard mishmash of narratives with no central organizing logic. A much more sensible approach would be to ensure that while "these additional views do not necessarily change the fundamental storyline, they can certainly add texture to make the narrative more complete and interesting".[33]

Adopting Multi-Perspectival Pedagogical Approaches to Singapore History

Second, the way the Singapore Story in particular and history in general is taught in our educational institutions should be carefully studied to see how the subject could be made more palatable to a younger well-educated, cosmopolitan, tech-savvy and increasingly politically influential "Generation Y" of Singaporeans.[34] Pluralizing the Singapore Story — whilst preserving the mainstream political master narrative at its core — could mean introducing new ways of framing the subject, such as adopting the "history from below" or "people's history" approach; the *Long Duree* (long duration) frame that views Singapore's history as part of the Malay archipelago going back between 200 to 700 years; or an even longer frame, locating the genesis of the Singapore Story in the distant geological past, when the island formed "one geographic unit" with what is now maritime Southeast Asia, embracing Malaysia, Indonesia and Borneo.[35] Moreover, in terms of historical research methodologies, source-based rather than textbook-based learning, "intended to get pupils to think about the evidence for history, and to look at it from different perspectives", represents global best practice at this time.[36] In addition, the many nuances of the Singapore Story 2.0 can be appreciated not just within the classroom but through "self-discovery in family and community efforts".[37] As Ann Low-Beer argues, a national history and a sense of identity is best appropriated by young people through their own respective voyages of discovery "fashioned from many sources", not only the classroom.[38] The Singapore Story 2.0 can and should be scrutinized with "rigorous research and intellectual honesty" so as to enable students — especially those from post-secondary levels onward — to "appreciate complexity" without succumbing to two-dimensional "propaganda".[39] In line with the emphasis on rigorous research, exciting new vistas can be opened up for tertiary-level students through the adoption of what Howard Gardner calls a strategy of "multi-perspectivalism"; that is, selectively blending historical research with the insights of the social sciences, such as, *inter alia*, evolutionary, social and cross-cultural psychology, as well as political science.[40]

However, such multi-perspectivalism should have limits. In particular, at the risk of stirring a hornet's nest, perhaps a bold and clear stand should be taken against the uncritical adoption of postmodernist approaches to history — a daunting but nonetheless necessary task, given how such perspectives have been allowed to make inroads into mainstream social sciences, the humanities and even the natural sciences.[41] As previously discussed, the Foucaldian, postmodernist turn, characterized by the assumption that all history is a text/fiction and irredeemably partisan, would make the study of history in general and the Singapore Story 2.0 in particular well nigh farcical. Those Alternate historians — not all of them, to be sure — who have been influenced by the postmodernist turn cannot by definition embrace the assumption by mainstream empirical historians of the three time-honoured objectives of history: "to record the truth about what happened in the past"; to "build a body of knowledge about the past"; and to pursue the study of the past "through a disciplined methodology".[42] How can they, when they argue that there are not one but several Singapore stories or "discourses, each with political and other motives"?[43] Other postmodernist-inclined Alternate commentators argue, unpersuasively, that:

> New Singapore History utilises *the processes, analytical tools, and logic of good historical research; however revisionist, the project is not political, the researchers being motivated to do good history, not politics* — even if the research may have potential, immediate political consequences (my emphasis).[44]

It seems worth asking, though, if politics is not a motivation, then why do some obviously postmodernist-inclined Alternates, rather than remaining as detached academic observers, consistently seem to act rather as partisan political commentators/activists, very publicly championing the causes of former detainees?[45] Further suggestions of a politically tinged rather than a detached scholarly agenda is, for instance, Thum Ping Tjin's public criticism in September 2014 of the decision by the Media Development Authority (MDA) to ban public screenings of the documentary *To Singapore With Love*, about Singaporean political exiles. MDA explained that it took its action because the documentary misconstrues the legitimate actions of security agencies to protect the stability of Singapore as acts that victimized the individuals in question. In response, Thum repeated the by now well-worn soliloquy that it was politics, not security that lay behind the MDA decision:

> The MDA's statement is wrong. *Research has proven that the primary aim of Operation Coldstore and other instances of repression was to remove political*

opposition to the Singapore government. If the MDA disagrees, they should ask the ISD to release documentary proof and allow us historians to revise our research. Having seen this film last week, the one thing that all the interviewees have in common is a deep, abiding love for Singapore. This movie **reinforces national security** by demonstrating the deep loyalty and commitment of Singaporeans to Singapore, even those forced unjustly into exile (italics are my emphasis).[46]

This "not-security-but-politics" stance however, is an argument that this study has demolished, thanks in no small measure to the ISDHC granting access to the current author to the very "documentary proof" Thum laments is unavailable. As the case of the current author and of other historians show, the ISD has evinced a willingness to open its Heritage Centre archives.[47] Hong Lysa has wondered "why these individuals were deserving of such trust".[48] Readers should consider: if certain postmodernist-inclined Alternates appear intent on pursuing what seems to observers as a partisan/adversarial rather than a detached academic agenda, would the ISD — like similar agencies even in the West, especially in light of the potentially destabilizing impact on national security of the activities of the likes of Wikileaks and Snowden[49] — grant "privileged access" to them?[50] It is worth reiterating that the perception of a politically motivated rather than merely a detached scholarly agenda on the part of some postmodernist-inclined Alternates is steadily growing. Former Permanent Secretary of the Foreign Affairs Ministry, Bilahari Kausikan, for instance, has taken Thum to task for asserting that the government has been guilty of "distorting the truth" about Singapore's past.[51] Even Chinese-educated former leftists very familiar with the workings of the CPM such as C.C. Chin, have come out to urge Hong to "speak impartially as a history scholar" and "restore history to its specific period in time rather than write about it based on contemporary 'political needs' or 'political correctness'". Tellingly, in regard to our earlier observation of the stock postmodernist tactic of distracting attention from the substance of a writer's argument by calling attention to his class position, Chin urges Hong to remember that individuals who have a different view from oneself should not automatically "be categorized as the authorities' spokesperson so as to totally negate their opinion".[52]

Recall again Richard Evans' complaint that postmodernist-inclined, partisan historians tend to fall prey to situations where "facts are mined to prove a case; evidence is twisted to suit a political purpose; inconvenient documents are ignored; sources deliberately misconstrued or misinterpreted".[53] In this respect, readers may want to consider asking why some Alternates, though cognizant of the huge significance of, and even citing, the accounts of the two crucial Barisan Sosialis meetings on 23 and 30 September 1962 that finally impelled Selkirk and Moore to accept that the BSS was heavily Communist-penetrated and guided, patently downplay the central point: that these documents persuaded these previously sceptical Singapore-based British officials that the Communist threat was in fact real and imminent?[54] Meanwhile other Alternates like Geoff Wade go even further, claiming that there was no evidence to substantiate the *volte-face* of Selkirk and Moore on the extent of CPM control of the BSS, and that this talk of "new evidence" was "possibly a pretext designed to validate the new British policy".[55] To reiterate: if one's methodology tends to reflexively encourage partisanship rather than academic detachment, one would find it a trifle challenging to prevent one's "political intent" from overwhelming one's "scholarship".[56]

It is thus difficult to escape the conclusion that elements within the Alternate constituency — in pushing for the widespread adoption of a "New Singapore History" — possess an academic agenda that is heavily tinged with a leftist political bias. This emerges even in Alternate works that explicitly assure readers that they possess no such orientation. Michael Barr and Carl Trocki, for instance, take pains to assure readers that they do not seek to "present an anti-PAP or anti-Lee Kuan Yew approach to the study of Singapore's social and political order".[57] Virtually in the same breath, however, they summarize the upshot of the chapter of one of the contributors to their volume, C.C. Chin, as that the CPM did not pose a serious threat to public order in Singapore as is generally supposed, when a closer reading of the Chin chapter indicates that the gist of what he was actually saying was that the CPM could not fully control the inferno they created — although they were certainly the ones that lit the match in the first place.[58] Readers would, ironically, thus be well advised — borrowing a much-used trope from postmodernist philosophy — to adopt the "hermeneutics of suspicion"[59] in scrutinizing the New Singapore History of the Alternates. The Alternate historian Loh Kah Seng gives the game away when in an unguarded moment he cheerfully acknowledges that he "will be the first to admit that the new Singapore histories are not immune from error and bias".[60]

That the postmodernist-influenced, leftist-tinged New Singapore History is not quite free of error and bias, is alas only part of the problem. From a more foundational, pedagogical perspective, if Foucault, Derrida and the postmodernist community are right and that reality is a state merely "constructed by the mind, not perceived by it", and that, as literary deconstructionists aver, nothing exists outside the text, then as the celebrated Harvard evolutionary biologist E.O. Wilson argues, we would have a big problem:

Each author's meaning is unique to himself, goes the underlying premise; nothing of his true intention or anything else connected to objective reality can be reliably assigned to it. His text is therefore open to fresh analysis and commentary issuing from the equally solipsistic world in the head of the reviewer. But then the reviewer is in turn the subject of deconstruction, as well as the reviewer of the reviewer, in infinite regress. That is what Jacques Derrida, the creator of deconstruction, meant when he stated ... (There is nothing outside the text).

The basic absurdity of this position is then exposed by Wilson:

At least, that is what I think he meant, after reading him, his defenders, and his critics with some care. *If the radical postmodernist premise is correct, we can never be sure that is what he meant.* Conversely, if that is what he meant, it is not certain we are obliged to consider his arguments further. This puzzle, which I am inclined to set aside as the "Derrida paradox", is similar to the Cretan paradox (a Cretan says "all Cretans are liars"). It awaits solution, though one need not feel any great sense of urgency in the matter (my emphasis).[61]

Wilson then administers the *coup de grace* to the entire creaky postmodernist edifice as a viable educational strategy, when he asserts that the difference between the Enlightenment and postmodernism is that while "Enlightenment thinkers believe we can know everything", "radical postmodernists believe we can know nothing"; and asserts — in a sentence that well applies to the postmodernist-oriented Alternate historians in particular, that there are "two kinds of original thinkers, those who upon viewing disorder try to create order, and those who upon encountering order try to protest it by creating disorder". Wilson insists in this connection that "in the Darwinian contest of ideas, order always wins, because" — in a further statement that the postmodernist-inclined amongst the Alternates should heed — "that is the way the real world works".[62]

Two Suggestions for the Postmodernist-inclined Alternates

Postmodernist-influenced, politically partisan Alternates should therefore take honest stock of their own root-and-branch intellectual premises and do two things: first, they should ask themselves: how can we be expected to take their real-world historical analyses seriously when — by their own foundational postmodernist, deconstructionist logic — neither they nor we can ever be sure of what historical documents are saying? After all, if everything is a text and nothing exists outside the text, what real-world use do their writings possibly have? For example, if Hong Lysa is serious in asserting that there is not one but many Singapore histories, each with its own political logic, and according to her very own Foucaldian power/knowledge paradigm there are no objective benchmarks for determining the veracity of each of these "discourses", on what possible basis should we believe the particularistic New Singapore History storyline that Coldstore was the government's "original sin"? Why should Thum be granted access to the Ministry of Home Affairs archives? What useful thing could he possibly do with them since — by his own obvious if not explicitly articulated postmodernist logic — there is no objective basis to discern the veracity of what the texts or for that matter he himself would be saying afterward?[63] Steven Pinker thus hits the nail on the head when he isolates the fundamental contradiction at the very core of the philosophical milieu that sustains the more postmodernist-oriented Alternates:

> It is ironic that a philosophy that prides itself on deconstructing the accoutrements of power should embrace a relativism that makes challenges to power impossible, because *it denies that there are objective benchmarks against which the deceptions of the powerful can be evaluated* (my emphasis).[64]

Perhaps postmodernist Alternates may wish to engage with Pinker's entirely fair assessment and seek to address the issue of how to recover the academic objectivity that their very own foundational philosophical roots appear to repudiate.

One other important effort appears apposite to prevent the postmodernist turn from being relegated to "history's curiosity cabinet alongside theosophy and transcendental idealism".[65] Apart from trying to resolve the fundamental contradiction at the very core of their philosophy as mentioned above, the postmodernist-inclined Alternates should help improve the general accessibility of some of their peers' output. This is to ensure that busy readers would not have to slowly and painfully pick their way through the self-indulgently dense verbiage of passages like the following:

> I would have used this (and other instances) to establish that there is no such thing as a master historical narrative arising *ex nihilo*. In the schema of critical theory, all narration and writing (including history as a narration, and the writing of history) is intertextual. Every "primary" text is already influenced, answering to, denying, being undermined by, or delegitimising previous and parallel narratives and discourses. While politicians are committed to maintaining the primal state of innocence of doxa, historians (and the historical endeavor) are committed to treating all texts as co-equal, if not co-complementary, alerting to readers the existence of competing possibles and the sum total of the alternatives not chosen by the established order.[66]

Passages like the above, by the way, are not at all the exception rather than the rule in the postmodernist canon; they form part of the latter's so-called "micro-political" rhetorical arsenal. That is to say, "incomprehensibility" is held to be "a sign of greatness" and that "clear writing is the sign of a reactionary". "Obscurity" in the postmodernist estimation, Keith Windschuttle adds, "is often assumed to equal profundity, a quality that signals a superiority over the thinking of the uneducated herd".[67] Pinker recalls that Foucault and his fraternity distrusted the demand for " 'linguistic transparency' because it hobbles the ability to 'think the world more radically' and puts a text in danger of being turned into a mass-market commodity". Little wonder then that because of such "pretentious and unintelligible scholarship", thoroughly baffled students are increasingly "staying away in droves".[68] To drive home the point: it would greatly aid the teaching of a Singapore Story 2.0 in particular and history in general in our educational institutions, if the very real limitations of the postmodernist turn are recognized and a genuine "back-to-basics" approach re-emphasized. This, recalling the great British historian Trevelyan, must simply involve a "mixture of the scientific (research), the imaginative or speculative (interpretation)" and last and by no means least, "the literary (presentation)".[69]

Getting the Balance Right Between Input and Output Legitimacy

A third way a freshened up and systematically pluralized Singapore Story 2.0 can be buttressed and strengthened, is in fact extraneous to its content: gently tweaking the time-honoured system of elite governance in Singapore with a view to structuring an updated social compact especially with the increasingly politically influential younger Generation Y of confident, cosmopolitan, restive and social media-savvy Singaporeans. The argument here is that the Singapore Story 2.0 is more likely to be embraced by this new politically conscious and vocal demographic, if the latter feels that not just the Story *per se*, but the political system it purports to explain, is inclusive enough to faithfully reflect their felt needs and aspirations as well. Put across more technically in the terminology of communication theory, the context (Singapore political system) impacts the ease with which the message (Singapore Story 2.0) is transmitted from sender (primarily the government) to receiver (the Singaporean Generation Y).[70] In contrast to previous generations, Generation Y Singaporeans need to feel meaningfully engaged with work and society and are far less tolerant of strictly hierarchical authority structures than their forebears.[71] The pioneer generation of Singaporeans would likely largely have — given the country's inclement internal and external environment of the 1950s and 1960s — viscerally accepted Lee's 1969 quip that to survive, Singapore must function "like a fine mechanism, like a chronometer and not just an ordinary watch",[72] and operate, as he more famously pointed out three years earlier, as a "tightly organized society".[73] A cursory glance at the social media nowadays, however, as well as the May 2011 election results, suggest that the current populace, Generation Y especially, require a different balance between what political scientists and systems theorists would call input and output legitimacy. Andrew Potter (himself drawing upon the work of Campbell Sharman) provides a concise explanation of these useful concepts:

> Input legitimacy relates to the functioning and machinery of an institution: how members are selected, the procedures by which decisions are made and power exercised, and so on. Output legitimacy refers to the public assessment of the relevance and quality of the institution's performance ... [both] forms of legitimacy express public assessment of the worth of an institution, but input legitimacy is a matter of the design of the institution while output legitimacy must be earned by the institution's performance.[74]

In short, we could say that while in the past overall system legitimacy was geared more towards the output end of the spectrum, today, the "input" element seems to have become more important. Hence to preserve and enhance overall system legitimacy, the Singapore government — while unapologetically maintaining the time-tested fundamentals of decisive, clean, meritocratic and efficient governance focused on managing the political and social order needed for economic growth in a highly competitive global environment [output] — must also intensify efforts to find creative ways to accommodate the energies, enthusiasms and aspirations of the younger generation [input].[75]

In this respect, the Our Singapore Conversation (OSC) exercise that ran from August 2012 to August 2013, in which 47,000 Singaporeans from all backgrounds engaged in "broad-based, free-ranging dialogue" on "every aspect of the Singaporean condition", certainly represents a promising step in the right direction.[76] Significantly, the OSC findings included popular aspirations for a "competent and trustworthy Government" that is "accountable to its citizens" and engaged in a "collaborative relationship" with Singaporeans built upon "mutual respect, sympathy and empathy".[77] This suggests that the citizenry would be happy to trust the Singapore government to maintain its strong societal leadership role, as long as it institutes a diversity of genuinely consultative mechanisms for public feedback on its policies. In this connection, American legal scholar and behavioural economist Cass Sunstein's ideas on "liberal paternalism" — in which policymakers act as "choice architects" by building up "the structures around which citizens make decisions about their lives" — suggest that policy-making for Generation Y should probably best evolve in the direction of "nudging instead of shoving",[78] hence gently and finely recalibrating the dynamic input-output balance needed for optimal system legitimacy.

Being Unapologetic for "Democracy, Singapore Style"

The fourth and final strategy for buttressing the Singapore Story 2.0 in the face of the assault by the Alternate constituency, is really, to cease being reflexively apologetic and bashful about how the Story helps explain the evolution of Singapore's unique and by any measure, robustly successful political system. Such an approach, characterized by quiet confidence rather than diffidence, is more likely to have a salutary impact in evolving a political context capable of incubating the richly textured, consensus-enhancing Singapore Story 2.0 that the nation needs in future. To elaborate: since the fall of global Communism at the end of the 1980s and the apparent victory of the West in the decades-long Cold War, the assumption — best popularized by American political scientist Francis Fukuyama in his famous *End of History* thesis — has been that in terms of ideas for optimally organizing human societies to attain their fullest potential, Western-style liberal democracy remains the "only game in town".[79] However, while many Alternates by and large have uncritically measured Singapore by this stock liberal democratic yardstick (a stance that colours their attitude towards Coldstore incidentally), Singaporeans should be clear that Fukuyama's argument has not been without its critics. First, in the twenty years since the publication of Fukuyama's celebrated book, rather than a gradual global synchronization of political systems with the liberal democratic model, we find instead "the return of national-specific values and increasing Balkanization of international relations", as well as — from Europe and China to Latin America — the rejection of the notion that the liberal democratic model is "the sole suitable variant of democracy for advancing their societies".[80] Second, as seen, in the wake of the 11 September 2001 terrorist attacks, the policy responses of even supposed exemplars of liberal democracy, like the United States, have fallen well short of the very standards they preach to others.[81]

Third — and most importantly — sociological, anthropological and cross-cultural psychological perspectives suggest that as there exist diverse cultures throughout the world, it should not be a surprise that there should similarly be a plurality of organically emergent political systems attuned to each geographical and ecological milieu.[82] If conditions are optimal, moreover, organically constituted political systems that reflect the wider political culture within which they are embedded, ought to be more stable than if such systems were imposed from outside without due regard for the idiosyncratic nuances of each sociocultural context. This is one reason why liberal democracy has so obviously failed to be consolidated in the intensely tribal political cultures of Iraq and Afghanistan since the U.S. invasions of both territories in the early 2000s. "The time has come", urges Leon Hadar therefore, "to recognize that the principles of liberal democracy are not universal" but "are embedded in unique historical and cultural conditions and cannot be pressed on other national societies that are not ready and perhaps not even interested in adopting them".[83] The Iranian psychologist Fathali M. Moghaddam concurs, arguing that democracy can only work if "local cultural characteristics supportive of democracy" are "appropriated, adapted, and utilized".[84] As the American political scientists Lawrence E. Harrison and Samuel P. Huntington once put it, "Culture matters."[85] Ironically, the argument that liberal democracy is pretty much a culture-bound construct and that there is a need for contextualization of democratic principles, has been one that the ever-pragmatic Lee Kuan Yew has been articulating for decades.[86]

In any case, by any measure, Singapore is a democracy characterized by free and fair elections, as the U.S. State Department has acknowledged.[87] However, while democratic, Singapore assuredly and quite openly is not liberal in the standard Western understanding of the term. If one recalls former Prime Minister Lee Kuan Yew's conviction that in Singapore, public order is the only framework within which the rule of law can effectively function — and add to that the extant presence of legislation such as *inter alia*, the Internal Security Act, Maintenance of Religious Harmony Act and Sedition Act, all of which impose certain restrictions on unfettered freedoms of speech and assembly — the idea that Singaporean democracy is one that is contextualized or customized to meet Singapore's needs, comes into focus. Hence as mentioned, there have been a veritable profusion of various appellations political scientists at home and abroad have used to describe Singapore, one of the relatively recent ones being "bureaucratic proxy democracy", or a sort of partial democracy, "the purpose of which is not merely to maintain power, but by deepening and broadening inputs from individuals, groups and civil society into the planning process — to optimise the planning, and the realization and development of, the 'nation'".[88]

It really needs re-asking though: why should Singapore be expected to mindlessly ape a Western-style liberal democracy anyway, when the nation's track record since Separation from Malaysia on 9 August 1965, which has been the envy of the developing world, clearly indicates that "democracy, Singapore style" has by and large delivered stability, growth and steadily increasing standards of living for a population once deeply mired in poverty and insecurity? Loh Kah Seng claims that the current writer "still lives in a Singapore that is content with the state of affairs (and the affairs dictated by the state) and the Singapore Story".[89] Well, recent figures indicate that Singapore's crime rate hit a twenty-nine-year low, reinforcing its "worldwide reputation for being safe"[90] — not insignificant when one thinks of the current sectarian bloodbath in Iraq and Syria at the time of writing, that has rendered innocent civilians, including entire families, bereft of basic human security.[91] Thus, the current "state of affairs" in Singapore, managed by a largely competent public bureaucracy, does seem heavenly in comparison. One therefore needs to maintain a sense of perspective: things could be worse — a lot worse. It is worth adding, in any case, that even-handed foreign observers do not honestly see why Singapore should do things too differently. Kamal Nath, a top official from India — the world's largest democracy — averred in 2008 that it was "inappropriate to compare Singapore with Western models of liberal democracy", because — to reiterate yet again, common sense dictates that "any system had to be adapted to a country's characteristics and background":

> Singapore has evolved its own model to suit its unique position as a small multiracial and multi-religious country. Pragmatism, meritocracy, multiracialism and an emphasis on community development have been important pillars of the governance structure of Singapore and they have done well to preserve this.[92]

Singaporean scholar-practitioner Bilahari Kausikan has argued that the government has never wanted, and does not want, to present its mode of governance as a universally applicable model. He argues — echoing Kamal Nath — that the state evolved its philosophy and style of governance in response to its own peculiar historical, political and strategic circumstances.[93] Nevertheless, such is the consistently high regard for the Singaporean model that, for example, mainland Chinese policymakers, pundits and politicians have studied it closely, viewing it as a "fascinating hybrid model which fused capitalistic, Western and Asian elements imbued with a pragmatic problem-solving approach".[94] For that matter, other knowledgeable foreign observers — while of course noting areas for improvement — on the whole envy Singapore and its citizens for what has been collectively achieved over the past five decades.[95] In sum, the apotheosis of the Singapore Story — the world-famous, highly globalized, politically stable and economically robust multi-racial, multi-religious city-state of Singapore — is something all Singaporeans, instead of being fashionably leery and cynical towards, can and should instead be justifiably proud of.

As discussed, certain governance tweaks in the direction of "nudging instead of shoving" could be made and a "new political culture based on compromise and consensus" be gradually nurtured.[96] Unfortunately, the evolution of such a political culture has been hampered in recent years by certain particularly loud and partisan Singaporean elements within the Alternate constituency. The latter have arguably if indirectly contributed towards the generalized coarsening of public discourse — especially evident in the social media — reflected in reflexive, adversarial cynicism towards both the Singapore Story and national institutions. In this writer's judgment, the indirect but nevertheless dystopian influence of such Alternate output — evinced once more at the time of writing in the criticism of the government's recent relaunch of former Prime Minister Lee Kuan Yew's *Battle for Merger* radio broadcasts — has helped foster a climate within some circles of generalized distrust and cynical permissiveness.[97] This is unfortunate, because as Singaporean diplomat Tommy Koh memorably avers, to move forward the nation really needs both "loving critics and critical lovers".[98] The *de facto* Alternate encouragement of reflexive cynicism towards those in authority, however, has on balance, been insalubrious. Alternate discourse has arguably contributed to the emergence of a counter-cultural milieu from which high profile, provocatively anti-establishment, special-interest offshoots, such as the so-called "looney fringe" of activists led by the controversial bloggers Roy Ngerng and Han Hui Hui, have arisen.[99] A corrective response, however, should not come from government, but rather from a maturing civil society. As moderate Muslim scholars and ordinary citizens have for several years now spoken out boldly against the virulently antisocial ideologies of the extremist Islamism of Jemaah Islamiyah and its Al Qaeda bedfellows, Singaporean community leaders, civil society organizations and ordinary citizens themselves should now take the lead in debunking and delegitimizing the political agenda underlying much of the so-called New Singapore History. Evidence in fact of such pushback by ordinary Singaporeans is beginning to emerge.[100]

Despite the protestations of the more politically activist Singaporean Alternates, therefore, there is no compelling reason why the basic political framework, which the country enjoys now, should not remain. It is after all, not for nothing that Jerry Hough, a specialist in Soviet Communism, once created global headlines when he declared that because of its highly successful adoption — not so much of liberal democracy, but rather market capitalism and by inference the uniquely contextualized political framework effectively accommodating it — "Singapore had actually won the Cold War"![101] Posterity should record therefore, that despite its undoubtedly regrettable unpleasantness, Operation Coldstore, rather than being simplistically and unfairly portrayed as the government's "original sin", represented a historic and necessary if difficult milestone. It was in the final analysis, an important element of the continually evolving Singapore Story — representing a fateful path taken on the city-state's eventful trajectory towards achieving political and economic viability as a globalized, multi-cultural nation-state in a rapidly evolving and not always friendly world.

Notes

1. "Report of Lim Chin Siong Interview", 15 December 1982, ISDHC.
2. "Report of Lim Chin Siong Interview", 27 January 1984, ISDHC.
3. "Report of Lim Chin Siong Interview", 25 August 1984; "Report of Lim Chin Siong Interview", 1 November 1984, ISDHC.
4. "Lim Chin Siong" paper.
5. Ibid.
6. Lee, *From Third World to First*, p. 135.
7. Chin, *Communist Party of Malaya*, p. 123.
8. Intelligence Bulletin dated 21 August 1969, ISDHC.
9. "Lim Chin Siong" paper.
10. Ibid.
11. Ibid.
12. Richard H. Crossman, ed., *The God That Failed*, with a Foreword by David C. Engerman (New York: Columbia University Press, 2001).
13. Zbigniew Brezezinski, *The Grand Failure: The Birth and Death of Communism in the Twentieth Century* (New York: Charles Scribner, 1989).
14. Kumar Ramakrishna, "Lim Chin Siong and that Beauty World Speech: A Closer Look".
15. *Straits Budget*, 9 February 1950; Rhodes House Library, Oxford: Operations Information Branch, Federal Police Headquarters, "Short History of the Emergency", 21 October 1952, A.E. Young papers, Box 1.
16. Sai and Huang, "The 'Chinese-educated' Political Vanguards", in Lam and Tan, eds., *Lee's Lieutenants*, p. 141.
17. Ibid., p. 144.
18. Yap, Lim and Leong, *Men in White*, pp. 199–200.
19. Wee, "The Vanquished: Lim Chin Siong and a Progressive National Narrative", in Lam and Tan, eds., *Lee's Lieutenants*, p. 185.
20. Ramakrishna, "Lim Chin Siong and that Beauty World Speech: A Closer Look".
21. Hong Lysa, "Back to the Basics: The Responsibilities of History-Writing in Singapore", *Sahabat Rakyat Malaysia*, 26 September 2014 <http://sahabatrakyatmy.blogspot.sg/2014/09/513_21.html> (accessed 7 October 2014). One wonders if by October 2014 Hong had shifted position on the existence of the historical CPM threat. If she now accepts that the CPM existed and the real

task is to ensure that the stories of Communists are properly and sympathetically told, does this mean that Coldstore in February 1963 — that was directed at the CUF — was justified and was in no way the PAP Government's "original sin" after all?

22. Kumar Ramakrishna, "Chin Peng: A Fanatic but no Hero", *Malaysian Insider*, 30 September 2013 <http://www.themalaysianinsider.com/sideviews/article/chin-peng-a-fanatic-but-no-hero-kumar-ramakrishna> (accessed 7 October 2014).

23. Waller, *Becoming Evil*, pp. 16–17.

24. Adrian G. Hayter, *The Second Step* (London: Hodder and Stoughton, 1962). During the early years of the Malayan Emergency, Hayter was Chief Instructor of Jungle Warfare at the Far East Land Forces Training Center. See Ramakrishna, *Emergency Propaganda*, p. 63.

25. <http://unravelling1987.blogspot.sg/2014/02/revising-revisionists-operation.html?showComment=1393664856045> (accessed 1 November 2014). See the response by "Mandy" at 17:07 on 1 March 2014, to the author's Coldstore piece reproduced in the link.

26. Tan Tai Yong, "History's Many Shades of Grey", *Straits Times*, 15 September 2014.

27. Chua, "Many Singapore Stories, One Resilient Nation".

28. James Francis Warren, *Rickshaw Coolie: A People's History of Singapore, 1880–1940* (Singapore: Oxford University Press, 1986); idem, *Ah Ku and Karayuki-san: Prostitution in Singapore 1870–1940* (Singapore: Oxford University Press, 1993).

29. <http://akikonomu.blogspot.sg/2014/07/living-with-myths-i-singapore-story.html> (accessed 17 September 2014).

30. Ann Low-Beer, "School History, National History and the Issue of National Identity", *International Journal of Historical Learning, Teaching and Research* 3, no. 1 (January 2003) <http://www.ub.edu/histodidactica/images/documentos/pdf/school_history.pdf> (accessed 1 November 2014).

31. Jonathan Eyal, "'Summer Camp Jihadists' Pose Challenge to the West", *Straits Times*, 25 August 2014.

32. Maria A. Ressa, "Southeast Asian Recruits Join Jihadist ISIS", *Rappler.com*, 19 June 2014 <http://www.rappler.com/world/regions/middle-east/60877-southeast-asia-terrorism-isis> (accessed 6 October 2014).

33. Tan, "History's Many Shades of Grey".

34. Generation Y refers to young people born after 1980. Preceding generations were the Traditionalists (born before 1946); Early Boomers (born between 1946 and 1954); Late Boomers (born between 1954 to 1965); and Generation X (born between 1965 and 1980). See Rajan Chettiar, "The Singapore Generation Y", n.d. <http://www.lawgazette.com.sg/2012-03/362.htm> (accessed 17 September 2014).

35. Hack, "Framing Singapore's History", in Tarling, ed., *Studying Singapore's Past*, pp. 30–37; Derek Heng, "Casting Singapore's History in the Long Duree", in

Singapore from Temasek to the 21st Century: Reinventing the Global City, edited by Karl Hack, Jean-Louis Margolin, with Karine Delaye (Singapore: NUS Press, 2010), pp. 55–75.

36. Low-Beer, "School History, National History and the Issue of National Identity", p. 3.

37. Tan, "History's Many Shades of Grey".

38. Low-Beer, "School History, National History and the Issue of National Identity", p. 6.

39. Tan, "History's Many Shades of Grey".

40. Howard Gardner, *Five Minds for the Future* (Boston: Harvard Business Press, 2008), pp. 71–72. Some Alternate historians somewhat retrogressively dismiss multi-perspectival approaches as an exercise in name-dropping. See Loh Kah Seng, "When Historians Deny New Research", *The Online Citizen*, 10 June 2014 <http://www.theonlinecitizen.com/2014/06/when-historians-deny-new-research/> (accessed 20 September 2014).

41. E.O. Wilson, *Consilience: The Unity of Knowledge* (New York: Vintage Books, 1999), pp. 43–48; Windschuttle, *Killing of History*, pp. 1–6; Steven Pinker, *The Blank Slate: The Modern Denial of Human Nature* (London: Penguin, 2003), pp. 197–98.

42. Windschuttle, *Killing of History*, p. 185.

43. Karl Hack, "Framing Singapore's History". In Tarling, ed., *Studying Singapore's Past*, p. 19.

44. <http://akikonomu.blogspot.sg/2014/07/living-with-myths-i-singapore-story.html> (accessed 17 September 2014).

45. Thum, Ping Tjin. "The 1963 Operation Coldstore in Singapore", 16 November 2013 <http://www.youtube.com/watch?v=GwviaaULeiY> (accessed 7 August 2014).

46. Jess C. Scott, "To Singapore with Love", 11 September 2014 <http://jesscscott.wordpress.com/2014/09/11/to-singapore-with-love/> (accessed 17 September 2014). Restricted screenings of the film under MDA's Not Allowed for All Ratings (NAR) guidelines are technically possible, and Yale-NUS College in fact received MDA's green light for use of the film in class. Yale-NUS subsequently dropped the idea however, following objections by the documentary producer Tan Pin Pin. See Kelly Ng, "Yale-NUS Shelves Plan to Screen 'To Singapore, With Love'", 20 September 2014 <http://www.todayonline.com/singapore/yale-nus-shelves-plan-screen-singapore-love> (accessed 29 November 2014).

47. For instance, Ramakrishna, *Freedom News*, as well as Wang Gung-Wu and Ong Weichong, eds., *Voice of Malayan Revolution: The CPM Radio War against Singapore and Malaysia* (Singapore: S. Rajaratnam School of International Studies, 2009), have been examples of the ISD releasing previously classified material to the public, in an attempt to "provide the basis for a fuller and more nuanced understanding of our recent past". See Kwa Chong Guan, "A Forgotten Voice of Revolution", *Straits Times*, 7 August 2009.

48. Hong, "The Battle for Merger Re-Staged".

49. While the full impact of the Wikileaks and Snowden phenomenon is still being debated, and the implications for the security-versus-privacy balance are certainly legitimate, a credible argument has been made that their unauthorized disclosures of the way national security bureaucracies carry out their counter-terrorism operations for instance, has been detrimental to national security. See Mark Hosenball, Matt Spetalnick and Peter Apps, "The 'Snowden Effect': US Spies Say Militants Change Tactics", Reuters, 25 June 2013 <http://www.reuters.com/article/2013/06/26/us-usa-security-tactics-idUSBRE95P00R20130626> (accessed 10 October 2014).

50. Hong, "Time to Understand Singapore's History in All it Complexity".

51. See "What Did the Communists Say about Operation Coldstore?", 7 October 2014 <http://unravelling1987.blogspot.sg/2014/10/what-did-communists-say-about-operation.html> (accessed 12 October 2014).

52. C.C. Chin, "Seeking the Truth from Facts, Being Objective and Impartial Are the Right Attitudes to History Research — Response to Hong Lysa's 'Back to the Basics: The Responsibilities of History Writing in Singapore'", 1 October 2014 <http://sahabatrakyatmy.blogspot.sg/2014/09/513_21.html> (accessed 8 November 2014).

53. Evans, *In Defence of History*, p. 219.

54. See Thum, *The Fundamental Issue is Anti-Colonialism, not Merger*, pp. 19–20.

55. Wade, Operation Coldstore", in Poh, Tan and Hong, eds., *The 1963 Operation Coldstore in Singapore*, p. 50, footnote 108. In fairness to Wade, it may have been a matter of timing as the documents were only released in 2013 and the Coldstore book came out later the same year. In any case, could Wade have been more circumspect in his assessment, rather than insinuating that talk of new evidence was nothing but a "pretext" to validate the new British policy?

56. Hong, "They Do Say the Darnest Things".

57. Barr and Trocki, "Introduction", in Barr and Trocki, eds., *Paths Not Taken*, p. 3.

58. See ibid., p. 8; and Chin, "The United Front Strategy", in Barr and Trocki, eds., *Paths Not Taken*, pp. 64–65.

59. Attributed to the French philosopher Paul Ricoeur, although he himself apparently felt uncomfortable with the way his term was subsequently employed by postmodernist philosophers as a means of the "dismantling" of "any stable reality whatsoever". See Alison Scott-Baumann, *Ricoeur and the Hermeneutics of Suspicion* (New York: Continuum, 2009), pp. 176–77.

60. Loh, "When Historians Deny New Research".

61. Wilson, *Consilience*, pp. 44–45.

62. Ibid., pp. 44–47.

63. Thum, in response to former senior Singapore diplomat Bilahari Kausikan's criticism of his selective citation of British documents in claiming that there was no CUF in Singapore at the time of Coldstore, insisted that he would

need access to Home Affairs documents concerning Coldstore. See "What did the Communists Say About Operation Coldstore?", 7 October 2014 <http://unravelling1987.blogspot.sg/2014/10/what-did-communists-say-about-operation.html> (accessed 12 October 2014).

64. Pinker, *Blank Slate*, p. 426.

65. Wilson, *Consilience*, p. 45.

66. <http://akikonomu.blogspot.sg/2014/07/living-with-myths-i-singapore-story.html> (accessed 17 September 2014).

67. See Windschuttle, *Killing of History*, pp. 5–6.

68. Pinker, *Blank Slate*, pp. 415–16.

69. Evans, *In Defence of History*, p. 25.

70. See, for instance, "The Communication Loop/Process of Communication", n.d. <http://communicationtheory.org/communication-loop-the-process-of-communication/> (accessed 4 October 2014).

71. See the insightful essay by two Singapore Armed Forces officers, Major Eugene Fu Wei'en and CPT Nah Jinping: "Understanding the Millennial Generation: Developing a More Effective Workforce for the Future SAF", *Pointer: Journal of the Singapore Armed Forces* 39, no. 1 (2013) <http://www.mindef.gov.sg/imindef/publications/pointer/journals/2013/v39n1/feature1.html> (accessed 1 November 2014).

72. Lee's interview in Vasil, *Governing Singapore*, p. 244.

73. Cited in Chan Heng Chee, "The PAP and the Structuring of the Political System", in *Management of Success: The Moulding of Modern Singapore*, edited by K.S. Sandhu and Paul Wheatley (Singapore: Institute of Southeast Asian Studies, 1989), p. 70.

74. Andrew Potter, "Two Concepts of Legitimacy", *MacLeans Canada*, 3 December 2008 <http://www.macleans.ca/general/two-concepts-of-legitimacy/> (accessed 10 October 2014).

75. A more detailed analysis of the input/output legitimacy schema within the overall framework of "interactive governance" can be found in Mijke Boedeltje and Juul Cornips, "Input and Output Legitimacy in Interactive Governance", n.d. <http://repub.eur.nl/pub/1750/NIG2-01.pdf> (accessed 10 October 2014).

76. Adrian W.J. Kuah and Lim Seok Hui, "After Our Singapore Conversation: The Futures of Governance", *Ethos*, Issue 13, June 2014 <https://www.cscollege.gov.sg/Knowledge/Ethos/Ethos%20-%20Issue%2013,%20June%202014/Pages/After%20Our%20Singapore%20Conversation%20The%20Futures%20of%20Governance.aspx> (accessed 17 September 2014).

77. <http://www.reach.gov.sg/Microsite/osc/index.html> (accessed 17 September 2014).

78. Chia Yan Min, "Pushing for the Art of Nudging the People", *Sunday Times*, 3 August 2014.

79. Francis Fukuyama, *The End of History and the Last Man* (New York: The Free Press, 1992).

80. Mark Varga, "Against the End of History", *Foreign Policy Association*, 30 April 2014 <http://foreignpolicyblogs.com/2014/04/30/against-the-end-of-history/> (accessed 19 September 2014).

81. Scheppele, "Law in a Time of Emergency".

82. For a seminal discussion of how ecological niches influence cultural evolution, see Geert Hofstede and Gert Jan Hofstede, *Cultures and Organizations: Software of the Mind: Intercultural Cooperation and its Importance for Survival.* 2nd ed. (New York: McGraw-Hill, 2005).

83. Leon Hadar, "The Arrogance of Universal Democracy", *The National Interest*, 19 February 2013 <http://nationalinterest.org/commentary/liberal-democracy-one-country-8096?page=2> (accessed 19 September 2014).

84. Fathali M. Moghaddam, *From the Terrorists' Point of View: What They Experience and Why They Come to Destroy* (Westport and London: Praeger Security International, 2006), p. 131. Moghaddam's insights, though applied to the terrorist phenomenon, are generally applicable enough to also retain relevance for our current study.

85. Lawrence E. Harrison and Samuel P. Huntington, eds., *Culture Matters: How Values Shape Human Progress* (New York: Basic Books, 2000). For a discussion of the national dimensions of different cultural systems, see Geert Hofstede, Gert Jan Hofstede and Michael Minkov, *Cultures and Organizations: Software of the Mind — Intercultural Cooperation and its Importance for Survival*, 3rd ed. (New York: McGraw-Hill, 2010).

86. Han, Fernandez and Tan, *Lee Kuan Yew: The Man and His Ideas*, pp. 372–75.

87. U.S. Department of State, *Country Reports on Human Rights Practices* (1999), cited in Cherian George, *The Air-Conditioned Nation: Essays on the Politics of Comfort and Control, 1990–2000* (Singapore: Landmark Books, 2000), p. 84.

88. Karl Hack, "Remaking Singapore, 1990–2004: From Disciplinarian Development to Bureaucratic Proxy Democracy", in *Singapore from Temasek to the 21st Century*, edited by Karl Hack and Jean-Louis Margolin, with Karine Delaye (Singapore: NUS Press, 2010), p. 345.

89. Loh, "When Historians Deny New Research".

90. Jalelah Abu Baker, "Singapore Crime Rate at a 29-Year Low", *Sunday Times*, 23 September 2013.

91. "Islamic State Killed 500 Yazidis, Buried Some Victims Alive", Reuters, 10 August 2014 <http://www.reuters.com/article/2014/08/10/us-iraq-security-yazidis-killings-idUSKBN0GA0DQ20140810> (accessed 6 October 2014).

92. Yap, Lim and Leong, *Men in White*, p. 662.

93. Bilahari Kausikan, "Governance that Works", *Journal of Democracy* 8, no. 2 (April 1997): 26–27.

94. Yap, Lim and Leong, *Men in White*, p. 664.

95. Tommy Koh, "To Singapore with Love and Diplomacy", *Straits Times*, 15 November 2014.

96. Kishore Mahbubani, "Nurturing the Art of Compromise", *Straits Times*, 13 September 2014.
97. Hong, "The Battle for Merger Re-Staged: SG50 and the Art of Shadow Boxing".
98. Koh, "To Singapore with Love and Diplomacy".
99. See, for instance, "Looney Fringe Han Hui Hui Calls Lee Kuan Yew a Traitor, Dog and Wishes Him Dead", *Anyhow Hantam*, 17 July 2014 <http://anyhowhantam.blogspot.sg/2014/07/looney-fringe-han-hui-hui-calls-lee.html?m=1> (accessed 4 October 2014). While no sane Singaporean — and government officials themselves for that matter — would deny that there are several areas of public policy that can always be improved, it is surely important to be able to have a discussion about these matters in a civilized, sober manner.
100. See the comments by netizens Jacob Koh and Jessica Chew, in response to Hong Lysa's reaction to the current author's criticisms of Thum Ping Tjin's original assertion that Lim Chin Siong's October 1956 arrest under the PPSO had been unjustified. Hong Lysa, "What is History: A Glance at 'Lim Chin Siong and that Beauty World Speech: A Closer Look'", 10 June 2014 <http://minimyna.wordpress.com/2014/06/10/what-is-history-a-glance-at-lim-chin-siong-and-that-beauty-world-speech-a-closer-look/> (accessed 5 October 2014).
101. Howard Wiarda, with Dale R. Herspring and Ester M. Skelley, *Development on the Periphery: Democratic Transitions in Southern and Eastern Europe* (Lanham: Rowman and Littlefield, 2006), p. 176.

BIBLIOGRAPHY

A. Books, Book Chapters, Journal Articles

Amrith, Sunil S. "Internationalism and Political Pluralism in Singapore, 1950–1963". In *Paths Not Taken: Political Pluralism in Post-War Singapore*, edited by Michael D. Barr and Carl A. Trocki. Singapore: NUS Press, 2008.

Anderson, Benedict. *Imagined Communities: Reflections on the Origins and Spread of Nationalism*. London: Verso, 1991.

Ball, S.J. "Selkirk in Singapore". *Twentieth Century British History* 10, no. 2 (1999): 162–91.

Bandura, Albert. "Mechanisms of Moral Disengagement". In *Origins of Terrorism: Psychologies, Ideologies, Theologies, States of Mind*, edited by W. Reich. Washington D.C: Woodrow Wilson Center Press, 1998.

Barr, Michael D. and Zlatko Skrbis. *Constructing Singapore: Elitism, Ethnicity and the Nation-building Project*. Copenhagen: NIAS Press, 2008.

Barr, Michael D. and Carl A. Trocki, eds. *Paths Not Taken: Political Pluralism in Post-War Singapore*. Singapore: NUS Press, 2008.

Barr, Michael D. and Carl A. Trocki. "Introduction". In *Paths Not Taken: Political Pluralism in Post-War Singapore*, edited by Michael D. Barr and Carl A. Trocki. Singapore: NUS Press, 2008.

Bloodworth, Dennis. *The Tiger and the Trojan Horse*. Singapore: Times Books International, 1986.

Bond, Christopher S. and Lewis M. Simons. *The Next Front: Southeast Asia and the Road to Global Peace with Islam*. New Jersey: John Wiley And Sons, 2009.

Brezezinski, Zbigniew. *The Grand Failure: The Birth and Death of Communism in the Twentieth Century*. New York: Charles Scribner, 1989.

Brown, David. *The State and Ethnic Politics in Southeast Asia*. London: Routledge, 1996.

Carew Hunt, R.N. *The Theory and Practice of Communism: An Introduction, with a Preface by Leonard Schapiro*. Aylesbury: Pelican, 1977.

Case, William F. "Can the 'Half-way House Stand'? Semidemocracy and Elite Theory in Three Southeast Asian Countries". *Comparative Politics* 28, no. 4 (July 1996): 437–64.

Chan, Heng Chee. "The PAP and the Structuring of the Political System". In *Management of Success: The Moulding of Modern Singapore*, edited by K.S. Sandhu and Paul Wheatley. Singapore: Institute of Southeast Asian Studies, 1989.

Cheah, Boon Kheng. "The Communist Insurgency in Malaysia, 1948–1989: Was it Due to the Cold War?". In *Cold War in Southeast Asia*, edited by Malcolm H. Murfett. Singapore: Marshall Cavendish International, 2012.

Chew, Ernest C.T. and Edwin Lee, eds. *A History of Singapore*. Singapore and New York: Oxford University Press, 1991.

Chew, Melanie. *Leaders of Singapore*. Singapore: Resource Press, 1996.

Chin, Aloysius. *The Communist Party of Malaya: The Inside Story*. Kuala Lumpur: Vinpress, 1995.

Chin, C.C. "The United Front Strategy of the Malayan Communist Party in Singapore, 1950s–1960s". In *Paths Not Taken: Political Pluralism in Post-War Singapore*, edited by Michael D. Barr and Carl A. Trocki. Singapore: NUS Press, 2008.

———— and Karl Hack, eds. *Dialogues with Chin Peng: New Light on the Malayan Communist Party*. Singapore: Singapore University Press, 2004.

Chin, Peng, with Ian Ward and Norma Miraflor. *Alias Chin Peng: My Side of History*. Singapore: Media Masters, 2003.

Chua, Beng Huat. *Communitarian Ideology and Democracy in Singapore*. London: Routledge, 1997.

Comber, Leon. *Malaya's Secret Police 1945–60: The Role of the Special Branch in the Malayan Emergency* (Singapore/Melbourne: Institute of Southeast Asian Studies/ Monash University Press, 2008).

Crossman, Richard H. ed. *The God That Failed*, with a Foreword by David C. Engerman. New York: Columbia University Press, 2001.

Drysdale, John. *Singapore: The Struggle for Success*. Sydney: Allen & Unwin, 1984.

Elton, G.R. *The Practice of History*. London: Fontana Press, 1987.

Evans, Richard J. *In Defence of History*. London: Granta, 1997.

Fong, Chong Pik. *Fong Chong Pik: The Memoirs of a Malayan Communist Revolutionary*. Petaling Jaya: SIRDC, 2008.

Fukuyama, Francis. *The End of History and the Last Man*. New York: The Free Press, 1992.

Gardner, Howard. *Five Minds for the Future*. Boston: Harvard Business Press, 2008.

George, Cherian. *The Air-Conditioned Nation: Essays on the Politics of Comfort and Control, 1990–2000*. Singapore: Landmark Books, 2000.

————. "Networked Autocracy: Consolidating Singapore's Political System". In

*Political Change, Democratic Transitions and Security in Southeast Asi*a, edited by Mely Caballero-Anthony. London: Routledge, 2009.

Hack, Karl. "Remaking Singapore, 1990–2004: From Disciplinarian Development to Bureaucratic Proxy Democracy". In *Singapore from Temasek to the 21st Century*, edited by Karl Hack and Jean-Louis Margolin, with Karine Delaye. Singapore: NUS Press, 2010.

———. "Framing Singapore's History". In *Studying Singapore's Past: C.M. Turnbull and the History of Modern Singapore*, edited by Nicholas Tarling. Singapore: NUS Press, 2012.

Han, Fook Kwang, Warren Fernandez and Sumiko Tan, eds. *Lee Kuan Yew: The Man and His Ideas*. Singapore: Times Editions, 1998.

Harper, T.N. "Lim Chin Siong and the 'Singapore Story' ". In *Comet in Our Sky: Lim Chin Siong in History*, edited by Tan Jing Quee and K.S. Jomo. Kuala Lumpur: INSAN, 2001.

Harrison, Lawrence E. and Samuel P. Huntington, eds. *Culture Matters: How Values Shape Human Progress*. New York: Basic Books, 2000.

Hayter, Adrian G. *The Second Step*. London: Hodder and Stoughton, 1962.

Healey, Denis. *The Time of My Life*. London: Penguin, 1990.

Heng, Derek. "Casting Singapore's History in the Long Duree". In *Singapore from Temasek to the 21st Century: Reinventing the Global City*, edited by Karl Hack, Jean-Louis Margolin, with Karine Delaye. Singapore: NUS Press, 2010.

Hofstede, Geert and Gert Jan Hofstede. *Cultures and Organizations: Software of the Mind: Intercultural Cooperation and its Importance for Survival*. 2nd ed. New York: McGraw-Hill, 2005.

———, Gert Jan Hofstede and Michael Minkov. *Cultures and Organizations: Software of the Mind — Intercultural Cooperation and its Importance for Survival*, 3rd ed. New York: McGraw-Hill, 2010.

Hong, Lysa and Huang Jianli. *The Scripting of a National History: Singapore and Its Past*. Singapore: NUS Press, 2008.

Humphreys, Stephen. "Legalizing Lawlessness: On Giorgio Agamben's *State of Exception*". *European Journal of International Law* 17, no. 3 (2006): 677–79.

Jones, Matthew. "Creating Malaysia: Singapore Security, the Borneo Territories, and the Contours of British Policy, 1961–63". *Journal of Imperial and Commonwealth History* 28, no. 2 (2000): 85–109.

———. *Conflict and Confrontation in Southeast Asia: 1961–1965*. Cambridge: Cambridge University Press, 2002.

Josey, Alex. *Lee Kuan Yew: The Crucial Years*. Singapore: Times Books International, 1980.

Kausikan, Bilahari. "Governance that Works". *Journal of Democracy* 8, no. 2 (April 1997): 24–34.

Lam, Peng Er and Kevin Y.L. Tan, eds. *Lee's Lieutenants: Singapore's Old Guard*. St Leonard's: Allen and Unwin, 1999.

Lau, Albert. *A Moment of Anguish: Singapore in Malaysia and the Politics of Disengagement.* Singapore: Times Academic Press, 1998.

Lee, Edwin. *Singapore: The Unexpected Nation.* Singapore: Institute of Southeast Asian Studies, 2008.

Lee, Kuan Yew. *The Battle for Merger.* Singapore: Government Printing Office, 1962.

———. *The Singapore Story: Memoirs of Lee Kuan Yew.* Singapore: Singapore Press Holdings and Times Editions, 1998.

———. *From Third World to First: The Singapore Story 1965–2000. Memoirs of Lee Kuan Yew.* Singapore: Singapore Press Holdings and Times Editions, 2000.

———. *The Battle for Merger.* Singapore: National Archives of Singapore/Straits Times Press, 2014.

Lee, Ting Hui. *The Open United Front: The Communist Struggle in Singapore, 1954–1966.* Singapore: South Seas Society, 1996.

Lim, Cheng Leng. *The Story of a Psywarrior: Tan Sri Dr C.C. Too.* Selangor Darul Ehsan: 2000.

Lim, Hock Siew. "Tribute to Lim Chin Siong". In *Comet in Our Sky: Lim Chin Siong in History*, edited by Tan Jing Quee and K.S. Jomo. Kuala Lumpur: INSAN, 2001.

Loh, Kah Seng. "Within the Singapore Story: The Use and Narrative of History in Singapore". *Crossroads: An Interdisciplinary Journal of Southeast Asia Studies* 12, no. 2 (1998): 1–21.

——— and Michael Fernandez. "The Left-Wing Trade Unions in Singapore, 1945–1970". In *Paths Not Taken: Political Pluralism in Post-War Singapore*, edited by Michael D. Barr and Carl A. Trocki. Singapore: NUS Press, 2008.

——— and Liew Kai Khiun, eds. *The Makers and Keepers of Singapore History.* Singapore: Ethos Books and Singapore Heritage Society, 2010.

Low, Donald. "What Went Wrong for the PAP in 2011?". In *Hard Choices: Challenging the Singapore Consensus*, edited by Donald Low and Sudhir Vadaketh. Singapore: NUS Press, 2014.

Martin Jones, David and M.L.R. Smith. *ASEAN and East ASIAN International Relations: Regional Delusion.* Cheltenham: Edwar Elgar, 2006.

Means, Gordon P. "Soft Authoritarianism in Malaysia and Singapore". *Journal of Democracy* 7, no. 4 (Oct. 1996): 103–17.

Mesenas, Clement. *Dissident Voices: Personalities in Singapore's Political History.* Singapore: Marshall Cavendish International, 2014.

Moghaddam, Fathali M. *From the Terrorists" Point of View: What They Experience and Why They Come to Destroy.* Westport and London: Praeger Security International, 2006.

Pinker, Steven. *The Blank Slate: The Modern Denial of Human Nature.* London: Penguin, 2003.

Poh, Soo Kai. "Living in a Time of Deception". In *The 1963 Operation Coldstore in Singapore: Commemorating 50 Years*, edited by Poh Soo Kai, Tan Kok Fang and

Hong Lysa. Petaling Jaya and Kuala Lumpur: Strategic Information and Research Development Centre and Pusat Sejarah Rakyat Malaysia, 2013.

———, Tang Jing Quee and Koh Kay Yew, eds. *The Fajar Generation: The University Socialist Club and the Politics of Postwar Malaya and Singapore*. Petaling Jaya: Strategic Information and Research Development Centre, 2010.

———, Tan Kok Fang and Hong Lysa, eds. *The 1963 Operation Coldstore in Singapore: Commemorating 50 Years*. Petaling Jaya and Kuala Lumpur: Strategic Information and Research Development Centre and Pusat Sejarah Rakyat Malaysia, 2013.

Poulgrain, Greg. "Lim Chin Siong in Britain's Southeast Asian De-Colonisation". In *Comet in Our Sky: Lim Chin Siong in History*, edited by Tan Jing Quee and K.S. Jomo. Kuala Lumpur: INSAN, 2001.

Rajakumar, M.K. "Lim Chin Siong's Place in Singapore History". In *Comet in Our Sky: Lim Chin Siong in History*, edited by Tan Jing Quee and K.S. Jomo. Kuala Lumpur: INSAN, 2001.

Ramakrishna, Kumar. "The Making of a Malayan Propagandist: The Communists, the British and C.C. Too". *Journal of the Malaysian Branch of the Royal Asiatic Society* 73, no. 1 (278) (2000): 67–90.

———. *Emergency Propaganda: The Winning of Malayan hearts and Minds 1948–1958*. Surrey: Curzon, 2002.

———. *Freedom News: The Untold Story of the Communist Underground Publication*. Singapore: S. Rajaratnam School of International Studies, 2008.

Sai, Siew Min and Huang Jianli. "The 'Chinese-educated' Political Vanguards". In *Lee's Lieutenants: Singapore's Old Guard*, edited by Lam Peng Er and Kevin Y.L. Tan. St Leonard's: Allen and Unwin, 1999.

Scheppele, Kim Lane. "Law in a Time of Emergency: States of Exception and the Temptations of 9/11". *University of Pennsylvania Journal of Constitutional Law* 6, no. 5 (2004): 1001–83.

Schmid, A.P. "Terrorism Research and Government", *International Center for Counter-Terrorism (ICCT) Commentary*, 18 April 2014.

———. *Violent and Non-Violent Extremism: Two Sides of the Same Coin?* The Hague: International Center for Counterterrorism (ICCT) Research Paper, 2014.

Scott-Baumann, Alison. *Ricoeur and the Hermeneutics of Suspicion*. New York: Continuum, 2009.

Stockwell, A.J. " 'A Widespread and Long-Concocted Plot to Overthrow the Government in Malaya?' The Origins of the Malayan Emergency", *Journal of Imperial and Commonwealth History* 21, no. 3 (September 1993): 66–88.

Tan, Jing Quee. "Lim Chin Siong: A Political Life". In *Comet in Our Sky: Lim Chin Siong in History*, edited by Tan Jing Quee and K.S. Jomo. Kuala Lumpur: INSAN, 2001.

——— and K.S. Jomo, eds. *Comet in Our Sky: Lim Chin Siong in History* Kuala Lumpur: INSAN, 2001.

———, Tan Kok Chiang and Hong Lysa, eds. *The May 13 Generation: The Chinese*

    Middle Schools Student Movement and Singapore Politics in the 1950s. Petaling
    Jaya: Strategic Information and Research Development Centre, 2011.

Tan, Kok Fang, Poh Soo Kai and Hong Lysa. "Introduction: Why Operation Coldstore
    Matters". In *The 1963 Operation Coldstore in Singapore: Commemorating 50
    Years*, edited by Poh Soo Kai, Tan Kok Fang and Hong Lysa. Petaling Jaya and
    Kuala Lumpur: Strategic Information and Research Development Centre and
    Pusat Sejarah Rakyat Malaysia, 2013.

Tan, Tai Yong. *Creating Greater Malaysia: Decolonization and the Politics of Merger*.
    Singapore: Institute of Southeast Asian Studies, 2008.

Thum, Ping Tjin. "The Limitations of Monolingual History". In *Studying Singapore's
    Past: C.M. Turnbull and the History of Modern Singapore*, edited by Nicholas
    Tarling. Singapore: NUS Press, 2012.

————. " 'Flesh and Bone Reunite as One Body': Singapore's Chinese-Speaking and
    their Perspectives on Merger". In *The 1963 Operation Coldstore in Singapore:
    Commemorating 50 Years*, edited by Poh Soo Kai, Tan Kok Fang and Hong
    Lysa. Petaling Jaya and Kuala Lumpur: Strategic Information and Research
    Development Centre and Pusat Sejarah Rakyat Malaysia, 2013.

————. *The Fundamental Issue is Anti-Colonialism, Not Merger: Singapore's 'Progressive
    Left', Operation Coldstore, and the Creation of Malaysia*. Singapore: Asia Research
    Institute Working Paper 211, November 2013.

Turnbull, C.M. *A History of Singapore, 1819–1988*. Singapore and New York: Oxford
    University Press, 1989.

Vasil, Raj. *Governing Singapore: Interviews with the New Leaders*. Revised ed. Singapore
    and Kuala Lumpur: Times Books International, 1988.

Wade, Geoff. "Operation Coldstore: A Key Event in the Creation of Modern
    Singapore". In *The 1963 Operation Coldstore in Singapore: Commemorating 50
    Years*, edited by Poh Soo Kai, Tan Kok Fang and Hong Lysa. Petaling Jaya and
    Kuala Lumpur: Strategic Information and Research Development Centre and
    Pusat Sejarah Rakyat Malaysia, 2013.

Waller, James. *Becoming Evil: How Ordinary People Commit Genocide and Mass Killing*.
    New York: Oxford University Press.

Wang, Gung Wu and Ong Weichong, eds. *Voice of Malayan Revolution: The CPM
    Radio War against Singapore and Malaysia*. Singapore: S. Rajaratnam School of
    International Studies, 2009.

Warren, James Francis. *Rickshaw Coolie: A People's History of Singapore, 1880–1940*.
    Singapore: Oxford University Press, 1986.

————. *Ah Ku and Karayuki-san: Prostitution in Singapore 1870–1940*. Singapore:
    Oxford University Press, 1993.

Wee, CJ W-L. "The Vanquished: Lim Chin Siong and a Progressive National
    Narrative". In *Lee's Lieutenants: Singapore's Old Guard*, edited by Lam Peng Er
    and Kevin Y.L. Tan. St Leonard's: Allen and Unwin, 1999.

Wiarda, Howard, with Dale R. Herspring and Ester M. Skelley. *Development on the Periphery: Democratic Transitions in Southern and Eastern Europe*. Lanham: Rowman and Littlefield, 2006.

Wilson, E.O. *Consilience: The Unity of Knowledge*. New York: Vintage Books, 1999.

Windschuttle, Keith. *The Killing of History: How Literary Critics and Social Theorists are Murdering Our Past*. New York: The Free Press, 1996.

Yap, Sonny, Richard Lim and Leong Weng Kam. *Men in White: The Untold Story of Singapore's Ruling Political Party*. Singapore: Straits Times Press, 2010.

Yeo, Kim Wah and Albert Lau. "From Colonialism to Independence, 1945–65". In *A History of Singapore*, edited by Ernest C.T. Chew and Edwin Lee. Singapore: Oxford University Press, 1991.

Zahari, Said. *Dark Clouds at Dawn: A Political Memoir*. Kuala Lumpur: INSAN, 2001.

Zhang, Taiyong. "Our Cohort's Commander — Lu Yexun". In *Mainstays of the Anti-Colonial Movement: The Legendary Figures of the Singapore People's Anti-British League*. Hong Kong: Footprints Publishing Company, 2013.

Zhong, Hua. "A Preliminary Study on the History of Singapore People's Anti-British League". In *Mainstays of the Anti-Colonial Movement: The Legendary Figures of the Singapore People's Anti-British League*. Hong Kong: Footprints Publishing Company, 2013.

Zhou, Guang. "First Anti-British League Group in Singapore Chinese High School". In *Mainstays of the Anti-Colonial Movement: The Legendary Figures of the Singapore People's Anti-British League*. Hong Kong: Footprints Publishing Company, 2013.

B. Online, Audiovisual and Newspaper Sources

Abu Baker, Jalelah. "Singapore Crime Rate at a 29-Year Low", *Sunday Times*, 23 September 2013 <http://akikonomu.blogspot.sg/2014/07/living-with-myths-i-singapore-story.html> (accessed 17 September 2014).

Bamford, James. "The Most Wanted Man in the World", *Wired.com*, 22 August 2014 <http://www.wired.com/2014/08/edward-snowden/> (accessed 2 October 2014).

Boedeltje, Mijke and Juul Cornips. "Input and Output Legitimacy in Interactive Governance", n.d. <http://repub.eur.nl/pub/1750/NIG2-01.pdf> (accessed 10 October 2014).

<http://www.brainyquote.com/quotes/quotes/g/georgesant101521.html> (accessed 2 October 2014).

"Brilliant, but a Bit of a Thug". *Life*, 16 July 1965.

Chettiar, Rajan. "The Singapore Generation Y", n.d. <http://www.lawgazette.com.sg/2012-03/362.htm> (accessed 17 September 2014).

Chia, Yan Min. "Pushing for the Art of Nudging the People", *Sunday Times*, 3 August 2014.

Chin, C.C. "Seeking the Truth from Facts, Being Objective and Impartial Are the Right Attitudes to History Research — Response to Hong Lysa's 'Back to the Basics: The Responsibilities of History Writing in Singapore'", 1 October

2014 <http://sahabatrakyatmy.blogspot.sg/2014/09/513_21.html> (accessed 8 November 2014).

Chua, Mui Hoong. "Many Singapore Stories, One Resilient Nation". *Straits Times*, 3 August 2014.

"The Communication Loop/Process of Communication", n.d. <http://communication theory.org/communication-loop-the-process-of-communication/> (accessed 4 October 2014).

Eyal, Jonathan. "'Summer Camp Jihadists' Pose Challenge to the West". *Straits Times*, 25 August 2014.

Fu, Wei"en, Eugene, Major and CPT Nah Jinping. "Understanding the Millennial Generation: Developing a More Effective Workforce for the Future SAF". *Pointer: Journal of the Singapore Armed Forces*, 39, no. 1 (2013) <http://www.mindef.gov.sg/imindef/publications/pointer/journals/2013/v39n1/feature1.html> (accessed 1 November 2014).

Hadar, Leon. "The Arrogance of Universal Democracy", *The National Interest*, 19 February 2013 <http://nationalinterest.org/commentary/liberal-democracy-one-country-8096?page=2> (accessed 19 September 2014).

"History of PAP (Part IV) — Lim Chin Siong — The Man Who Almost Became Prime Minister", 6 July 2006 <http://singaporegovt.blogspot.sg/2006/07/history-of-pap-part-iv-lim-chin-siong_06.html> (accessed 20 August 2014).

Hong, Lysa. "Rejoinder on 'Alternative Narratives: The Danger of Romanticising the Other'", *RSIS Commentary* 117/2010, 17 September 2010 <http://www.rsis.edu.sg/wp-content/uploads/2014/07/RSIS11720103.pdf> (accessed 7 October 2014).

———. "In Memory of Tan Jing Quee", *The Online Citizen*, 14 June 2014 <http://www.theonlinecitizen.com/2014/06/in-memory-of-tan-jing-quee/> (accessed 7 August 2014).

———. "A Tale Outrageously Told: Days of Rage on the Hock Lee Riots", 23 February 2014 <http://minimyna.wordpress.com/2014/02/23/a-tale-outrageously-told-days-of-rage-on-the-hock-lee-riots/> (accessed 7 August 2014).

———. "Time to Understand Singapore's History in All it Complexity", *The Online Citizen*, 25 March 2014 <http://www.theonlinecitizen.com/2014/03/time-to-understand-spores-history-in-all-its-complexity/> (accessed 7 October 2014).

———. "What is History: A Glance at 'Lim Chin Siong and that Beauty World Speech: A Closer Look'", 10 June 2014 <http://minimyna.wordpress.com/2014/06/10/what-is-history-a-glance-at-lim-chin-siong-and-that-beauty-world-speech-a-closer-look/> (accessed 7 August 2014).

———. "They Do Say the Darnest Things: What a To-Do About Operation Coldstore", 29 September 2014 <http://minimyna.wordpress.com/2014/09/29/they-do-say-the-darnest-things-what-a-to-do-about-operation-coldstore/> (accessed 2 October 2014).

———. "The Battle for Merger Re-Staged: SG50 and the Art of Shadow Boxing", *The Online Citizen*, 7 November 2014 <http://www.theonlinecitizen.com/2014/11/

the-battle-for-merger-re-staged-sg-50-and-the-art-of-shadow-boxing/> (accessed 8 November 2014).

Hosenball, Mark, Matt Spetalnick and Peter Apps. "The 'Snowden Effect': US Spies Say Militants Change Tactics", Reuters, 25 June 2013 <http://www.reuters.com/article/2013/06/26/us-usa-security-tactics-idUSBRE95P00R20130626> (accessed 10 October 2014).

"How Lee Kuan Yew Stole Democracy from Lim Chin Siong and the People of Singapore", 18 November 2013 <http://therealsingapore.com/content/how-lee-kuan-yew-stole-democracy-lim-chin-siong-and-people-singapore> (accessed 20 Aug. 2014).

"Islamic State Killed 500 Yazidis, Buried Some Victims Alive", Reuters, 10 August 2014 <http://www.reuters.com/article/2014/08/10/us-iraq-security-yazidis-killings-idUSKBN0GA0DQ20140810> (accessed 6 October 2014).

Kassim, Ismail. <http://nohardfeelingsmemoir.wordpress.com/category/1/page/2/> (accessed 13 September 2014).

Koh, Tommy. "To Singapore with Love and Diplomacy", *Straits Times*, 15 November 2014.

Kuah, Adrian W.J. and Lim Seok Hui. "After Our Singapore Conversation: The Futures of Governance", *Ethos*, Issue 13, June 2014 <https://www.cscollege.gov.sg/Knowledge/Ethos/Ethos%20-%20Issue%2013,%20June%202014/Pages/After%20Our%20Singapore%20Conversation%20The%20Futures%20of%20Governance.aspx> (accessed 17 September 2014).

Kwa, Chong Guan. "A Forgotten Voice of Revolution". *Straits Times*, 7 August 2009 <http://leewatch.info/quotes/> (accessed 13 September 2014).

Lim, Raymond. "Staying Relevant in the Midst of Globalisation", 26 July 2006 <http://www.mfa.gov.sg/content/mfa/media_centre/special_events/pedrabranca/press_room/sp_tr/2006/200607/press_200607_1.html> (accessed 18 August 2014).

Loh, Kah Seng. "When Historians Deny New Research", 10 June 2014 <http://www.theonlinecitizen.com/2014/06/when-historians-deny-new-research/> (accessed 6 October 2014).

———. "Singapore Histories: Titles, Reputations, Bosses and Subordinates in a Little Town", 1 October 2014 <https://www.facebook.com/notes/kah-seng/singapore-histories-titles-reputations-bosses-and-subordinates-in-a-little-town/10152729122973887?pnref=lhc> (accessed 1 November 2014).

"Looney Fringe Han Hui Hui Calls Lee Kuan Yew a Traitor, Dog and Wishes Him Dead", *Anyhow Hantam*, 17 July 2014 <http://anyhowhantam.blogspot.sg/2014/07/looney-fringe-han-hui-hui-calls-lee.html?m=1> (accessed 4 October 2014).

Low-Beer, Ann. "School History, National History and the Issue of National Identity". *International Journal of Historical Learning, Teaching and Research* 3, no. 1 (January 2003) <http://www.ub.edu/histodidactica/images/documentos/pdf/school_history.pdf> (accessed 1 November 2014).

Mahbubani, Kishore. "Nurturing the Art of Compromise", *Straits Times*, 13 September 2014.

Ng, Kelly. "Yale-NUS Shelves Plan to Screen 'To Singapore, With Love'", 20 September 2014 <http://www.todayonline.com/singapore/yale-nus-shelves-plan-screen-singapore-love> (accessed 29 November 2014).

"Obituary of Lord Moore of Wolvercote". *Daily Telegraph*, 28 April 2009.

Ong, Weichong. "Alternative Histories: The Danger of Romanticising the Other", *RSIS Commentary* 113/2010, 14 September 2010 <http://www.rsis.edu.sg/wp-content/uploads/2014/07/RSIS11320103.pdf> (accessed 7 October 2014).

Potter, Andrew. "Two Concepts of Legitimacy", *MacLeans Canada*, 3 December 2008 <http://www.macleans.ca/general/two-concepts-of-legitimacy/> (accessed 10 October 2014).

Purser, Philip. "Obituary: Lord Moore of Wolvercote". *The Guardian*, 5 May 2009.

Ramakrishna, Kumar. "Chin Peng: A Fanatic but no Hero", *The Malaysian Insider*, 30 September 2013 <http://www.themalaysianinsider.com/sideviews/article/chin-peng-a-fanatic-but-no-hero-kumar-ramakrishna> (accessed 7 October 2014).

———. "Revising the Revisionists: Operation Coldstore in History", *IPS Commons*, 19 February 2014 <http://www.ipscommons.sg/index.php/categories/featured/159-revising-the-revisionists-operation-coldstore-in-history> (accessed 7 August 2014).

———. "Lim Chin Siong and that Beauty World Speech: A Closer Look", *IPS Commons*, 4 June 2014 <http://www.ipscommons.sg/index.php/categories/featured/177-lim-chin-siong-and-that-beauty-world-speech-a-closer-look> (accessed 7 August 2014).

<http://www.reach.gov.sg/Microsite/osc/index.html> (accessed 17 September 2014).

Ressa, Maria A. "Southeast Asian Recruits Join Jihadist ISIS", *Rappler.com*, 19 June 2014 <http://www.rappler.com/world/regions/middle-east/60877-southeast-asia-terrorism-isis> (accessed 6 October 2014).

Riding the Tiger: The Chronicle of a Nation's Battle Against Communism [dvd] (Singapore: Ministry of Information and the Arts, 2001).

Scott, Jess C. "To Singapore with Love", 11 September 2014 <http://jesscscott.wordpress.com/2014/09/11/to-singapore-with-love/> (accessed 17 September 2014).

Sha, Ariffin. "Youth of Singapore: It's Time to Rise", 31 July 2014 <http://ariffin-sha.com/arise-young-singaporeans/> (accessed 7 August 2014).

"Sir Geofroy Tory". *The Telegraph*, 10 October 2012 <http://www.telegraph.co.uk/news/obituaries/politics-obituaries/9600062/Sir-Geofroy-Tory.html> (accessed 27 August 2014).

Straits Budget, 9 February 1950.

Tan, Bah Bah. "The Lim Chin Siong Story: Clash of the Singapore Historians", *The Independent* (Singapore), 13 June 2014 <http://theindependent.sg/

blog/2014/06/13/lim-chin-siong-story-clash-of-the-singapore-historians/> (accessed 7 August 2014).

Tan, Tai Yong. "History's Many Shades of Grey". *Straits Times*, 15 September 2014.

Thum, Ping Tjin. "The 1963 Operation Coldstore in Singapore", 16 November 2013 <http://www.youtube.com/watch?v=GwviaaULeiY> (accessed 7 August 2014).

———. "Lim Chin Siong was Wrongfully Detained", *The Online Citizen*, 8 May 2014 <http://www.theonlinecitizen.com/2014/05/lim-chin-siong-was-wrongfully-detained> (accessed 7 August 2014).

"United Front Were no Communists: British Intelligence", 6 December 2013 <http://www.theonlinecitizen.com/2013/12/united-front-were-no-communists-british-intelligence/> (accessed 25 August 2014).

<http://unravelling 1987blogspot.sg/2014/02/revising-revisionists-operation.html?showComment=1393664856045> (accessed 1 November 2014)

Varga, Mark. "Against the End of History", *Foreign Policy Association*, 30 April 2014 <http://foreignpolicyblogs.com/2014/04/30/against-the-end-of-history/> (accessed 19 September 2014).

Wade, Geoff. "Singapore's History Wars", 30 April 2014 <http://www.eastasiaforum.org/2014/04/30/singapores-history-wars/> (accessed 7 August 2014).

"What did the Communists Say About Operation Coldstore? 7 October 2014 <http://unravelling1987.blogspot.sg/2014/10/what-did-communists-say-about-operation.html> (accessed 12 October 2014).

<https://wikileaks.org/About.html> (accessed 2 October 2014).

C. Miscellaneous Talks/Lectures/Papers

Rajaratnam, S. Senior Minister (Prime Minister's Office), "Is God a Liberation Theologian?" National University of Singapore Lecture Theatre 13, Friday, 14 August 1987.

Thum Ping Tjin. "Merger, Acquisition, or Takeover? Singapore's Progressive Left, Merger and the Enduring Consequences of Operation Coldstore", Lecture, Oxford University, United Kingdom, 31 January 2014.

Wade, Geoff. " 'Operation Cold Store': A Key Event in the Creation of Malaysia and in the Origins of Modern Singapore", paper presented at the 21st Conference of the International Association of Historians of Asia, 21–25 June 2010.

D. Government Sources

Internal Security Department Heritage Centre, Singapore

"Statement of Seet Chay Tuan", 19 December 1955.

"Statement of Koh Thong Eng", 1 October 1956.

"The Security Threat to Singapore (Communism and Nationalism)", 24 July 1959.

"Surveillance Report", 18 July 1961.
"Report on Barisan Sosialis: AM Azahari's "Government"; Political Asylum; Protest Demonstration and Recruitment of Volunteers", 13 December 1962.
"Report of Lim Chin Siong Interview", 5 February 1963.
"Note on Interrogation of Lim Chin Siong at Changi Gaol, 28 April 1963, 0950 – 1150 hours", 10 May 1963.
"Translation of a comment on Lim Chin Siong's statement", 8 June 1963.
"Report on Barisan Sosialis: Pasting [sic] Up Posters", 11 February 1964.
"Report of Lim Chin Siong Interview", 1 April 1964.
"Communist Party of Malaya Organisation from 1960–1968", 29 March 1969.
"Intelligence Bulletin", 21 August 1969.
"Report of Lim Chin Siong Interview", 15 December 1982.
"Report of Lim Chin Siong Interview", 27 January 1984.
"Report of Lim Chin Siong Interview", 25 August 1984.
"Report of Lim Chin Siong Interview", 1 November 1984.
"Lim Chin Siong", 27 February 2014.

The National Archives/ Public Record Office, Kew, London, UK

"The Communist Threat in Singapore", Cmd. 33 of 1957, 23 August 1957.

CO 1030   Colonial Office and Commonwealth Office:
            Far Eastern Department and Successors, Registered Files.
CO 1035   Colonial Office: Intelligence and Security Departments, Registered Files.
DO 169   Commonwealth Relations Office and Commonwealth Office: Far East and Pacific Department, Registered Files.
FO 1091   Commissioner General for the United Kingdom in South East Asia, and United Kingdom Commissioner for Singapore and South East Asia: Registered Files.
FCO 141   Foreign and Commonwealth Office and predecessors: Records of Former Colonial Administrations: Migrated Archives.

Rhodes House Library, Oxford University, Oxford, UK

Operations Information Branch, Federal Police Headquarters, "Short History of the Emergency", 21 October 1952, A.E. Young Papers, Box 1.

INDEX

Note: Pages numbers followed by "n" refer to notes.

ABOUT THE AUTHOR

Kumar Ramakrishna is Associate Professor and Head of the Centre of Excellence for National Security at the S. Rajaratnam School of International Studies, Nanyang Technological University. A historian by background, he has written extensively on counter-extremism as well as psychological warfare during the Malayan Emergency. He is the author of *Emergency Propaganda: The Winning of Malayan Hearts and Minds, 1948–1958* (2002) and editor of *Freedom News: The Untold Story of the Communist Underground Publication* (2008).

www.ingramcontent.com/pod-product-compliance
Lightning Source LLC
Chambersburg PA
CBHW070243290326
41929CB00046B/2419